STATISTICAL
PROFILES
OF WOMEN'S
AND MEN'S
STATUS
IN THE
ECONOMY
SCIENCE AND
SOCIETY

T0315086

STATISTICAL
PROFILES
OF WOMEN'S
AND MEN'S
STATUS
IN THE
ECONOMY
SCIENCE AND
SOCIETY

Edited by
Ewa Okoń-Horodyńska
Anna Zachorowska-Mazurkiewicz

Jagiellonian University Press

The book has been financed from Norway Grants in the Polish-Norwegian Research Programme operated by the National Centre for Research and Development, Pol-Nor/200588/60

REVIEWER
Dr hab. Paweł Kawalec, Professor at the John Paul II Catholic University of Lublin

COVER DESIGN
Andrzej Pilichowski-Ragno

ISBN 978-83-233-4007-2

www.wuj.pl

Jagiellonian University Press
Editorial Offices: Michałowskiego St. 9/2, 31-126 Cracow
Phone: +48 12 663 23 82, Fax: +48 12 663 23 83
Distribution: Phone: +48 12 631 01 97, Fax: +48 12 631 01 98
Cell Phone: +48 506 006 674, e-mail: sprzedaz@wuj.pl
Bank: PEKAO SA, IBAN PL 80 1240 4722 1111 0000 4856 3325

Table of Contents

Introduction

The universality of the opinion that the most effective route to economic progress is research skilfully oriented and used to develop innovation, particularly technological, probably needs no more repetition. Science, which determines a society's intellectual level and prosperity, has become the driving force behind the development of the new economy. Stimulation of scientific research and practical application of the results is the subject of the economic policy of any modern state. Both the scientific and technical requirements are now valuable and sought-after around the world because they are a competitive commodity and may be a source of significant revenue windfalls. It should be emphasized, however, that technological innovations do not grow and spread like the proverbial plague. They are created, developed and used as a result of decisions and actions taken by specific actors and the relationships between them. "Technological innovations are hard, deliberate, focused work that requires knowledge, diligence, perseverance, and commitment; they require innovators to use their greatest assets, and this work is the result, caused in the economy and society, because it causes a change in the behaviour of both businesses and consumers" (Drucker, 1992, pp. 152–153). So the speed, direction, and even the randomness of technological innovation, implemented in the specific formulas of innovation processes, is caused by an existing or evolving institutional structure, as well as market expectations and users of already applied technologies. The institutional structure is, admittedly, a framework for creating an innovative environment in a given economy, but the innovation process itself takes place in the organization that positively or negatively affects the involvement of existing potentials and successes achieved. Technological changes are not achievable by a simple transfer of knowledge (e.g. new technology) between different countries, because it is not always the case that the transfer is absorbable; on the contrary, the essence of technological change and the creation of innovation lies in the national and organizational specifics, with their roots in skills, abilities, and level of accumulated knowledge. Nations and organizations are not only differentiated by various quantitative levels of innovation, but also by the ways in which this innovation is accepted in its fragmentary compositions. The European Union has still not recorded the success in the growth of innovation forecast for years, remaining

consistently in the world rankings behind the US and Japan, and more impor-
tantly, new potential competitors are emerging, e.g. China. The European Commission also constantly creates successive offensives and strategies to intensify
the development of research and innovation in all EU member states, and the
failure of previous programmes in this area is explained by the lack of political
will and conviction of heads of state, that the objectives were too ambitious,
and that so far the cohesion strategy between the entire European Union and
policies of member states has been absent, which is further compounded by the
poor state of public finances in many EU countries and the crisis in 2008. The
Europe 2020 programme, especially the Innovation Union and the shifting of the
trust and support of innovative activity to the regions, once again provides the
opportunity for huge financial and institutional support for the development of
innovation in the EU. Will yet another programme trigger innovation in the EU?
Polish entrepreneurs argue that EU regulations harm innovation, and universities
that the use of EU support hitherto, which, it is true, has enabled a leap forward
in improving the quality of infrastructure, but in the long run will lead to the
financial collapse of higher education institutions that dramatically take out loans
for their own contribution to projects and maintaining this infrastructure, while
for its research, it is already no longer sufficient. Under these conditions, which
have been assessed ambiguously, a further search for the sources of a creative base
for the development of innovation has become a necessary challenge. This was
one of the research tasks of 'Innovative Gender' as a New Source of Progress,[1] to
whose introduction the proposed report is related. Of interest is the search for
the wider sourcing of creative ability, because traditional methods have failed to
solve a variety of problems, which, since it is unconventional and has practical
applications, becomes innovations. We begin with the assumption that achieving
the ability to develop innovation depends on the multidimensional predisposition
to tackle these problems, and therefore those inherent in people, and herein lies
the significance of gender, or motivated by the market, organized or spontaneous,
as well as those supported or inhibited by state policy in different countries or
regions. In view of the growing importance of gender studies, justified for many
by economic and social phenomena, the introduction of gender roles in the innovation process seems obvious and requires exploration. As a contribution to
the objective of the research project, this book is in essence made up of multiple
threads. In the first place we introduce a discussion on the understanding and
the ability to describe gender, which is essential as a category of analysis in the
social sciences. Later come considerations focused around women's and men's
professional, political and social situation, business, time use, activity in the R&D
and patent sector. Using theoretical and practical knowledge, an attempt is made
to determine the profiles of men and women at the same time using as a filter the

---

1   'Innovative Gender' as a New Source of Progress project is funded from Norway Grants in the
     Polish-Norwegian Research Programme operated by the National Centre for Research and
     Development, Pol-Nor/200588/60.

psychological aspects of innovation. These profiles have ultimately been used to determine the scope of the category Innovative Gender, as a key concept of the proposed research project, by which, as it is assumed, we can capture the role of women and men in the process of innovation. On this basis, it will be possible to develop research methods which will enable assessment of the strength of this relationship symbolically defined in the InnoGend project.

Ewa Okoń-Horodyńska

Preface

The papers in this collection have provided answers to many important questions about the status of women and men in various areas of activity – politics, science, the economy, and society – and in more detail in creative and innovative activity. Although the results of the analysis could be used in a number of thematic discussions, the authors treat them primarily as a contribution to the study of the influence of gender relations on the creative and innovative activities of men and women. The research results summarized in this monograph are part of the 'Innovative Gender' as a New Source of Progress (InnoGend) project conducted by a team of researchers from the Jagiellonian University, the University of Warsaw, and Ostfold University College. One of the project's main research questions is: whether and how gender can contribute to the growth of social creativity and the development of innovation, and whether in any dimension support of innovative activity is reflected in state policy. It may be assumed that if the policy of promoting creativity and innovation is neutral in terms of gender roles, this means that either gender does not matter in the innovation process, or that the impact of gender in this process is avoided. Highlighting the positive (or negative) relationships between gender and the creativity and innovativeness of men and women may indeed be helpful in the search for new sources of progress.

The need to define the most important categories of gender and its "environment" thus arises from the specifics of the project. Gender is a time-variable social phenomenon, constituting the superstructure of biological sex, which is reduced to a set of traits, behaviours, attitudes, roles and attributes assigned by the wider culture to one sex and expected by society, appropriately from a woman or a man, as well as the closely related relationships between them, which includes a hierarchy. Gender is rooted in social institutions, which translates on the one hand into a lack of awareness, and on the other to its variability over time (Magdalena Jaworek and Anna Zachorowska-Mazurkiewicz).

In economics in defining the categories of gender the main emphasis is on the disclosure of new reserves and incentives for development – on local and global levels. Increasing participation of women in economy and society is a real action, revealing unexploited gains, which sophisticated mathematical models cannot grasp. Gender equality functioning in practice is the main issue of economic participation. For example: "economic citizenship" – own income and access to paid work /self-employment so participation in decision making (in politics & business) are the main pillars of equality in Norway, which in the chapter is used as a benchmark (Danuta Tomczak).

The positions of women and men in society from the point of view of their role in academia and politics is not optimistic even in countries at the highest level of development. Both in the United States and in Europe, despite the fact that women make up almost half of those receiving a doctoral degree, among professors they are barely one-fifth. As a point of reference for the action to equalize the situation of women and men in academia, Nordic solutions and the guidelines of European institutions have been adopted in the chapter. A significant gender imbalance persists for years also in politics. Complex determinants of women's participation in government institutions at various levels have an impact on this. Solutions oriented on the equalization of women's representation in the numerical sense (which are results of quotas or parities) do not necessarily contribute to the achievement of gender equality in the area of policy (Marta du Vall and Marta Majorek).

The professional situation of women in Poland is analysed in the context of existing legislation indicating the need to preserve equal professional rights. However, the situation of women in the labour market in the period 2000–2012 was unfavourable compared to that of men, which means that labour market realities differ significantly from declarations of gender equality. What could be the reasons for this? Danuta Kopycińska looks for the causes of this in existing traditions and sociocultural norms.

A comparative analysis of the entrepreneurship of men and women shows that women entrepreneurs are a minority in most developed countries; and there is also a negative correlation between the probability of becoming an entrepreneur and female gender. Among entrepreneurs in Poland signs of occupational segregation can be demonstrated – women entrepreneurs run companies mainly in the service sectors, while men dominate in sectors related to the construction, transport and cars (Katarzyna Białek).

Analyses relating to time use show the time allocated to paid and unpaid work among women and men in Poland. As in other countries, these show that the traditional division of labour has been maintained in which men are active in the labour market and women work in the household. If you treat work extensively as paid work performed in the labour market and unpaid in the household, women work much longer than men. Women's workload, both unpaid and paid, requires some skill in order to combine these duties, which translates into innovative solutions (Katarzyna Mroczek, Anna Zachorowska-Mazurkiewicz).

The results of surveys of the profile of men's and women's values, with particular emphasis on creativity, have shown a relative absence of strong polarization of values based on gender, except for two areas. Firstly, overall women rate values more than men, both at the individual and organizational levels. Women give greater importance to personal values and perceive their environment to be more focused on values. Secondly, women give greater importance to creativity, but only at the level of the organization, which may suggest that women perceive their environment as more conducive to creativity than men (Anna Dyląg, Marcin Szafrański).

Regarding attempts to measure the achievements of men and women in science, technology and innovation activity, based on an analysis relating to the limitations and possibilities of using patent information to study gender in the context of technological creativity, it was found that the development of methods to measure the effects of scientific, scientific and technical and innovative activity in its present form does not help in obtaining answers to the question of whether the social roles and relationships between men and women affect creativity and innovation. The effects of the complex process of innovation in terms of gender relations still require a dedicated measurement methodology to be defined which is capable of being performed primarily at the microeconomic level (Rafał Wisła).

Analysis of the patent creativity of women and men in Poland in the years 1999–2013 shows that in the totality of inventors among the Polish population, women conducted approximately three times the growth rate of creative patent activity than men. The patent activity of men and women in Poland shows signs of segregation. Despite the existence of common areas of activity – production of chemicals, chemical products and manmade fibres, and manufacture of food products, beverages and tobacco – in areas such as mining and quarrying of non-energy raw materials or manufacture of leather and leather products there is significant gender segregation. By extending this analysis to countries such as Germany, France, the UK, and Italy in the years 1999–2013, it was determined that the highest average rate of change in all countries analysed the number of women innovators is increasing, with the greatest change in Italy and the smallest in the UK (Tomasz Sierotowicz).

As for the psychological aspects of innovation, analysis referred to the most important psychological factors divided into levels: individual, team, and organisation. It was shown that in the former, impact on innovation activity was displayed by: intelligence, openness to experience, low agreeableness and conscientiousness, and also intrinsic motivation. The factors affecting the team level on the process of innovation include group norms and team composition. Finally, at the organizational level, an important role in the innovation process was played by appropriate leadership, autonomy and workload (Magdalena Jaworek, Anna Dyląg).

Innovation, and thus unconventional solutions, which, however, have found practical application, provide an entrance to and a path to follow in economic development. Among the many features determining the innovation process, gender have not yet been taken into account. This omission has become both a major topic of research in this project, which uses the concept of Innovative Gender, ascribing to women and men equal measure, opportunities and situations included in the model of the innovation genome. Focusing on differences was usually in the studies taken as the basis of claims arising from the different dimensions of gender discrimination, in the Innovative Gender approach there is a basis for the formulation of postulates for process changes, which in creation, implementation and dissemination involve various cooperating teams of men and women belonging to different social groups. And perhaps that is the secret to successful innovation (Ewa Okoń-Horodyńska).

Chapter 1

Gender as a category of analysis in the social sciences

Magdalena Jaworek, Anna Zachorowska-Mazurkiewicz

Abstract

Gender is a broader category than the simple distinction between the sexes – it shows the relationship and the influence of social institutions on perceptions and the development through socialization of femininity and masculinity. The term *gender* is not clearly understood, making it necessary to accurately define the category that will be used in the studies carried out in the framework of the 'Innovative Gender' as a New Source of Progress project. The purpose of this chapter is to develop a definition of gender which can become the basis of the concept of *innovative gender*. To this end, we show the origins of the concept of gender as established in psychology. Then, considerations are transferred to the social sciences, which introduces a new aspect, namely the concepts of gender are shifted to the level of social relations from the previously studied level of the individual. In the social sciences, economics is highlighted, and the opportunities that the introduction to this science of the analysis of gender are opening up.

Key words: gender, psychology, social sciences, economics

Introduction

The term "gender" is not clearly understood, both in society and scientific considerations it appears with numerous interpretations. Gender can be translated as the differentiation between women and men, as the social relations established in the differences between the sexes, or as a set of specific characteristics attributed to individuals. This ambiguity makes it necessary to accurately define the category that will be used in the studies carried out in the framework of the 'Innovative Gender' as a New Source of Progress project. The purpose of this chapter is to develop a definition of gender which can become the basis for the concept of innovative gender.

The first part of the chapter presents the genesis of the concept of gender established in psychology and disseminated by the feminist movement. This section focuses on the achievements of the psychological sciences. In the second section, considerations are transferred to the social sciences, which introduces a new aspect, namely the concepts of gender are shifted to the level of social relations from the previously studied level of the individual. In the social sciences, economics is highlighted, and the opportunities that the introduction to this science of the analysis of gender are opening up. The chapter ends with a short presentation of the research on Innovative Gender and the definition of gender used in this research.

1.1. Gender – genesis[1]

In English, the terms sex and gender can be used interchangeably. However, since the 1970s, thanks to the psychologist Rhoda Unger, the concept of gender in the social sciences and humanities has gone beyond the traditional understanding and taken on a new dimension. Unger recognized that there is a need to distinguish between biologically determined sex, closely related to the characteristics of genital anatomy, sex hormones and chromosomes (sex), and gender, as determined by culture, attributing the word 'gender' that can be used to describe those components of sex that are not associated with human biology, but normally considered masculine or feminine attributes (Unger, 1979).

The need to introduce two separate terms (sex and gender) relating to masculinity and femininity to science has its origins, inter alia, in the approach to research and reflection on gender differences at the turn of the 20th century, often biased to the disadvantage of women. In the field of psychology, it was leading and renowned psychologists, such as Edward Thorndike and Sigmund Freud, who argued in their publications for the inferiority of women to men in intellectual, emotional, moral and physical terms (in: Brannon, 2002, pp. 24–30; Bem, 2000, pp. 63–66). Most researchers drew on biology while claiming this, simultaneously ignoring the issues of education and related cultural factors, or even the interaction between nature and the environment in shaping the individual. Such an approach was, on the one hand, the result of even more unequal relationships between woman and man than is currently the case, and on the other contributed to the strengthening of existing gender stereotypes, as well as the conviction of a clear division between typically female and male roles inherent in nature; there was also a strong argument against the admission of women to fields previously reserved for men, such as politics,[2]

---

1   The concept of gender has grown on the basis of Western culture, hence most of the discussion on this topic in this paper refers to the same cultural background.

2   Women gained the right to vote in 1869 in Wyoming, a year later in Utah, in the United Kingdom women over 30 years of age were given the right to vote in 1918, the same year as women in independent Poland. American women were granted the right to vote two years later. More on how the right to vote was obtained and the development of women's movements, see Sanders, 2001; Ślęczka, 1999; Zachorowska-Mazurkiewicz, 2006.

science,[3] or even sports. On the other hand, increasingly active feminists objected to such a perspective, and the number of women scientists started to grow, challenging the methods and sometimes the validity of the study of gender differences, as well as some of the findings or their interpretation relating to this subject (Shields, 1975; Unger, 1979). In this instance, psychologists made an important contribution: Helen Bradford Thompson and Leta Stetter Hollingworth (in: Benjamin, 2008), whose very diligent research in the early twentieth century undermined the general perception of significant heterogeneity (in favour of the male) between men and women in terms of a variety of physical and psychological factors (speed of learning, motor fatigue, memory, etc.). In the ensuing period of activity of feminist movements and research on the issue of gender differences, attention was also drawn to the limitations and implications posed by the "traditional" division of social roles (Bem, 2000).

For women, the effect of imposing roles due to biology was to block their path to an education, and a further consequence of its exercise in the fields of academia was the belief that they were less intelligent than men and lost valuable energy that should be spent on motherhood.[4] Economists, too, saw a threat to women's maternal functions if they took paid work. Therefore, Pigou and Marshall were supporters of a total ban on the employment of mothers (Pujol, 1995, pp. 20–24; Zachorowska-Mazurkiewicz, 2012, p. 310). Another burning issue which the suffragettes fought in the late nineteenth and early twentieth century was the barring of women's access to politics and the possibility of co-decision on the fate of the country/community in which they lived. It should be noted, however, that the negative consequences of rigidly binding social roles with biological sex lie not just with women. The widespread belief in the superiority of females over males regarding suitability to care for children results in the not always fair judgments of family courts, who in cases of judgments on parental rights entrust the vast majority these to mothers, to the displeasure of some fathers.[5]

The increasing emancipation of women combined with the growing awareness of the obstacles and limitations originating in gender prejudices and stereotypes, often based on the belief of the crucial role of biology in shaping the individual,

---

3   In the UK, the first College for women opened in 1869 in Hitchin, in 1873 in Girton College, Cambridge. However, the degrees awarded to women in Cambridge were equated with the titles awarded to men in 1948. The first German universities began to accept women in 1901. In Poland, the first female students were given the right to participate in classes at the University of Jan Kazimierz Lwów and the Jagiellonian University in Kraków in 1895. However, the latter university did not employ Maria Skłodowska, who was trying to take work in Kraków after graduation in Paris. For more information, see: Sanders, 2001, and Zachorowska-Mazurkiewicz, 2006.

4   E. Clarke's concept, included in his book *Sex in Education* (1873), was supported by H. Spencer, one of the leading philosophers of the second half of the 20th century, or G.S. Hall, acclaimed psychologist, the first president of the American Psychological Association (following: Bem, 2000).

5   Fathers' opposition to judgments in which parental rights are granted mainly to women is reflected in numerous associations and organizations for the rights of the father, e.g. the Central Association and Protection of the Rights of the Child of the Father, Dzielnytata.pl., TataDzieciom. org, Fundacja Ojców Pokrzywdzonych przez Sądy, and many others.

his/her behaviours, attitudes, needs, etc., led to the concept of what is today called 'gender'. In psychology, the term refers primarily to the characteristics and behaviours that in a given culture are seen as suitable for a man or woman (Brannon, 2002, p. 42). The American Psychological Association defines gender more broadly – as acquired characteristics – the attributes, attitudes, social roles and behaviours assigned to boys and men or girls and women by the wider culture (APA, 2013). That set of features will include various aspects of personality such as "masculine" assertiveness and "feminine" passivity, temperament, e.g. "feminine" lability and "masculine" emotional stability, or intelligence. In turn, behaviours relate to how people react in different situations, e.g. aggression in males and female tears. Attributes are defined here as the properties associated with a particular sex, and may refer to psychological traits (above), associated with the physiognomy (breasts for women, beards for men), or objects, such as gender-appropriate clothing and accessories. However, that which stands out as part of gender are the roles assigned to men and women, not because of their individual capabilities, but allied to predispositions – allegedly biologically determined.

The clear division of roles has been tried and tested for millennia in a much less complicated way, though paradoxically – because of the more numerous risks to life and the more difficult circumstances compared with the current, wherein physical strength and endurance (the domain of the male) and "the number of hands" to work, to defend against the enemy or to war (the reproductive function of women) were the basis of existence, representing the survival of the community and the individuals associated with it. Currently, due to social, political, and economic changes, in the age of information and modern technology, in the most developed countries, mental abilities (including the creative thinking underlying innovation) and the 'soft' skills that can earn you high social status and independence take on special value. Gender differences regarding the intellectual capacity of women and men, contrary to the common belief of a large part of scientists from the turn of the previous century, if they even exist (inconsistent research results) are small, and to a greater extent refer to specific abilities (structure of intelligence) than the general intellectual level. The soft skills are acquired and more dependent on personality, not gender, so assigning e.g. caring abilities to women and leadership to men is a mistake, reducing the possibility of individual development. In conclusion, the rigid division of social roles does not have as strong a foundation as in the past, and locking the individual into the framework of biological sex can lead to non-use of their full potential.

It should be noted that the term 'gender' is a relatively fluid concept, depending as it does on changing culture. As over the years the professed system of values changes (e.g. Generations X, Y, Z), the patterns of behaviour associated with this or that role, or age (e.g. passive vs. active lifestyle, the growing number of over-sixties), in the same way it will touch on categories closely associated with culture, such as gender (see Hoffman and Borders research, 2001).

In the psychological literature, there is also the concept of gender identity, which is the identification of oneself as a representative of the female or male

(Brannon, 2001, p. 210).[6] At the beginning of research on gender differences, gender was considered one-dimensional, where one pole meant masculinity, the second – femininity. Any deviation from the biological sex at that time was treated at the same time as a pathology (after: Bem, 2000). The first tool for investigating the level of masculinity-femininity (M-F test) was constructed in the 1930s by Terman and Miles. Further questionnaires examining masculinity and femininity, in terms of the basic assumptions, differed little from their version, treating it one-dimensionally, as one aspect of personality.[7]

In the 70s and 80s, the subject of gender, on a wave of popularity, developed theories in which even the gender dichotomy between male and female was questioned, where the largest contribution was a psychologist Sandra Lipsitz Bem (1974, 1976, 2000). In her view, each unit may have (or claim to) the characteristics of both male and female, and thus fit within one of four groups:
- whose psychological gender is consistent with biological sex ("manly men" – "female women"),
- manifesting characteristics different from their own biological sex ("masculine women" – "feminine men"),
- showing no (or little) of the characteristics of either sex (undifferentiated type/indefinite),
- having characteristics commonly attributed to both men and women (defined as androgynous type).

Such an understanding of gender identity is relatively fixed, and to some extent independent of biological sex, gender identity, or sexual orientation. Table 1.1 contains characteristics that, on the basis of 600 characteristics, as a result of a suitable research procedure, have been assigned to the highest degree of masculinity and femininity. Items which received roughly the same number of points are included in a neutral group (Bem, 1974). The final results are shown in Table 1.1.

It should be noted that the set of defining characteristics of masculinity or femininity fixed by Bem and associates refers only to American culture and a few decades ago. Today, ongoing research is making changes to this list – a good portion of the characteristics decisively attributed to masculinity or femininity are becoming more neutral character (e.g. Hoffman and Borders, 2001). An additional variable to include would be the cultural factor – whether the same features would be assigned to masculinity and femininity by representatives of different countries, nationalities, religions, etc., and how much.

The concept of gender was a simple reaction to the unequal treatment of women next to men, and leading their social function primarily to motherhood, raising children, and taking care of the home. At the same time the role of mother, wife, housekeeper, nanny, were deprecated and/or roles played by men as head/

---

6 In Polish literature the concept functions of psychological gender (e.g. Kuczyńska, 1992, 2002; Szpitalak and Prochwicz, 2013), which seems to be the same as the term *gender identity*.

7 Masculinity-Femininity is one of the dimensions of personality questionnaires examined by, for example, the MMPI (Minnesota Multiphasic Personality Inventory).

Table 1.1. Characteristics assigned to one psychological gender tool using the BSRI (Bem Sex-Role Inventory)

Masculinity	Femininity	Neutral
Independence	Tractability	Willingness to help
Defending their views	Serenity	Sorrow
Confidence in their own strength	Shyness	Conscientiousness
Athleticism	Tenderness	Theatricality
Assertiveness	Adulation	Happiness
Strong personality	Loyalty	Unpredictability
Effectiveness	Femininity	Reliability
Analyticity	Friendliness	Jealousy
Leadership tendencies	Sensitivity to the needs of others	Truthfulness
Willingness to take risks	Forbearance	Mystery
Ease in decision-making	Compassion	Sincerity
Self-sufficiency	The desire to mitigate hurtful feelings	Conceit
Domination	Mild tongued	Pleasant disposition
Masculinity	Warmth	Seriousness
The desire to take a stance	Delicacy	Friendly attitude
Aggressiveness	Naivety	Incompetence
Leadership activities	Childlike	Adaptability
Individualism	Non use of harsh language	Inconsistency
Competition	Love of children	Tact
Ambition	Gentleness	Conventionality

Source: E. Głażewska (2001). "Androgynia – model człowieka XXI wieku," *Annales Universitatis Mariae Curie-Skłodowska*, Lublin – Polonia, Vol. XXVI, No. 2, p. 22.

breadwinner/leader/warrior were elevated.[8] This order was also supported by scientists[9] (mostly men) through not always reliable studies, or misinterpretation of the results. Feminist achievements such as winning the right to vote or ever wider access to education among women and their participation in science, coupled with socioeconomic changes that were favourable for them – a growing demand for professions that did not require physical strength, which allowed some women to taste the independence offered by "their own" money, in addition to stimulating the appetite for better paid and more prestigious jobs (Sanders, 2001; Zachorowska-Mazurkiewicz, 2006). And here again, they encountered resistance

---

8   According to Bem (2000), this is not about the fact that for some reason a gender is better or worse, but the establishment *a priori* of a certain standard, whose determinant is masculinity. Any deviation from this standard is regarded as a departure from the ideal.

9   It should be noted that to this day, science indicates a relatively strong inequality between men and women, see chapters included in this volume.

in obtaining higher and more responsible positions, which in the literature has been called the "glass ceiling."[10]

Psychologists, in the formation of what was already being called gender theory, played a very significant role, undermining of the research related to gender differences, the results of which were usually interpreted in favour of males. In their research on gender they focus on issues related to the essence and causes of the differences in terms of cognitive processes, intelligence, emotions, personality, sexuality, education and upbringing, and even the psychopathology and treatment of mental disorders, as well as functioning in the working environment, and interpersonal relations (see: Brannon, 2002). In this, they pay far more attention than 100–150 years ago to environmental factors in the development and shaping of the individual, with particular emphasis on prejudices and stereotypes, emphasizing the negative consequences of closing the individual within the framework of their role. However, the term gender does not just operate in the field of psychology. Increasingly, it is used in the context of other disciplines.

1.2. The category of gender in the social sciences, with particular emphasis on economics

The concept of gender in the social sciences, as in psychology, is different from the concept of biological sex, and refers to the socially constructed roles, learned behaviours, and expectations of women and men. However, in the social sciences, including economics, gender is interpreted not only as a property of individuals, but also as a social phenomenon (Bradley, 2008, p. 11). Gender is the social importance given to biological differences between the sexes (Ferber, Nelson, 1993, pp. 9-10, for: Dijkstra and Plantega, 2003). By using this term, we focus on the system of social relations that produce the differences between men and women (Klamer, 1992, p. 323, for: Dijkstra and Plantega, 2003). Gender thus refers to a social phenomenon, the processes of creating a socio-cultural models of *femininity* and *masculinity*, and above all, the corresponding patterns of social roles (Klimowicz et al., 2009, p. 14).

Gender refers to the diverse and complex relationships between men and women, including the reproductive system, the division of labour based on gender and cultural definitions of femininity and masculinity. It is to draw attention to the cultural superstructure of biological sex, to the complex of attributes and behaviours expected of men and women and seen as useful in their social functioning (Titkow, 2011, pp. 38–39). The primary function of gender is to articulate the social organization of gender differences. Organization understood as the principles of

---

10 More on this in Titkow (2003).

providing the meaning and scope of these differences, and consequently constituting the rules that define relationships between men and women in a given culture and society (p. 40). Gender is socially constructed, and is used by people as a structuring element of the world they perceive, giving it a specific meaning. A simple statement like "she's a woman," or "he's a man" does not tell us anything about their sex beyond the accepted dimension of biological sex. This meaning of gender has a specific value and is used as a variable in social studies (Bradley, 2008, p. 11–16).

Women and men are different biologically, but all cultures and societies interpret and amend these differences in terms of a set of social expectations of appropriate behaviour and actions taken by them (UNIFEM, 2002, p. 188). The social roles assigned to men and women change over time, are culturally conditioned, and depend on ethnicity, religion, education, class, and the geographical, economic and political environments. Thus gender specifies a set of attributes and behaviours expected by society from men and women and builds their social identity (Klimowicz et al., 2009, p. 14). These expectations are translated into law, access to resources, and power relations between men and women. While societies differ in terms of expectations for women and men, in all there is an asymmetry, which is well established, but not static (UNIFEM, 2002, p. 188). Being a social construct, gender is not fixed, it is variable and depends on time, place and culture. Since the concept of gender includes all those features of men and women which are changeable and vary depending on social context, it thus contains everything that is variable and socially determined (Titkow, 2011, p. 41). Gender must be understood dynamically as a social practice, constantly created and reconstructed through the activities of women and men, as well as social institutions such as family, welfare state, and the labour market (Daly and Rake, 2003, p. 37, cited in: Warzywoda-Kruszyńska and Bunio-Mroczek, 2011). One of the most important contemporary changes is due to community of experience of women and men, the similarity of the resources available, and the roles they perform. The result is a multiplicity of images of women and men, which – when it comes to identity – can no longer be considered as typically masculine or feminine elements, and begin to be seen as common[11] (Siemieńska, 2011, p. 197).

If gender is the product of humanity and the social structures and relationships it has created, the status quo can be changed. But in order to change them, you first have to know the "content" of gender (Titkow, 2011, p. 41). Gender is deeply rooted in social institutions such as the family, the labour market, the media, the education system, and so on. Therefore, in order to bring about a change in the character of the relationship between the sexes, it is not enough to change the individual attitudes of specific people – you have to influence the social impact of the institution (Anderson and Collins, 1998, p. 83, for: Warzywoda-Kruszyńska and Bunio-Mroczek, 2011). Gender is the term for a theoretical perspective,

---

11 This is changing in part, the specificity of the roles previously considered separate for men and women is blurring in the awareness and at the behavioural level, making them androgynous (Siemieńska, 2011, p. 197).

a source of the instruments needed for the analysis of socio-political phenomena and their transformation (Titkow, 2011, p. 37). Gender differences contain a hierarchy, and since gender is a relational term, which refers to the interaction between male and female roles, the study of one gender automatically entails study of the other (Barker, 1999, p. 391). Therefore, according to Anna Titkow (2011, p. 37) the category of gender is synonymous with the theoretical revolution in the manner of research not only of the situation of women, but of the whole of social life. Gender becomes a major category only when we examine the relationship between women and men, as well as the world of wider relationships, in which their lives take place (Bradley, 2008, p. 16).

Economics as one of the social sciences, opened up to the category of gender relatively recently, as a result, inter alia, of historical conditions.[12] The origins of economics as a scientific discipline are directly related to the creation and development of the capitalist system. Production processes then shifted from households to factories and converted to for-profit activities with the use of hired labour. The main focus of economics was considered to be the relationship between economic agents (England, 1993). This historically evolved tendency to focus exclusively on the relationship between the people in the market led to the complete omission of productive and reproductive work done free of charge for households, local communities, the non-profit sector, and the public, and therefore to miss the economic role of women (Albelda, 1997, pp. 160–161).

Some of the first economists dealing with issues related to gender are Gary Becker, Jacob Mincer and Soloman Polachek. In considerations called "new household economics," they worked on the production, marriage, divorce, fertility and the division of labour between the genders. According to their model, men have a comparative advantage in the labour market, while women in activities related to raising children and running the household. These advantages are partly due to biological conditions, and partly to the different experiences (Becker, 1981). Their consequence, however, are lower investment in human capital made by women, and lower wages for their work (Mincer and Polachek, 1974). The models developed by Becker, Mincer and Polachek certainly bring gender into mainstream economics (neoclassical economics), but based on stereotypical assumptions. This approach contributes to an incomplete understanding of gender relations in the economy, but also in society. For a better understanding of these relationships, gender would appear to be a useful category. The use of the category of gender in economic analyses enables us to extend the understanding of economic processes and the operation of institutions by exploring ways to develop opportunities by people, their choices and limitations, which are affected by diverse and often conflicting factors. Exploring the ways of constructing universal categories can help in discovering methods to create and reproduce the social hierarchy and inequality (Barker, 1999, p. 395).

Both mainstream economic theory and the economic policy based on it, despite the fact that they appear to be neutral on grounds of gender, in fact, favour men.

---

12 For more information, see Zachorowska-Mazurkiewicz, 2011.

This is because the concepts, theories and methodologies neutral in terms of gender often hide, naturalise, and protect the privileges of one of them. An illustration of this is the persistent pay gap between men and women. In neoclassical economics, this phenomenon is explained by the rational decisions of women. An analysis that takes into account the category of gender includes the social expectations of women and men. Women are seen as wives and mothers, and this in turn affects their employment decisions (Barker, 1999, p. 391). Critical economy, constituting an alternative to the mainstream, opens the possibility of developing theory and economic policies taking into account gender relations. The critical perspective in economics easily engages in an analysis of gender inequalities at the micro level. However, most progressive economists, despite the fact they view individual market participants by their gender (especially in the case of the analyses of households), do not define the market itself in a similar way, or relationships in companies, although both companies and the market can operate in a way that is particularly restrictive or unfair to women (Elson, 1994, p. 38–39). The monetary economy cannot grow without the unpaid contribution shaped by the structure of gender relations, which is ignored in macroeconomic aggregates (p. 40). Thus, information on production for their one's own needs, informal paid work, work for the household, as well as the work of volunteers, is essential for understanding the economy as a whole and the changes taking place within it (MacDonald, 1995, p. 164).

1.3. Instead of a conclusion – InnoGend and a definition of gender

'Innovative Gender' as a New Source of Progress (InnoGend) is a study designed to demonstrate the link between gender, the roles assigned to women and men in society, and the processes of creativity and innovation. The research aims to answer the question of whether gender translates into creativity and innovation, what are the symptoms, and whether state policy by supporting creativity and innovation processes actually take all these aspects into account. If the policy to promote creativity and innovation is neutral on grounds of gender, is it because gender does not play a role in these processes, or rather that the impact of gender is skipped? Understanding the relationship between gender, and creativity and innovation of women and men, and the influence of the state may be helpful in promoting progress and may even point to its new source.

Policies promoting creativity and innovation are gender-neutral. However, this neutrality may not correspond to actual relationships. If women's and men's innovation and creativity manifests itself in different ways, and a model based on only one gender is taken as a template, this assumed neutrality leads to the domination of one gender only, leaving the other in the shade, or even introducing obstacles to the process of creating innovation. If certain manifestations of innovation are made difficult, this will no doubt affect economic growth and development. Support for non-obvious manifestations of creativity and innovation may produce a comparative advantage, contribute to the progress of civilization, and also promote equality between the sexes.

The aspects to be highlighted as particularly important in the concept of gender are:
- gender is not only a property of individuals, but also a social phenomenon,
- gender is the social meanings attributed to the biological differences between the sexes,
- it is the cultural superstructure on biological sex, a complex of attributes and behaviours expected of women and men and perceived as useful in their social functioning,
- social roles assigned to women and men vary over time,
- the concept of gender includes all those features of men and women which are changeable and vary depending on social context, and thus contains everything that is variable and socially determined,
- gender is deeply rooted in social institutions and social mentality, often unconsciously, and is thus not subject to any reflection,
- gender differences contain a hierarchy, and because gender is a relational term, referring to the interaction the of male and female roles, studying one sex entails also studying the other,
- gender to some extent determines the life choices regarding education, occupation, and interests, which may impede or prevent the realization of the individual's potential,
- it determines the direction of education and socialization, sets social standards, and contributes to the strengthening of stereotypes and prejudices leading to discrimination.

Therefore, our proposed definition is:

Gender is a time-variable social phenomenon, constituting the superstructure of biological sex, which is reduced to a set of traits, behaviours, attitudes, roles and attributes assigned by the wider culture to one sex and expected by society, appropriately from a woman or a man, as well as the closely related relationships between them, which includes a hierarchy. Gender is rooted in social institutions, which translates on the one hand into a lack of awareness, and on the other to its variability over time. Rooting gender in the social mentality, and its frequent unconsciousness, means that the average individual does not give this category any deeper reflection or consideration. The status quo is considered to be the norm, and the attempt to change it raises a general fear and resistance, just as feminist circles' fight in the mid-19th century to grant women the right to vote.

Gender research is not easy to carry out. In the first stage, we can just look for information on the activity of men and women in a specific area. However, reaching such information is not always easy. Data sets may not present data disaggregated by gender, because this element could have been considered negligible at the stage of building the study. The absence of women (or men), however, may be due to social relations which statistics do not show. Thus selection of appropriate research methods is important, although it is not the only problem. Gender is a category that shows the relationship and the influence of social institutions on perceptions and the development through socialization of femininity and masculinity. The perception of such links is difficult, because it requires the researcher to understanding a relationship of which they are part.

Literature

Albelda, R. (1997), _Economics & Feminism; Disturbances in the Field_, New York: Twayne Publishers.
Anderson, M., Collins P. H. (1998), _Race, Class and Gender: An Anthology_, Belmont: WadsWorth.
APA (American Psychological Association), http://www.apa.org/topics/sexuality/transgender. aspx?item=2 [accessed 28.12.2013].
Barker, D.K. (1999), "Gender," [in:] J. Peterson, M. Lewis (eds.), _The Elgar Companion to Feminist Economics_, Cheltenham, Northampton: Edward Elgar.
Becker, G.S. (1981), _A Treatise on the Family_, Cambridge: Harvard University Press.
Bem, S.L., Martyna, W., Watson, C. (1976), "Sex typing and androgyny. Father explorations of the expressive domain," _Journal of Personality and Social Psychology_, No. 34, pp. 1016–1023.
Bem, S.L. (2000), _Męskość – kobiecość. O różnicach wynikających z płci_, Gdańsk: Gdańskie Wydawnictwo Psychologiczne.
Bem, S.L. (1974), "The measurement of psychological androgyny," _Journal of Consulting and Clinical Psychology_, No. 42, pp. 155–162.
Benjamin, L.T., Jr. (2008), _Historia współczesnej psychologii_, Warszawa: Wydawnictwo Naukowe PWN.
Bradley, H. (2008), _Płeć_, Warszawa: Wydawnictwo Sic!.
Brannon, L. (2002), _Psychologia rodzaju. Kobiety i mężczyźni: podobni czy różni?_ Gdańsk: Gdańskie Wydawnictwo Psychologiczne, pp. 24–30.
Callamard, A. (2001), _Metodologia badań nacechowanych wrażliwością na społeczno-kulturową tożsamość płci_, Warszawa: Amnesty International Polska.
Daly, M., Rake, K. (2003), _Gender and the Welfare State. Care, Work and Welfare in Europe and the USA_, Cambridge: Polity Press.
Dijkstra, G.A., Plantega, J. (2003), _Ekonomia i płeć. Pozycja zawodowa kobiet w Unii Europejskiej_, Gdańsk: Gdańskie Wydawnictwo Psychologiczne.
Elson, D. (1994), "Micro, meso, macro: Gender and economic analysis in the context of policy reform," [in:] I. Baker (ed.), _The Strategic Silence: Gender and Economic Policy_, London: Zed Books, pp. 33–45.
England, P. (1993), "The separative self: Androcentric bias in neoclassical assumptions," [in:] M.A. Ferber, J.A. Nelson (eds.), _Beyond the Economic Man: Feminist Theory and Economics_, Chicago: University of Chicago Press.
Ferber, M., Nelson, J.A. (1993), "Introduction: The social construction of economics and the social construction of gender," [in:] M.A. Ferber, J.A. Nelson (eds.), _Beyond Economic Man: Feminist Theory and Economics_, Chicago, London: University of Chicago Press.
Głażewska, E. (2001), "Androgynia – model człowieka XXI wieku," _Annales Universitatis Mariae Curie-Skłodowska_, Lublin – Polonia, Vol. XXVI, No. 2, pp. 17–28.
Hoffman, R.M., Borders, L.D-A. (2001), "Twenty-five years after the Bem SEX-Role Inventory: A reassessment and new issues regarding classification variability," _Measurement and Evaluation in Counselling and Development_, No. 34, pp. 39–55.

Klamer, A. (1992), "Commentary," [in:] N. de Marchi (ed.), *Post-Popperian Methodology of Economics*, Boston: Kluwer Scientific Publishers.

Klimowicz, M., Pacześniak, A., Wiktorska-Święcka, A. (2009), *Płeć w społeczeństwie, ekonomii i polityce*, Toruń: Wydawnictwo Adam Marszałek.

Kuczyńska, A. (1992), *Inwentarz do oceny płci psychologicznej. Podręcznik*, Warszawa: Pracownia Testów Psychologicznych PTP.

Kuczyńska, A. (2002), "Płeć psychologiczna idealnego i rzeczywistego partnera życiowego oraz jej wpływ na jakość realnie utworzonych związków," *Przegląd Psychologiczny*, No. 4 (45), pp. 385–399.

MacDonald, M. (1995), "Feminist economics: From theory to research," *Canadian Economics Association*, XXVIII, No. 1, pp. 159–176.

Mincer, J., Polachek, S. (1974), "Family investments in human capital," *Journal of Political Economy*, No. 82, pp. 76–108.

Nelson, J.A. (1992), "Gender, metaphor, and the definition of economics," *Economics & Philosophy*, No. 8, pp. 103–125.

Nelson, J.A. (1995), "Feminism and economics," *Journal of Economic Perspectives*, Vol. 9, No. 2, Spring, pp. 131–148.

Pujol, M. (1995), "Into the margin," [in:] E. Kuiper, J. Sap, S. Feiner, N. Ott, Z. Tzannatos (eds.), *Out of the Margin: Feminist Perspectives on Economics*. London and New York: Routledge, pp. 20–24.

Sanders, V. (2001), "First wave feminism," [in:] *The Routledge Companion to Feminist and Postfeminism*, London and New York: Routledge, pp. 16–28.

Shields, S.A. (1975). "Functionalism, Darwinism, and the psychology of woman: A study in social myth," *American Psychologist*, No. 30, pp. 852–857.

Siemieńska, R. (2011), "Kontrakt płci. Między sfera prywatną i publiczną," [in:] K. Slany, J. Struzik, K. Wojnicka (eds.), *Gender w społeczeństwie polskim*, Kraków: Nomos, pp. 196–224.

Strassmann, D. (1999), "Feminist economics," [in:] J. Peterson, M. Lewis (eds.), *The Elgar Companion to Feminist Economics*, Cheltenham: Edward Elgar, pp. 360–373.

Szpitalak, M., Prochwicz, K. (2013), "Płeć psychologiczna osób z depresją kliniczną. Doniesienia wstępne," *Psychiatria Polska*, Vol. XLVII, No. 1, pp. 53–64.

Ślęczka, K. (1999), *Feminizm*, Katowice: Książnica.

Titkow, A. (ed.) (2003), *Szklany sufit; bariery i ograniczenia karier kobiet*, Warszawa: ISP.

Titkow, A. (2011), "Kategoria płci kulturowej jako instrumentarium badawcze i źródło wiedzy o społeczeństwie," [in:] K. Slany, J. Struzik, K. Wojnicka (eds.), *Gender w społeczeństwie polskim*, Kraków: Nomos, pp. 36–56.

Unger, R.K. (1979). "Toward a redefinition of sex and gender," *American Psychologist*, No. 34, pp. 1085–1094.

UNIFEM (2002), *Gender Budget Initiatives: Strategies, Concepts, and Experiences*, Brussels: UNIFEM.

Warzywoda-Kruszyńska, W., Bunio-Mroczek, P. (2011), "Gender w badaniach nad welfare state. Wyzwanie dla polskiej socjologii," [in:] K. Slany, J. Struzik, K. Wojnicka (eds.), *Gender w społeczeństwie polskim*, Kraków: Nomos, pp. 162–173.

Zachorowska-Mazurkiewicz, A. (2006), *Kobiety i instytucje. Kobiety na rynku pracy w Stanach Zjednoczonych, Unii Europejskiej i w Polsce*, Katowice: Śląsk.

Zachorowska-Mazurkiewicz, A. (2011), "Kobiecość i męskość w teorii ekonomii," [in:] B. Bartosz (ed.), *Kobiecość i męskość – komunikacja, relacje, społeczeństwo*, Warszawa: Eneteia, pp. 373–386.

Zachorowska-Mazurkiewicz, A. (2012), "Dobrobyt w ujęciu ekonomii feministycznej," [in:] U. Zagóra-Jonszta (ed.), *Dokonania współczesnej myśli ekonomicznej. Teoretyczne ujęcie dobrobytu. Studia Ekonomiczne 101*, Katowice: Uniwersytet Ekonomiczny, pp. 308–316.

Chapter 2

Gender in economics

Danuta Tomczak

Abstract

The severe consequences of the economic crisis of 2007/2008 – caused by the expansion of financial sector, high risk exposure and over-dimensioned speculation – call for a new economic design. The intense search for appropriate solutions opens space for innovative ideas for smart and fair socioeconomic progress. The increasing participation of women in the economy and society is real, revealing unexploited gains which sophisticated mathematical models cannot grasp. The aim of this paper is to show how a gender approach in economics reveals new reserves and incentives for development – at the local and global levels. The research question is how gender equality contributes to achieving these results. The Norwegian experience is used here as a case study. It shows the development of gender equality in Norway from a historical perspective, its challenges both before and now, and finally, the positive results it has produced, by comparison with selected European countries and the US. "Economic citizenship" – one's own income and access to paid work/self-employment and thus participation in decision making (in politics & business) are the main pillars of equality in Norway.

Key words: gender, economics, equality, Norway

2.1. Which problems in a global economy need serious response?

2.1.1. The increasing marketization of the economy and society: What is a good society?

Michael Sandel's book *What Money Can't Buy. The Moral Limits of Markets* (2013b) raises the problem of the monetization of our lives, where human values are converted into commodities and given a value in money (surrogate mothers, organs for transplantation, blood).

> The classical economists, going back to Adam Smith, conceived of economics as a branch of moral and political philosophy. But the version of economics commonly taught today presents itself as an autonomous discipline, one that does not pass judge-

ments on how income should be distributed or how this or that good should be valued. The notion that economics is a value-free science has always been questionable. But the more markets extend their reach into noneconomic aspects of life, the more entangled they become with moral questions (Sandel, 2013b, p. 122).

The modern capitalist economy is a market economy, with variation in the operation of the market mechanism; nevertheless, there are limits to markets' expansion into other spheres of life and society, which should not be managed by markets. A good society does not have a price. Life is not a commodity.

Sandel's lecture and the discussion raised about the question of "money and morality" can be followed on the web (http://www.justiceharvard.org/2012/08/st-pauls-institute-join-the-debate-video), where the subject – the role of money and markets in a good society – is the main issue. Many scholars and citizens share Sandel's view questioning the advancing commercialization of public and private life in a modern society and concluding that it should be limited.

2.1.2. Growing inequality – income and wealth disparities

Thomas Piketty in his book – *Capital in the Twenty-First Century* (French edition 2013; English translation 2014) raises the question of the sharply growing inequality in liberalised 21st-century capitalism, where the share of capital income in GDP is steady increasing while the labour income shrinks. His conclusions apply to many countries, as OECD, PIIE, and World Bank reports confirm. Piketty analyses historical changes in income and wealth in the 19th and 20th centuries and attempts to find an answer as to why economics has failed to alter this rising trend in inequality.

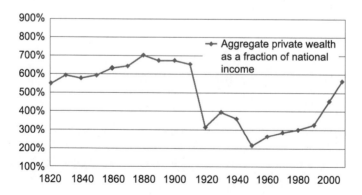

Figure 2.1. Wealth-income ratio in France 1820–2008
Source: Th. Piketty (2010), "On the long run evolution of inheritance: France 1820–2050," *PSE Working Papers*, September, Appendix.

What have we learned from this paper? In our view, the main contribution of this paper is to demonstrate empirically and theoretically that there is nothing inherent in the structure of modern economic growth that should lead to a long run decline of inherited (non-human) wealth relative to labour income. The fact that the "rise of human capital" is to a large extent an illusion should not come as a surprise to macroeconomists. With stable capital shares and wealth-income ratios, the simple arithmetic of growth and wealth accumulation is likely to operate pretty much in the same way in the future as it did in the past. In particular, the r>g logic implies that past wealth and inheritance are bound to play a key role in the future (Piketty, 2010, p. 78).

2.2.3. The disparity of economic theory and policy – competing schools and lobbyists

Krugman in his publications and comments in the NYT has often criticized economic policies that have been recommended and applied as dogmatic solutions, not appropriate for solving the severe problems of national economies in crisis. He has questioned the austerity 'packages', served up by the EU and IMF for Greece and Spain, and other dominant practices, like inflation targeting in monetary policies. The point here is a critique of simplified universal solutions which do not work properly in economies with different structures, conditions and problems. So the conclusion is: less textbook – more local knowledge in designing goal-determined policies. Comment to Paul Krugman "Why Economics failed:" "It's not that economics failed. It's that the cult of Mammon succeeded," writes one of the student bloggers (NYT, 2.05.2014).

2.1.4. A shrinking labour force supply – aging societies

Most of the developed economies are experiencing aging– fewer births, and higher life expectancy – which creates a gap for balancing labour market participation and state budget balances. Figure 2.2 illustrates the projection for Norway, but the trend is similar for other countries, as are the problems it creates.

These four selected problems are important drawbacks of contemporary capitalism. They will serve here as the backdrop for a search for new sources of progress, upgrading of societies and individuals' well-being, better micro and macro management mechanisms, and similar.

How can solutions be found for improving the competitiveness of national economies, which makes society better off and more effective? One of the possible paths is the gender approach, comprising the behaviour and choices of individuals, groups and public institutions in societies which vary because of different gender-related attitudes. In the functioning models of a market economy in diverse societies, "gendered solutions" are expected to bring interesting results.

Accordingly, the concept of economics as a value-neutral science seems somewhat implausible in this context. Human behaviour and choices are based on

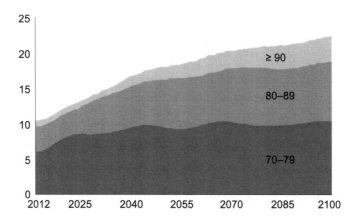

Figure 2.2. People over 70 years old – projection 2012–2100 for Norway, as a percentage of population
Source: Statistics Norway: http://www.ssb.no/a/publikasjoner/pdf/oa_201204/brunborg3.pdf [accessed May 2014].

values, so the study of selected problems from a gender perspective will enhance an interdisciplinary and normative approach to economics. The research questions in this chapter will concentrate on gender as a factor contributing to the solution of the current economic dilemmas such as the examples mentioned above.

2.2. Why does gender matter?

2.2.1. Gender: what it is and what it isn't

There is no intention to discuss definitions here, just a short ingress to avoid confusion. As the term "gender," from the Latin "genus," has a parallel word in only a few languages, it is translated by the expression "the state of being male or female," which is not a precise expression, as it does not say what factors constitute "the state of being" a man or a woman in a given society. Quite often "gender" is misunderstood and/or associated with radical feminism, which obviously does not apply here. Gender as a research subject is – in the author's understanding – concerned with **how men and women,** individuals and groups, **perform and contribute,** due to their capabilities, roles and positions in a society/functioning economic system, to achieve the best results. These individuals, groups and institutions always function in real socio-political structures.

Gender refers to the cultural and social attitudes that together shape and sanction "female" and "male:" behaviour – networking – experience and more, so it – per definition – brings a new value-based dimension into scientific disciplines, economics included. The "economic value" of the "gendered approach" is a better use of a society's resources. Let's start with labour market participation.

2.2.2. Labour market participation and self-employment – a gender gap

There is clear evidence that the GDP growth and use of all available and capable labour are closely correlated. National economies where the rates of female employment are high achieve higher growth rates, dynamic increases in GDP per capita, and rising welfare. Groups which are not fully represented in the labour market, i.e. the unemployed, are quite often the young and elderly people and women, which means that potential macroeconomic gains are not attained (Elborgh-Woytek et al., 2013).

How well or badly the potential of women's employment has been exploited is illustrated in Figure 2.3 (OECD, 2014) by the gap in employment of male and female labour. The gender employment gap has been reduced between 1992 and 2012, which is positive, but there are still examples of countries where the gap is between 30–40%, which reflects a social structure typical for a century ago, but not today. Thus, gender mainstreaming is a source of potential socioeconomic gains in many countries. A close look at the disparities illustrated by the Figure 2.3 asks for an explanation of what the reasons might be for the spread from 3% to 40%. Therefore, it is recommended to review "the best cases."

The questions following the data in Figure 2.3 are many, but in this paper I will concentrate on two:

1. what are the main factors generating differentiated "gendered" labour market participation,
2. what is the advantage of the gender inclusion potential in a national economy.

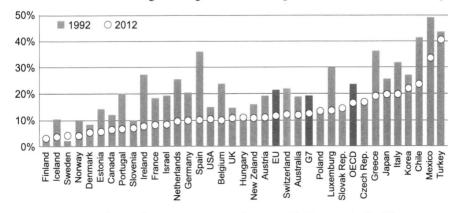

Figure 2.3. The gender employment gap 1992 and 2012 in OECD countries (in %)
Source: OECD estimates based on Labour Force Statistics, OECD report *All on Board: Make the Inclusive Growth Happen*, OECD 2014, p. 30; http://www.oecd.org/inclusive-growth/All-on-Board-Making-Inclusive--Growth-Happen.pdf [accessed July 2014].

The working hypothesis is that gender equality is the main factor contributing to the above presented differences in gender employment gaps, therefore the theory and practice of gender equality should be analysed thoroughly. This hypothesis comes from a very simple relationship: the top four countries with the lowest gender employment gap – Finland, Iceland, Sweden and Norway are also the four with the best ranking in the global gender gap index, which suggests that the Nordic model has gender promoting features.

2.3. Gender equality

2.3.1. Gender equity and gender equality – different meanings

The terminology used by European Union institutions will be applied here. Accordingly, gender equity is defined as fairness of treatment by gender – rights, benefits, opportunities, obligations – and is also known as equal treatment. Gender equality is more than equal treatment, it is the freedom to develop personal abilities for all humans, without the limitations set by adopted or inherited gender roles.

The above definition does not give a common understanding of what gender equality is and how it is practised, so the point of departure has to be the formulation of the relevant topics to be considered:

a) formal equal rights for men and women,
b) access to education,
c) family, marriage and child-care rights and obligations,
d) employment and "economic citizenship,"
e) political social participation.

Historical perspective, ethnicity, social position – all give a different picture of the state of affairs in a given society.

2.3.2. Gender equality – an accord of theory and practice

Gender equality – as the above formulation points out – has many dimensions, not all measurable and not all transparent to disclose. Therefore it is important to state that gender equality here should not be mixed up with the sex-based roles of males and females in a society. Gender – not biology and sex roles – is the subject of study in this discourse.

The theoretical framework for gender equality comprises sociology, law, political science and economics, so it is, as Nancy Fraser formulates, "a bridge discourse" (Fraser, 1989), where scientific deliberations often intersect with political regulation and family structures. Scientific studies alone do not provide an answer to how human needs evolve and who or what shapes citizens' needs – family, clan, religion, organizations, state or market – and what justice and equality really is or should be. Governments use experts and set up commissions before drawing up legislation, so in practice scientific discourses make a framework for policy formulation (Roman, 2008, p. 103). Which policy topics are regarded as essential will, naturally, depend on the functioning economic system and political priorities, determined by place and time.

Each decade has had its "flagship-issues" – equality has been one of these since the 1960s, but the focus has changed. At the beginning wage earners were the group of concern, so "state feminism" and radical emancipation was prioritized in the 1970s–1980s, followed by gender equality and equal opportunities for men and women. The focus on family and new family policy was developed in the 1990s, where attention was switched to the economic independence of women: the model of "dual breadwinner" and the concept of "economic citizenship" were on the agenda (Carlsson-Wetterberg and Melby, 2008). Economic independence became a key issue. In the countries where these targets have almost been accomplished the equality issue changed focus again – towards equal participation of men and women in decision making and to ethnicity and disability as prejudices to be tackled. It is important to emphasise that the conceptualisation of equality differs by country and changes with time (Carlsson-Wetterberg and Melby, 2008, p. 56).

The increasing economic inequality in recent decades is especially challenging for forming counterbalance procedures, and advocating access to equality for all disadvantaged groups and individuals. A successful approach towards all aspects of equality requires broad social support, well-functioning public institutions and strong government. Well-functioning institutions are crucial for achieving positive policy results.

2.3.3. Gender equality in Europe/EU

European countries have a long record of progress towards common rights for all citizens, improving step by step since the French Revolution of 1789. In the post-war period equality was legitimised for the group of countries in the Treaty of Rome in 1957. The European Commission now has a work programme on gender equality for 2010–2015, where policies include following thematic priorities:
   – equal economic independence for women and men,
   – equal pay for work of equal value,
   – equality in decision-making,
   – dignity, integrity and ending gender-based violence,
   – promoting gender equality beyond the EU,
   – horizontal issues (gender roles, including the role of men, legislation and governance.

What the portrait of European equality looks like in statistics is clearly illustrated on the interactive map of the EU 34, EEA and candidate countries, where the data presented have been collected for 2010/2011. In Table 2.1 a sample of four indicators for nine countries have been selected to view the differences.

Table 2.1. Selected equality indicators 2010/2011; all numbers in percentage

Country	Women rate of employment	Women in tertiary education	Women in supervisory boards	Pay gap on equal position
Norway	73.4	32.1	42	16.0
Sweden	71.8	34.6	25	15.8
Denmark	70.4	31.3	16	16.0
Finland	67.4	37.9	28	19.4
Germany	67.7	21.5	16	23.1
UK	64.5	34.0	16	19.5
Poland	53.1	24.4	12	9.8
Serbia	38.3	11.6	16	–
Turkey	28.8	11.3	11	–

Source: EC http://ec.europa.eu/justice/gender-equality/equality-pays-off/spotlight-on-your-country/ index_en.htm [accessed June 2014].

As Scandinavian countries attain the top ranking in gender equality and several other international comparisons, it is plausible to analyse more closely why gender equality became important and how it has been built up and shaped. Norway will serve here as a case study.

2.4. Norway – a gender equality trendsetter

2.4.1. Historical reflections: what has happened since 1913

In 2013 the 100-year anniversary of voting rights for women was celebrated, so much space was naturally devoted to debates on the evolution of equality – from non-discrimination towards equal treatment and to discussions on various dimensions of "real" equality. The Ministry of Equality, Children and Inclusion prepared a report for the Parliament (Stortinget) for this occasion (Meld-St.44, 2012–2013) with the reflective title: "Gender equality does not come by itself"! The report states:
  a) gender equality is beneficial,
  b) it does not happen "naturally,"
  c) government and public institutions must act,
  d) Norwegian society supports strongly the concept of equality,
  e) new challenges come up all the time, so the process is not over.
  To grasp the different dimensions of gender equality, three main categories have been selected:
  1) Democracy – political rights, political participation – decision making.
  2) Family policy – rights to inherit, public child care and care for the elderly, sharing of duties.
  3) Labour market participation – access, flexibility, rights to equal pay and career.

Table 2.2. The progress of gender equality in Norway – selected events

1884	1913	1915	1930	1950/ 1997	1966	1975	1978/ 2013	1993
Women's society established	Voting rights to all citizens	New family law	Maternity leave	Convention on equal pay adopted	Social security law	Abortion law	Gender equality law	Fully paid maternity leave 42 weeks
1900	**1921**	**1945**	**1946**	**1964**	**1970**	**1978**	**1986**	**2009**
30% women employed	First female member of Parliament	First female minister	Children allowance	Public care work law	32% women employed	Fathers right to paternity leave	8 (of 18) women in government	Right to kindergarten

Source: own selection of data from Meld-St.44, 2012–2013.

Education is not shown in Table 2.2 due to the limited space, but, of course, it plays an important role in gender equality progress and will be addressed later.

2.4.2. Welfare state – a key to equality in the Nordic model concept

The role of the state in the economy has been contested since the 1980s, when liberal economic theories (Hayek, 2006) spread from country to country, fostering privatization of public property, supporting individual freedom, free movements of capital, and downscaling state interventions in the economy and society. This process has brought about a Copernicus-like revolution in the capitalist market economy – the gravitation centre has been relocated from factory/corporation – the central operation unit in classic capitalism – to the financial market, the centre of the economic system today (Davis, 2009, p. 5). This individualisation of society has changed the former functions of the state; many of these functions have been privatized, outsourced or disbanded.

In Scandinavia this process of state power pulverisation has been less intense, due to strong community feeling, common responsibility and a high level of trust within the society and towards the state and public institutions. The "citizen-friendly" Nordic model, with its emphasis on full employment, fairness, and a generous welfare system, was the main factor contributing to the maximization of women's economic independence (Esping-Andersen, 1999). There is no doubt that appropriate policy has been decisive in terms of results.

The Scandinavian model of the economy is not uniform; solutions in each Nordic country differ and have also changed in the recent years, due to conservative parties' entry to government offices. What do they have in common and what is important? Work for all: a high rate of employment both men and women, strong public institutions – both central and local, mutual trust among citizens and between citizens and institutions.

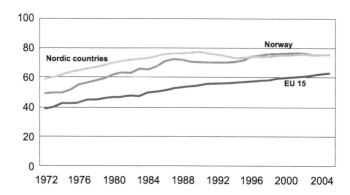

Figure 2.4. Female labour participation: Nordic countries and EU 15
Source: Norges Bank, http://www.norges-bank.no/pages/60251/EN/charts-2007-02-15.pdf [accessed April 2014].

The Norwegian welfare state offers a full salary under sickness for up to one year, 12 days of paid leave for a sick child, a minimum social security pension for all residents, child benefits for all inhabitants, a guaranteed place in kindergarten at a fixed price (approx. 400 USD per month), free access to all education, tertiary included, scholarship & study loans, also for studies abroad, free public health care and more.

2.4.3. Gender equality – economic independence

As already mentioned, "economic citizenship" has been an important issue in gender equality discourse and demonstrated itself over the years of women's struggle for:
- equal status in marriage (custody, right to inherit, valuation of unpaid housework to pension,
- right to full time work (parental leave, child care system – kindergarten & after school activities),
- equal pay for equal work,
- access to education and system of promotion to higher positions.

Economic independence is directly linked to paid work and own income. Here both law and collective institutional solutions have helped to progress towards the target – especially right to get/obligation for municipalities to offer – a kindergarten place for children when a family applies, the joint responsibility of father and mother for childcare in the family (divided parental leave for mother and father). The income gap is still present, mainly due to the part-time jobs undertaken by women and professions/positions held. Increasing migration brings new challenges to equality, triggered by ethnic diversity, religion and controversies on what means are proper for assimilation and integration into Norwegian society (Pringle, 2008). Also horizontal and vertical gender segregation in the labour market persists.

The statistical overview of gender equality in Norway is presented in the Appendix.

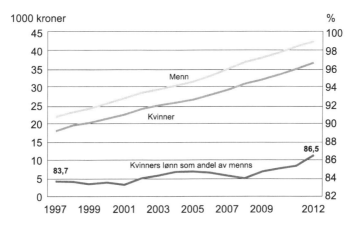

Figure 2.5. Average gross month income (left: in 1000 of NOK, right: in percentage)
Source: Central Statistical Office of Norway, May 2014.

2.4.4. Political participation and integration in civil society

Rights – civil, political and social – are complementary. Civil rights – such as individual freedom, freedom of religion, the right to own property, the right to work and "… follow the occupation of one's choice and the place of one's choice …" (Marshall, 1950, p. 10) – create opportunities, but it is not obvious whether and how these opportunities are exploited. Norwegian women, well backed by a public institutional framework and networks, have utilized their opportunities and entered the public arena. A few numbers may illustrate this:

Table 2.3. Division of power in Poland and Norway 2014 (in percentage)

Members	Parliament 2014		Government 2014		Central Bank Executive Board	
	PL	N	PL	N	PL	N
Men	76	60	84	50	80	67
Women	24	40	16	50	20	33

Source: own data selection from official statistics.

2.4.5. Equality in decision making – controversy over a quota-based system

Favouring certain social groups, for some reason neglected or discriminated, is always controversial, because there is no consensus as to what "equal status" actually means. It can relate to equality of opportunity, living conditions, type of work, the amount of allowances received, salaries and incomes, i.e. different aspects of the functioning social order.

The long-lasting traditional forms of distortion in employment and payment between men and women forced the government to a radical move – promoting women to managerial positions by introducing gender quotas:

- Minimum 40% representatives of each sex on the boards of public limited liability companies; passed by the parliament (Storting) in 2003, put into effect January 1, 2006.
- Favouring the employment of women in positions with male domination, if the female candidate has the same qualifications as the male one (e.g. professors in universities, directors in large institutions).
- Regarding gender quotas – not introduced up to now - in electoral tickets (right now each political party has its own "equality policy").

Norway was the first country to introduce gender quotas in all public limited liability company boards, which provoked many protests and debates questioning the legality of gender quotas. Before – as in 2002, women represented only 6% of board's members. The same rule on 40% of women in boards of public companies was introduced in 2010 in Iceland and France (for companies with more than 500 employees), 33% rule in Belgium in 2011, and Italy should increase women quota to 30% within 2015 (Danielsen et al., 2013, p. 369).

Table 2.4. Women in managerial positions in 500 largest corporations in Nordic countries 2004 and 2009 (in percentage)

Country	2004	2008/2009
Norway	12.4	20.7
Sweden	15.0	17.8
Finland	11.7	17.2
Denmark	5.9	13.9

Source: The Nordic 500 Project, Centre for Corporate Diversity, http://www.corporatediversity.no [accessed July 2014].

Heated debates discrediting gender quotas calmed down as it turned out that women's active presence in managing the public limited liability companies had no negative effect on results. On the contrary, it improved the setting and the decision-making process was better. Training and exams have been organized for female candidates for company boards. A database has been also created where potential female candidates with appropriate qualifications can be found.

If there is a negative side to the gender quota policy, it is, in my view, the pressure on already highly exposed female managers. Many of them are members of the boards of several companies, and the resulting time overload can lead to the reproduction of the same experiences ("business as usual"), instead of the expected "breath of fresh air" that women's participation was expected to ensure. Generally, introducing the gender quota policy is met with approval and is no longer a source of controversy (Tomczak, 2012).

2.5. The impact of a "gendered approach" in economics

2.5.1. Gender-related gains

"There is ample evidence that when women are able to develop their full labour market potential, there can be significant macroeconomic gains" (Elborgh-Woytek et al., 2013, p. 4). The main factors which the paper lists are:
- aging economies – the growth rate rises if the female labour participation increases,
- women's income contributes to development – home investments & better education for girls,
- equal access raises productivity in female-owned companies,
- better use of talent in a society with higher work participation.

The IMF analyses family benefits for advanced economies and emerging economies, which relates the results to different conditions in the member countries and the relevant gender equality "state of affairs." There is still room for potential gains. A selection of indicators for 5 countries presented in Table 2.5 illustrates the differences and potential.

Table 2.5. Selected macroeconomic indicators and social rankings

Country	GDP growth rates		Unem- poyment rate	Globalization ranking	Gini coefficient		Employ- ment of women %	Taxes in sta- te budget %	HDI rank	Gender gap rank
Year	2010	2013	2012	2013	1985	2011	2012	2010/ 2011	2013	2012
Germany	3.9	0.5	5.5	22	0.25	0.29	68.0	36.6	5	13
Norway	0.5	0.6	3.2	20	0.23	0.25	73.8	42.8	1	3
Estonia	2.6	0.8	12.8	25	–	0.31	62.8	34.0	33	60
USA	2.5	1.9	8.1	34	0.34	0.38	62.2	24.8	3	22
Poland	3.9	1.6	10.1	26	0.25	0.30	53.1	31.8	39	53

Sources: OECD, Eurostat, http://www.oecd.org/els/soc/49499779.pdf, s. 45 (Gini), Human Development Report 2013; 16 (HDI index) http://www.globalization-index.org/static/pdf/rankings_2013.pdfhttp://www3.weforum.org/docs/WEF_GenderGap_Report_2012.pdfhttp://www.oecd.org/statistics/compare-your-country.htm [accessed July 2014].

The above developed market economies USA, Germany and Norway represent three different models of a market economy, so do the two transition countries – Poland and Estonia. The countries with the social model of market economy receive better scores in gender equality than those with the liberal model (USA, Estonia), and following, higher economic and social benefits (Germany, Norway). A strong state and public institutions enforce gender equality and contribute to higher female participation in the labour market, and so receive better macroeconomic effectiveness and a higher level of citizens' well-being/life satisfaction. The gap revealed between developed economies and emerging economies opens up new opportunities, if properly understood and directed.

2.5.2. Learning from the Scandinavian experience

What is quite clear is that gender equity and equality is a process which takes time – perhaps not a 100 years, but many. Political declarations, charters of rights and law – these indicate just the start of a long and challenging route of implementing decisions and solutions which work in practice. Steps towards equality have a proven "step by step" logic:

1. Equal political rights and open access to education.
2. Access to paid work or self-employment – own income/economic independence.
3. Public focus on family – sharing of duties, equal obligations and rights.
4. Social participation outside home – cooperating, networking.
5. Participation in decision making – political and corporate involvement & career open up.
6. Ethnicity factor – migrants and minorities integration to the "status of equality."
7. Tackling of controversies equality/religion/tradition in multicultural society.

Each step needs new solutions and rearrangements, but brings new value added, such as higher work participation, higher family income and social gains and more. Children of active mothers have also better prospects for their own achievements. How to use the Norwegian experience to progress and gain? The local conditions – culture and quality of institutions, in general, are main factors of the potential for progress.

Here Poland might be a good example of a paradox: a European economy doing relatively well, with low indicators for gender equality, which means an unexploited resource uncovered – a new potential push to growth. What an opportunity! But – before the next step was taken a fierce discussion over the term "gender" has arisen. "Gender" has been discredited, misunderstood and banned by the Catholic Church. For many social groups gender serves now as something evil, immoral and suspicious, so this may result in a step back instead of a step forward towards equality and equality-related gains. The governing authorities have a new challenge – if the political response is not firm and consistent there is a danger of hibernation for gender initiatives in Poland.

Conclusions

1. The global economy has advantages and disadvantages, therefore it is important to analyse the gains and losses it brings to a single country and to different population groups within a country.

2. Marketization of non-market relations (Sandel, 2013a) – growing inequality (r>g; Gini; Piketty, 2014) – persistently dogmatic economic theory and – following – inadequate economic policy (Krugman, 2009, 2013, 2014) – these are serious drawbacks which call for new compound solutions.
3. When financial acrobatics destabilized the world economy and pushed many countries into a blind gate, a search for new initiatives, such as a change in economic policy (Krugman, 2014), local governance (Ostrom, 2009) or a gender-related approach are important contributions.
4. The last – gender approach – is the matter addressed in this paper. The increasing participation of women in the economy is real, revealing unexploited gains that sophisticated mathematical models cannot grasp.

Gender equality functioning in practice is the main issue of economic participation. The conditions for creating gender equality are presented based on Norway's experience and compared with selected data for EU countries. "Economic citizenship" – one's own income and access to paid work/self-employment and therefore participation in decision making (in politics & business) are the main pillars of equality in Norway. The extent to which the Norwegian experience may help other countries to form their strategies and policies in this field will be a task for separate studies.

Literature

Brunborg, H., Texmon, I., Tønnessen, M. (2012), *Befolkningsframskrivninger 2012–2100: Resultater*, Økonomiske analyser 4, Statistics Norway, Oslo http://www.ssb.no/a/publikasjoner/pdf/oa_201204/brunborg3.pdf [accessed May 2014].

Carlsson-Wetterberg, Ch., Melby, K. (2008), "The claim of economic citizenship: The concept of equality in a historical context," [in:] *Gender Equality and Welfare Politics in Scandinavia: The Limits of Political Ambition?* Bristol: Policy Press, University of Bristol, pp. 43–62.

Danielsen, H., Larsen, E., Owesen, I.W. (2013), *Norsk Likestilinshistorie 1814–2013*, Bergen: Fagbokforlaget.

Davis, G.F. (2009), *Managed by the Markets. How Finance Re-shaped America*, Oxford: Oxford University Press.

Elborgh-Woytek, K., Newiak, M., Kochhar, K., Fabrizio, S., Kpodar, K., Wingender, P., Clements, B., Schwartz, G. (2013), *Women, Work, and the Economy: Macroeconomic Gains from Gender Equity*, Washington: IMF Staff Discussion Notes.

Esping-Andersen, G. (1999), *Social Foundations of Post-industrial Economies*, Oxford: Oxford University Press.

Esping-Andersen, G., Gallie, D., Hemerijck, A., Myles, J. (2002), *Why We Need a New Welfare State*, Oxford: Oxford University Press.

Fraser, N. (1989), *Unruly Practices: Power, Discourse and Gender in Contemporary Social Theory*, Minneapolis, MN: University of Minnesota Press.

Fraser, N. (2003), "Social justice in globalisation. Redistribution, recognition, and participation," *Eurozine magazine*, Revista Crítica de Ciências Sociais, http://www.eurozine.com/articles/2003-01-24-fraser-en.html [accessed July 2014].

Hayek, F.A. von (2006), *The Constitution of Liberty*, London: Routledge.

Holst, C. (2008), "Gender justice in the European Union. The normative subtext of methodological choices," *ARENA Working Paper*, 18, University of Oslo, Oslo.

Krugman, P. (2009), *Finanskriser og depresjonsøkonomi – og hva kan gjøres med finanskrisen*, Oslo: Hegnar Media.

Krugman, P. (2013), *End This Depression Now!*, London: WW Norton & Company Inc.

Krugman, P. (2014), articles and blog in NYT ("New York Times").

Marshall, T.H. (1950), *Citizenship and Social Class*, London: Pluto Press.

OECD report: *All on Board: Make the Inclusive Growth Happen*, OECD 2014, p. 30, http://www.oecd.org/inclusive-growth/All-on-Board-Making-Inclusive-Growth-Happen.pdf [accessed July 2014].

Ostrom, E. (2009), Beyond Markets and States: Polycentric Governance of Complex Economic Systems, Nobel Prize Lecture, 8.12.2009, Stockholm.

Piketty, Th. (2010), "On the long run evolution of inheritance: France 1820–2050," *PSE Working Papers*, September.

Piketty, Th. (2014), *Capital in the Twenty-first Century*, Cambridge, Mass.: Belknap Press of Harvard University.

Pringle, K. (2008), "Future research on gender equality in the Scandinavian countries," [in:] *Gender Equality and Welfare Politics in Scandinavia: The Limits of Political Ambition?* Bristol: Policy Press, University of Bristol, pp. 223–230.

Rogg Korsvik, T., Stø, A. (2011), *The Nordic Approach*, Oslo: Kolofon Forlag.

Roman, Ch. (2008), "Scientific discourse in social policy and the construction of new families," [in:] *Gender Equality and Welfare Politics in Scandinavia: The Limits of Political Ambition?* Bristol: Policy Press, University of Bristol, pp. 101–116.

Sandel, M.J. (2013a), "Market reasoning as moral reasoning: Why economists should re-engage with political philosophy," *Journal of Economic Perspectives*, Vol. 27, No. 4, Fall, pp. 121–140.

Sandel, M.J. (2013b), *What Money Can't Buy*, Farrar, New York: Straus and Giroux.

Schumpeter, J.A. (1994), *History of Economic Analysis*, London: Routledge.

Tomczak, D. (2012), "Channels to innovation in regions – can equality policy contribute?," Conference Paper, IV Międzynarodowa Konferencja Wydziału Ekonomii WSEI "Zarządzanie Rozwojem Regionu," 24–25.05.2012, Lublin.

Tomczak, D., Tufte, G.C. (2011), "The impact of social participation on human development – Poland compared with six European countries," [in:] D. Tomczak (ed.), *Wellbeing and Competences of Individuals in Local Communities in Poland*, Warsaw: Warsaw University Press, pp. 13–34.

Zak, P.J. (2006), *Values and Value: Moral Economics*, Gruter Institute Project on Values and Free Enterprise, SSRN Economics Research Network, http://papers.ssm.com/sol3/JEL-JOUR_Results.cfm?form_name=journalBrowse&journal_id-926595 [accessed July 2014].

Appendix 2.1. Indicators for gender equality. Source data. The whole country

	2011	2012
Share of 1–5 years olds in kindergarten (per cent)	89.7	90.1
Share of women among municipal county members (per cent)	38.2	38.2
Share of men with higher education (per cent)	25.6	26.0
Share of women with higher education (per cent)	30.7	31.6
Share of men (20–66 years) in the work force (per cent)	82.5	82.9
Share of women (20–66 years) in the work force (per cent)	76.7	76.8
Average gross income, men (NOK)	453 300	470 500
Average gross income, women (NOK)	299 900	313 100
Share of employed men (20–66 years) working part-time (per cent)	13.8	13.7
Share of employed women (20–66 years) working part-time (per cent)	35.5	34.5
Share of fathers taking the full fathers quota or more (per cent)	64.6	68.1
Level of gender balanced business structure (score)	0.60	0.60
Share of women among employees (20–66 years) in public sector (per cent)	70.6	70.7
Share of women among employees (20–66 years) private sector (per cent)	36.8	36.5
Share of women among leaders (20–66 years) (per cent)	34.7	35.2
Level of gender balance in educational programmes in upper secondary school (score)	0.66	0.66

Source: http://www.ssb.no/en/befolkning/statistikker/likekom [accessed July 2014].

Chapter 3

Taking gender seriously. Present trends and recommendation for scientific environment

Marta Du Vall, Marta Majorek

Abstract

This report deals with the issues of women's participation in the science and research sector. Analysis of the statistical data shows that both in the United States and in Europe, despite the fact that women make up almost half of those receiving a doctoral degree, among professors they are barely one-fifth. This issue is presented in geographical terms, divided into the countries of the European Union, Poland and Scandinavia. Common to them is the situation in which women scientists encounter more barriers than similarly qualified men on their career path. In Poland, too, despite a significant increase in the number of women studying at the further stages of the scientific career, the situation of women is not satisfactory. The last part of the paper is devoted to the policy of the Nordic countries in eliminating the phenomenon of gender inequality in the scientific sector. Although the countries in this region all run their own policy on gender balance in society, they are conducting a far-reaching consultation on a common strategy in this area, and action on gender equality in the Nordic scientific research sector is based primarily on anti-discrimination legislation. The solutions adopted in this region and the guidelines of European institutions will be treated as a kind of reference point for action to eliminate inequalities based on gender in the scientific sector.

Key words: science, gender, the European Union, Nordic countries, Poland

Introduction

In taking on the issue of equality considerations in science, it must first be noted that all the available statistics and research on a global, regional or national scale provide hard evidence of continuous underrepresentation of women in science. In almost all parts of the world the difference in the representation of women and men in the scientific environment is truly substantial. This situation is perfectly illustrated by the map given below, where we see sharp disparities and

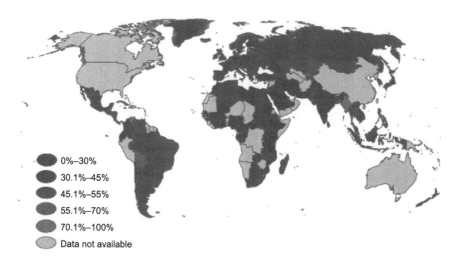

Map 3.1. Women as a share of total researchers, 2010 or later available year
Source: http://www.uis.unesco.org/ScienceTechnology/Documents/sti-women-in-science-en.pdf [accessed March 2014].

under-representation of women scientists, even in some of the most developed countries – where the struggle for women's rights and equality has been going on for decades, including France, Germany and Japan (where women represent less than one-third of academics).

The definition of scientist/women scientists or academics adopted for this report is in part proposed in the document entitled "Women in Science" prepared by the UNESCO Institute of Statistics, which states that a scientist is a person engaged in the creation of new knowledge, initiation and conduct of research, discovery of products, methods and systems, as well as the person managing such projects (UNESCO, 2012). Due to the nature of scientific work, those involved in teaching at universities, having degrees, and performing management functions in higher education institutions should also be included here. Higher education, according to the category adopted by Eurostat, provides a level of education offered by universities, colleges, institutes of technology and other institutions that grant degrees or professional diplomas (Eurostat, 2013).

This paper presents a descriptive analysis of secondary data contained in collected statistical materials (prepared by international and national institutions) and scientific studies. The content is divided into main sections, presenting the title issue observed geographically (World and the European Union, Poland, Scandinavia). Data presentation is enriched with tables and graphs. The methodology used in the study provides clarity and transparency of the presented material and provides an easy way to match readers' interest in levels of gender representation and underrepresentation in the scientific community.

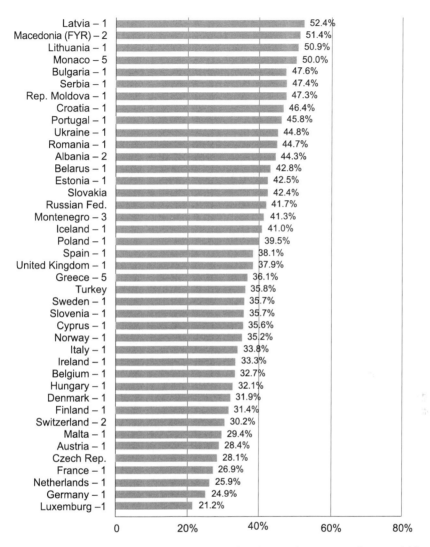

Figure 3.1. Female researchers as a percentage of total researchers, 2010 or later available year
Source: http://www.uis.unesco.org/ScienceTechnology/Documents/sti-women-in-science-en.pdf [accessed March 2014].

3.1. The World and the European Union

A report prepared by Thomson Reuters in collaboration with Times Higher Education showing surprising levels of gender inequality in the world's top universities is unusually interesting. The Global Gender Index 2013 was prepared on the basis of data provided voluntarily by the scientific institutions included in the ranking of top 400 universities in the world. According to the report, the biggest difference in gender representation is in Japan, where women make up only 12.7% of scientists in the top-rated universities in the country. Immediately after Japan ranks Taiwan, where only 21.3% of lecturers employed in seven national universities are women. Against this background, the United Kingdom (48 UK research institutions participated in the survey) is decidedly better, and women constitute 34.6% of the scientific staff. Right above the British we should note the United States, where the proportion of women is 35.9%, based on the 111 scientific institutions included. A country that comes close to achieving equal gender division is Turkey, where 47.5% of workers in the top five national universities are women. It is worth noting that we are still dealing with an scientific gender gap in the Nordic countries (often regarded as the most progressive in the world on issues of equality), and so, for example, women scientists in Sweden are 36.7%, 31.7% in Norway, and in Denmark 31% (Grove, 2013). Further information on the region can be read below.

It is worth noting also looking at a series of analyses of the phenomenon of discrimination against women in the scientific community included in a special issue of the journal *Nature* in March 2013 (Nature, 2013). This includes known markers that both in the United States and in Europe, women account for about half of those receiving a doctoral degree, but only one-fifth of professors. Despite some progress, women scientists continue to earn less, are less likely to be promoted, earn fewer grants, and are more likely to abandon scientific careers than similarly qualified men. Few women are invited to participate in the scientific advisory committees at various enterprises and companies. Also scientific conferences where even half the speakers are women are not a common occurrence. The question arises why is progress on gender equality in the education system not progressing? Motherhood is certainly one of the factors why women decide not to pursue a career. However, this is a practical question which in theory it is easy to deal with if the political will is there. There is, however, another, much more serious problem: overt or unconscious bias and stereotypical recognition of male and female roles. Unfortunately, such attitudes are even met among women scientists, and furthermore, common among those who actively promote learning as a women's issue.

Before we get into the presentation of statistical data on the proportion of men and women in science in the European Union perspective, it is worth considering the education system itself and the question of whether the underrepresentation of women is not the result of mistakes made at an earlier stage of education. This problem is presented clearly by the *Gender Equality Index* drawn up by the European Institute for Gender Equality (Gender Equality Index, 2013). One of the areas that are analysed is the area of knowledge, which clearly shows inequalities between men and women in the field of education and training. The analysis demonstrates that gender differences in education continue to occur, for example, if we take into account the preferences in the selection of courses studied and success achieved. The aim of the report was to measure the disparities in participation of women and men in tertiary education and learning. The results show that at the EU level since 2008 there has been a reversal of gender participation rates in education at the higher level. Historically, more men than women achieved higher education, but since 2008, there has been a noticeable change in trends. Now, women predominate among people in tertiary education (Grove, 2013). In 2010, the percentage of women students (55%) and graduates (59%) were higher than the percentage of male students, but among PhD students and graduates men were more numerous than women (where the percentages were 49% and 46% respectively) (European Commission, 2013). Statistics on the underrepresentation of women and men in certain areas, such as education for men or engineering and manufacturing for women, however, remain mostly unchanged. This is important insofar as these differences translate into inequalities in participation in the labour market.

Analysing the situation of women and men in the scientific environment from the EU perspective, it should be noted that the promotion of gender equality is one of the key priorities identified by the European Commission for the European Research Area (ERA). The Commission sent Member States a recommendation for the removal of barriers to recruitment, retention in the profession, and career development for women scientists. The Commission is also trying to solve the problem of the gender gap in managerial positions in the higher education sector (European Commission, 2013). Current information on the situation of women in European science and research is contained in the report *She Figures 2012*, drawn up by the European Commission (DG. Research and Innovation and Eurostat) in cooperation with the statistical correspondents of the Helsinki Group on Women and Science.

The basic conclusions of this report can be summarized in a few points. In 2010, the proportion of women among those employed at universities was 45%, where (unfortunately) women accounted for 53% of the personnel of lower rank, employed as specialists or technicians; while women accounted for only 32% of teaching scientists and engineers; however, the share of women in activities related to research work was 44%. The data indicate a significant improvement over previous years, where, for example, in 2009, the share of women in research work was 33%. Also the percentage of female scientists is growing faster than men – corresponding to 5.1% in 2002–2009 for women and 3.3% for men. Among engineers an increase in the proportion of women on average by 5.4% per year (in 2002 and 2010) can also be seen, while the same rate for men is 3.2%. On average in the European Union, women account for 40% of all scientists in higher education (European Commission, 2013, p. 5).

In 2010 in the European Union, 46% of all PhD graduates were women. In the period 2002–2010 the average number of PhD graduates grew at a rate of 3.7% per annum (for men this rate amounted to 1.6%). In the same year the number of women PhD graduates outnumbered men in almost all fields of science, with the exception of: mathematics and computer science (40% female graduates), and engineering, manufacturing and construction (26% female graduates). In the years 2002–2009, women scientists generally gain in all fields of science and in the higher education system itself, but at a very different pace in different countries. The greatest progress has been made especially in the humanities, as well as in engineering and technology (European Commission, 2013, p. 5).

Table 3.1. Number of researchers in the higher education sector (HES), by sex, 2002–2009

	2005		2006		2007		2008		2009	
	Women	Man	Women	Man	Women	Man	Women	Man	Women	Man
BE	9 437	16 662	9 998	16 831	10 580	17 422	11 262	18 083	11 835	18 519
BG	1 451	2 443	1 446	2 463	2 022	2 895	2 210	3 095	2 839	3 736
CZ	5 633	11 148	5 949	11 222	6 493	12 175	6 619	12 391	6 878	12 541
DK	5 591	10 091	5 919	10 151	6 106	10 222	:	:	9 359	13 569
DE	52 272	122 351	57 968	126 404	62 675	128 936	67 381	130 470	74 816	140 658
EE	1 583	2 035	1 763	2 183	1 987	2 333	2 000	2 357	2 062	2 423
IE	3 630	5 870	3 852	6 216	4 070	6 530	4 493	7 117	4 605	7 295
EL	9 106	14 878	:	:	:	:	:	:	:	:
ES	41 376	67 447	43 318	69 757	45 959	72 810	47 689	74 478	49 790	75 340
FR	36 704	70 652	37 538	71 225	37 425	71 003	37 705	71 508	36 250	69 258
IT	24 311	45 876	25 721	46 683	26 482	47 257	27 507	47 433	29 170	47 915
CY	270	537	276	554	293	578	295	580	360	626
LV	2 259	2 109	2 533	2 412	2 889	2 523	2 985	2 683	2 631	2 417
LT	4 524	4 600	4 632	4 604	5 412	4 783	5 528	4 797	5 663	4 970
LU	54	151	67	192	75	212	124	243	197	353
HU	6 979	12 107	6 928	12 000	6 857	11 688	6 840	11 741	6 644	11 751
MT	181	495	191	523	179	530	214	554	183	438
NL	6 917	13 837	7 124	13 728	7 292	13 731	7 765	13 912	8 321	14 236
AT	:	:	8 190	15 419	9 465	16 502	:	:	10 965	18 074
PL	29 652	42 609	29 171	41 160	29 607	41 116	29 379	40 992	29 744	40 848
PT	10 025	11 359	11 383	12 661	12 741	13 962	21 497	24 959	28 715	29 166
RO	4 701	6 791	6 436	8 161	7 417	9 093	7 858	9 721	8 279	9 858
SI	1 291	2 273	1 374	2 235	1 348	2 275	1 619	2 545	1 723	2 508
SK	5 268	6 981	5 832	7 547	6 177	7 741	6 381	8 002	7 359	9 126
FI	8 088	10 407	9 226	11 141	9 471	11 099	9 612	11 036	9 987	11 463
SE	16 882	18 060	:	:	15 510	19 652	:	:	16 712	20 854
UK	106 839	148 210	:	:	116 018	155 342	:	:	124 310	159 967
HR	2 884	3 742	2 857	3 727	3 214	4 102	3 434	4 322	3 389	4 077
TR	25 968	41 536	27 770	43 249	31 654	47 466	32 308	47 875	33 802	49 479
IS	543	706	606	775	559	702	584	734	658	846
NO	7 121	10 966	:	:	8 349	11 463	8 877	11 713	9 392	11 923
CH	:	:	9 455	20 185	:	:	11 408	22 195	:	:
JP	63 407	232 069	66 584	234 609	68 738	233 754	71 402	234 445	:	:

Data unavailable: EU-27, EU-25, EU-15, MK, IL, US.
Break in series: DK 2007, IT 2005, SE 2005.
Others: „:" not available. Head count.

Source: Eurostat – Statistics on research and development (online data code: rd_p_persocc).

The *She Figures 2012* report also points out the major differences in the careers of women and men. The scientific career for women is characterized by a distinct vertical segregation. The percentage of women students (2010 – 55%) and graduates (2010 – 59%) were higher than for men, but men are overrepresented among PhD students and graduates (female students represent 49% and PhD graduates

46%). Moreover, women make up only 44% of the faculty of class C (postdoctoral), 37% of scientific staff Class B (with the degree of doctor habilitated) and only 20% of the Class A scientific staff (professors). It is easy to see that we are dealing here with a classic pyramid of inequality, where at lower levels, at the base, there is an overwhelming number of women. The underrepresentation of women is even more striking in the field of the hard sciences and technology, where the share of women increased from only 31% of the student population at the first level to 38% of doctoral students and 35% of PhD graduates. Among Class C scientists with degrees in the field of science and technology only 32% are women, in group B women account for 23%, while among professors they are only 11%. In general, the proportion of female professors is the highest in the humanities and social sciences, respectively, 28.4% and 19.4%, and lowest in engineering and technology – 7.9%. The estimated European Union indicator of the "thickness" of the glass ceiling in the scientific community in 2010 was 1.8, which is a slight improvement over the last few years, because in 2004 it was 1.9. Regarding decision-making bodies and management in 2010, the average in the European Union was 15.5% of institutions in the higher education sector directed by women, and only 10% of women held the position of rector. Women, on average, account for 36% of the members of governing bodies in higher education institutions (European Commission 2013b, p. 6).

In conclusion, there can be no doubt that the problem of inequality between men and women in the scientific community in the European Union exists, although the situations of individual countries varies slightly (the latter part of the paper presents the situation in Poland and the Scandinavian countries). The European Commission clearly indicates, however, that we cannot wait with arms crossed, hoping that women automatically "catch up" with men. A proactive policy is needed to reduce the existing inequalities significantly. The report highlights the necessity of finding solutions for combining work and family life. Interestingly, statistically scientific and research sector employees belong to the group that is still more likely to have children than those working in other industries. Hence, the question of the appropriate balance between work and home becomes crucial, according to the European Commission, in the creation of solutions for the scientific sector and equal opportunities for men and women in science (European Commission, 2013, p. 7).

3.2. Poland

Regarding Poland, it should be noted that since the early 1990s society's level of education has been rising extremely fast, especially for women. In 2002, among people aged 15 years and more, the percentage of people who had incomplete basic, basic, completed secondary school, post-secondary or tertiary education with a master's degree was higher among women than among men. Among women, however, there were fewer than among men who had the vocational and secondary vocational education. Among the population with higher education in the cities, women accounted for 54.0% (men – 46.0%) and 59.4% in rural areas. Among the total number of people with higher education, the participation of women increased in the period 1988–2002 from 47.0% to 54.8%.

At the same time, the percentage of women with secondary vocational education, general secondary, and post-secondary education decreased. The percentages of women with higher education were higher among those aged 20–49, calculated relative to the total number of women with higher education, than the men's percentages, calculated in relation to all men. Young men much more often than their female contemporaries had only incomplete basic education or no school education; 21.5% of men and 9.2% of women aged 15–19 in 2002. In total, 10.7% of women and 9.7% of men in Poland had a higher education.

Much greater differences occurred when it came to the group with basic vocational education. First of all, significantly fewer women had this type of education (17.5% of all women in Poland) than men (31.3% of all men). Poland is doing much worse when it comes to education of adults. The percentage of women was 5.4%, and men – 4.3% in 2005, while in Sweden, where the education of adults is most popular when it comes to EU countries, it came to 35.6% women and 27.9% of men. Slightly fewer people were educated in the UK, Denmark and Finland, where the percentages of women in education were a few percentage points higher than among men (CSO, 2007, pp. 24–25).

In the period 1990–2005, the number of Polish women students has increased fivefold; the number of men – fourfold. As far back as 1990 women accounted for more than half of all students. In 2005/06, they were 56.5% of the total student population and 65.0% of graduates. They were most strongly represented among students of medical schools (75.6% of the total enrolled in these universities), and teacher education schools (71.8%). Their percentage was the lowest among students of the Ministry of Internal Affairs and Administration (13.3%), Ministry of National Defence (23.8%) and higher technical schools (31.7%).

Comparison of the percentage of women studying various groups of subjects shows that the differences in the choice of directions are even greater when comparing the percentages of men and women than when compared to their presence in different types of schools. In the field of information technology in the school year 2005/06, women accounted for only 12.1% of the total enrolment. The courses included in the technical and transport services groups were still strongly masculine. Course that were already very feminine, such as social work, education, social, humanities, and biological sciences remained the same. There was a marked increase in the number of women in fields related to business and administration, as well as services to the population. It should be added that in the 1990s in general, the number of students in the fields of business and administration also increased significantly for men, due to the large employment opportunities in this area at this time.

The participation of women is even higher for postgraduate studies; in the school year 2000/01 they represented 70.6% of all students, and in 2005–06 – 68.4%. Poland had one of the highest rates of students in higher education among the countries of the European Union. In the school year 2003/04 there were 597.1 female students per 10 thousand of the total number of women, and 469.4 men per 10 thousand of the total number of men. There were higher rates for women in Latvia (635.3) and Finland (600.4). For men – in Finland (547.6) and Greece (527.6). In most European countries, such as, Germany, France, the UK, and Italy, the absolute number of students were similar to the number of students in Poland, but 10 per thousand women or men, they were significantly lower (CSO, 2007, pp. 24–25).

Table 3.2. Women in doctoral studies by fields of science

Field of sciences	1995/96	2000/01	2005/06	1995/96	2000/01	2005/06
	In absolute numbers			In % of total participants in a given field of sciences		
TOTAL	3995	11315	16131	38,1	44,2	49,3
Natural sciences	1014	1896	2689	44,5	49,2	52,4
Technical sciences	299	1367	1506	15,8	23,6	28,9
Medical sciences	282	1017	1738	50,2	51,2	60,2
Agricultural sciences	306	1274	981	48,6	57,5	60,5
Social sciences	2094	5761	9217	40,9	48,9	51,6

Source: Central Statistical Office (2007), *Women in Poland*, Warsaw, p. 119.

During the school years 1995/96–2005/06, there was a large increase in the number of women in doctoral studies from 3995 to the 16 131. The balance between men and women also changed. In the school year 2005/06, they accounted for nearly half (49.3%) of those in doctoral studies. In particular, there were many doctoral students in arts and medical schools, and schools of physical education, where they accounted for more than 60%. Analysis by areas of science in the school years 1995/96–2005/06 differentiates courses of study to a more or less rapid increase in the percentage of women among doctoral students. In the case of science in areas such as life, medical, agricultural, or social, the percentage of women among doctoral students at the beginning of the period was 40% or more. This increased in the next few years to more than 60% in the case of medical and agricultural studies. They almost doubled in the case of technical sciences, showing that this field, traditionally regarded as masculine, is starting to change, but women still accounted for only a small group (CSO, 2007, pp. 24–25).

As a result of the changes, there was a systematic increase in the percentage of women receiving doctoral and habilitated doctor degrees. The number of women also increased from 22.4% to 27.0% of all those granted professorial titles in 1991–2005. Women were almost absent among members of the Polish Academy of Sciences. Their participation changed slightly over this period, despite the increase in the number of scientific staff at different levels. In 1990 they accounted for 2.2%

of the total number of members (10 people), and in 2005 – 2.7% (15 people). In 2005, women accounted for nearly half of the employees working in research and development (42.7%), 19.6% of all employees with the title of professor, 28.7% with a habilitation degree and 42.4% – as a doctor. It is easy to see that this share resembles a pyramid; reflecting the number of degrees and titles granted to women in previous years. Among those employed in research and development, women in Poland and other countries in Central and Eastern European countries were generally a higher proportion than in the old EU member states. In 2004, in Poland they accounted for 43.4% of total employment, while In Germany – 28.0%, the Netherlands – 23.6%, France – 32.4%, Sweden – 36.1%, Estonia – 48.6%, Latvia – 54.2%, and in the Czech Republic – 34.6%. For research workers, these differences were even more pronounced. In Latvia, in 2004 women accounted for 52.8%, Poland – 38.9% (CSO, 2007, pp. 24–25).

Table 3.3. Women employed in research and development activities by groups of posts

Occupation	2000	2005	2000	2005
	In absolute numbers		In % of total employment in a given occupation	
TOTAL	54326	52645	43,2	42,7
Researchers	33572	38426	38,1	39,3
Technicians and equivalent staff	10578	6613	52,1	47,3
Other supporting staff	10176	7606	59,4	65,8

Source: Central Statistical Office (2007), "Women in Poland," Warsaw, p. 120.

As shown by the data published by the European Commission in 2007, women accounted for 37% of scientists in Poland. This percentage is slightly higher than the average in the European Union, where it is 30%. In 2009, a slight increase was observed that at the European Union level was 33%, while in Poland it was 40%. Comparative data for the Poland and the 27 countries of the European Union in 2009, indicating the percentage ratio of scientific staff to the total labour force, shows that in Poland women in science account for 42% of all employed women, while among men it is only 25%. Among those with a doctorate, women account for about half (in the European Union this percentage is 44%), but for post-doctoral degrees it is 26% (for the European Union, this percentage is 37%), and for the titular professorship level reaches only 17% (in the European Union it is 20%). Even fewer women manage to take leadership positions in scientific research institutions: in the EU, women account for an average of 15%. In Poland, women are an exception at the position of rector: according to data for 2006, there were 3, and in 2009 – 4. As regards the remaining positions in the executive ranks of university, here also men predominate overwhelmingly: At the position of vice-rector in 2006 15.3% were women, and in 2009 – 17.1%. For deans, in 2006 9.8% were women, while in 2009 the ratio was 13.8%. The same trend can be observed in relation to the function of Deputy Dean: in 2006 it was exercised by 30.1% of women, and the situation was similar in 2009, with a slight decrease to 30%. Also in the case of decision-making bodies in Polish science, the representation of women is around 7% (du Vall and Majorek, 2013, p. 3).

Statistics show that more Polish women than men gain a higher education, but in the later stages of the scientific career the situation of women is not satisfactory. Undoubtedly a positive impulse for the developments in the Polish science and research sector is the policy of the European Union. The Polish Ministry of Science and Higher Education is working with a special unit of the Directorate General of R&I (Gender and Ethics) in the context of the work of the Committee of the 7th Framework Programme *Science in Society* and the Helsinki Group (*Helsinki Group on Gender in Research and Innovation*). The promotion of gender equality, as has been indicated earlier, is one of the key priorities of the European Research Area (ERA). Thanks to the EU's policy, the Polish government and institutions responsible for the science and research sector are obliged to take action to remove the barriers to recruitment, retention in the profession, and the career development of women scientists and efficient use of their skills.

3.3. Scandinavia

Despite the undisputed leadership position occupied by the Nordic countries in the area of balanced participation of women and men in society, there are still spheres in which a gender imbalance is observable. Reference should made to be a field that is broadly understood as the scientific sector. Although the will to act in these countries is visible and the visions of its implementation widely discussed, there are still insufficient concrete solutions that would boost the numerical representation of women in the field.

The issue of gender equality in the scientific sector in the countries of the region became a subject of wider interest somewhat earlier than was the case in most European countries. However, the Nordic countries run their own policy on gender balance in society, and national differences in the approach to this problem are visible, and hence, in the perception of its importance and place in the list of political and social priorities of the individual governments. The scope of monitoring and political will to monitor the phenomenon of gender inequality in the scientific sector also varies from country to country.

Although so far no common mechanisms have been developed which would be implemented at the regional level, this subject is important to the extent that consultations on the implementation of joint strategies are carried out at the regional level. These consultations were initiated by the Norwegian Ministry of Education and Research, which at the moment of taking over the leadership of the Nordic Council of Ministers in 2012, directed the attention of Member States of the Council on the need to develop a strategy and the tools necessary to promote gender balance in the research sector in Scandinavia.

Within the Nordic Council of Ministers NordForsk operates, which is an organization that funds and coordinates research and scientific cooperation in the Nordic region, as well as providing consultancy in the field. In 2010 NordForsk accepted a submission that the gender perspective should be a factor in its funding of research programs: "NordForsk seeks to promote the participation of both men and women in the activities it finances and to increase the participation of the underrepresented gender at any given time" (NordForsk, 2014). The Top-level Research initiative requires researchers applying for funding for research to demonstrate the extent to which they have taken the gender perspective into account in their application. Moreover, in 2012, NordForsk and the Secretary General of the Nordic Council of Ministers together with the European Commission adopted a Memorandum of Understanding, which refers to paying particular attention to issues of gender equality and gender perspectives in research (Geoghegan-Quinn, 2012).

In the 1970s and 1980s, a number of Nordic institutions of higher education, as well as leading research institutes, organized activities for gender equality, and implemented mechanisms to promote this idea in the coming decades. A characteristic phenomenon was the shift from the realm of recruitment mechanisms and activities aimed at women as individuals to the actual implementation of the principle of gender equality in the daily operation of scientific institutions.

Activities on gender equality in the Nordic scientific research sector are primarily based on anti-discrimination legislation. Crucial in this regard are the legal solutions to combatting discrimination on grounds of sex, and thus of equal treatment and neutrality of gender in the labour market and the provisions relating to equal pay. In each of the countries in the region in the basic law there is a clear formulation of *a prohibition against discrimination on the basis of sex*, followed by extension ordinary legislation which prohibits any difference in treatment of the sexes.

These same principles apply to the education sector, regardless of level. Both educational institutions and other actors in the labour market are obliged to promote gender equality through preparing reports on action carried out in this area over a given period, as well as submitting planned strategies to be implemented to the appropriate authorities. Such regulations apply also equally to universities and research institutions, so that in Denmark, Finland, Iceland and Sweden an employer of a certain number of employees, irrespective of the sector it represents, is obliged to draw up a plan of action in the area of gender equality. The form and extent of the detail of these plans vary from country to country. In addition, the obvious question arises as to what extent these plans have a real impact on the conditions in a specific workplace (Bergman and Rustad, 2013, p. 25).

Analysis of the effectiveness of such instruments should primarily take into account the issue of independence of research institutions, particularly universities, which have a wide range of autonomy and independence. And therefore, as long as there is no climate conducive to change towards greater gender balance within scientific institutions, regulation at the level of government will not bring the desired results.

This does not mean, however, that the ministries responsible for research and higher education have no impact on the policy of scientific institutions in the field of gender balance. Due to the fact that modern scientific research and higher education more often go hand in hand with the need for the development of innovation, the ministries which are responsible for innovation and development in the broad sense, including economic, can also take more active part in promoting the idea of equality in the scientific sector.

In Finland, the broadly defined issue of equality is the responsibility of the Ministry of Social Affairs and Health, and implementing specific strategies in this regard is the responsibility of the following bodies: Ombudsman for Equality, the Gender Equality Unit and the Council for Equality (Ministry of Social Affairs and Health Finland, 2014). The Academy of Finland, which developed an Equality Plan for 2011–2013, is mainly responsible for funding research activities. In accordance with the regulations contained therein, the sex that remains in the minority should occupy at least 40% of the posts as researchers, experts and appointed members of working groups. The plan also provides that "if the percentage of the underrepresented gender falls below 40 per cent for the position in question, of two applicants who are equally qualified or only slightly differ in their level of qualification, the representative of the underrepresented gender shall be selected" (Academy of Finland, 2014). Most universities established a network of cooperation among their Committees on Gender Equality, and the University of Helsinki has appointed an Adviser on Gender Equality (Ruest-Archambault, 2008, pp. 72–73).

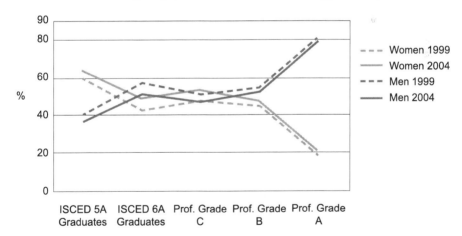

Figure 3.2. Relative share of women and men in a typical scientific career (Finland)
Source: E. Ruest-Archambault (2008), *Benchmarking Policy Measures for Gender Equality in Science*, Brussels: European Commission, p. 72.

In Denmark, however, the policy on gender equality in higher education is somewhat less restrictive. The Ministry for Gender Equality is responsible for the equality of opportunity in the broad sense, and the Ministry of Science, Technology and Innovation together with the Ministry for Gender Equality has established a *Think Tank on More Women in Research*. Its responsibilities include developing recommendations to increase the participation of women in science and research (Pedersen, 2005, pp. 5–6). The Danes have not set up bodies responsible for monitoring the implementation of the principles of equality in scientific institutions. However, legislation has been amended to address this issue. And so, the amendments which were incorporated in 2011 into The Danish Act on Universities provide that the Ministry of Education and the specific university shall enter a 3-year agreement, known as a development contract, which can also include an entry on gender equality, but this is not obligatory, which should undoubtedly be regarded as a sign of respect by the executive for the autonomy of universities and their independence on the prioritization of their own development, including in the field of scientific staff (The Danish Act on Universities, 2011).

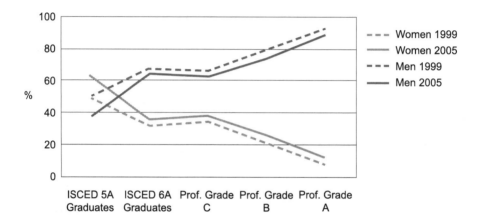

Figure 3.3. Relative share of women and men in a typical scientific career (Denmark)
Source: E. Ruest-Archambault (2008), *Benchmarking Policy Measures for Gender Equality in Science*, Brussels: European Commission, p. 69.

The Swedish government in turn has adopted a system of regulation (*regulation letters*), which includes requirements for the recruitment of professors and the obligation to submit to the competent authorities reports on the progress that the institution has made in the implementation of gender equality. It is worth noting that in 1997, the Swedish National Assembly set a target of achieving a proportion of women in professorial positions of professors in universities and colleges at a minimum of 36% in 2012–2015.

In Sweden, the issue of gender equality until 2010 lay in the competence of the Ministry for Integration and Gender Equality. After the election and the reorganization of the government the Ministry of Education and Research took over the responsibility for gender equality (Government Institutions in Sweden in 2014). The Swedish government established a Delegation for Gender Equality in Higher Education (2009–2011) in order to promote gender equality in the scientific sector, carried out a review implemented by research institutions and universities on activities in this field. This agenda has also initiates research on this issue, publishes reports, and organizes conferences and seminars. Until 2013, these activities were supported by the Swedish National Agency for Higher Education, and they were subsequently incorporated within the competence of new bodies – the Swedish Council for Higher Education and the Swedish Higher Education Authority (Swedish Council for Higher Education, 2013).

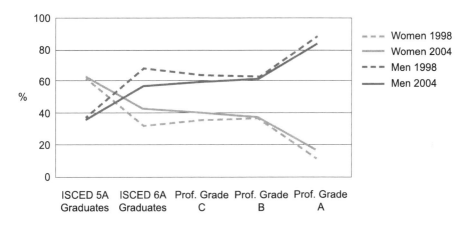

Figure 3.4. Relative share of women and men in a typical scientific career (Sweden)
Source: E. Ruest-Archambault (2008), *Benchmarking Policy Measures for Gender Equality in Science*, Brussels: European Commission, p. 123.

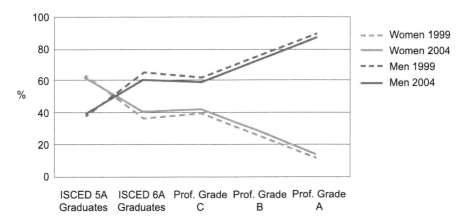

Figure 3.5. Relative share of women and men in a typical scientific career (Norway)
Source: E. Ruest-Archambault (2008), *Benchmarking Policy Measures for Gender Equality in Science*, Brussels: European Commission, p. 139.

In Norway, attention should be paid to the Norway Committee for Gender Balance in Research, bought to life in 2004 and formerly bearing the name of the Committee for Mainstreaming – Women in Science. The name change, it seems, reflects the change of emphasis in the approach to gender issues in science, where in place of the integration of women into the mainstream of scientific life, the need has appeared to balance the presence and activities of women and men in the field.

Among the tasks that it is committed to, the Committee was to promote gender equality in the field of higher education and to provide universities and research institutions with recommendations, the implementation of which could be helpful in terms of achieving a better balance in this respect. One of the objectives of the Committee is also to raise awareness in society of the seriousness of the problem of the imbalance in the numerical representation of both sexes in the scientific sector (Committee for Gender Balance in Research Norway, 2014).

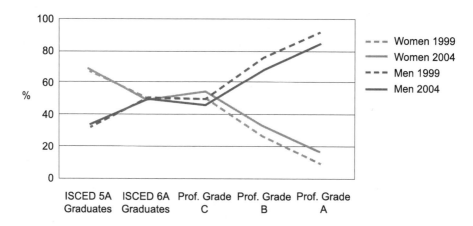

Figure 3.6. Relative share of women and men in a typical scientific career (Iceland)
Source: E. Ruest-Archambault (2008), *Benchmarking policy measures for gender equality in science*, Brussels: European Commission, p. 133.

In the case of Iceland, the Minister of Education, Science and Culture appointed a woman in science committee for their department in 2004. Its job is to monitor the implementation of gender equality policy, based on the government draft socially aware Women in Science, the implementation of which fell on 2004–2008 (Ministry of Education, Science and Culture Iceland, 2004). The Committee examines data on the presence and activities of women in the scientific sector, and identifies barriers to the implementation of the principle of equality, offering solutions in this area and suggesting desirable directions of reforms. In addition, Iceland has the Centre for Gender Equality, which is responsible for the implementation of the Act on the Equal Status and Equal Rights of Women and Men. As the *Parliamentary resolution on a four year gender equality action program* in 2011 states, in 2013 and 2014, those research institutions that demonstrate the greatest progress in the field of gender equality, will receive Equality Awards (The Centre for Gender Equality Iceland, 2011).

In the case of participation of women in research and committee councils a kind of balance is clearly noticeable, which places the Nordic countries slightly above the EU (in 2010 for the 27 EU member states this was 36%). The difference is noted with respect to the positions of rector, where in the case of the European Union in 2010 this amounted to 15.5%, and outside Denmark in all other Nordic countries this percentage is clearly higher.

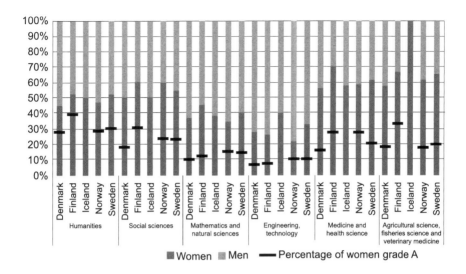

Figure 3.7. The percentage of doctorates broken down by gender and discipline and the percentage of women with a professorial title (grade A) in the Nordic countries (2010)
Source: S. Bergman, L.M. Rustad (2013), *The Nordic Region – A Step Closer to Gender Balance in Research? Joint Nordic Strategies and Measures That Promote Gender Balance among Researchers in Academia*, Copenhagen: Norden, p. 21.

Table 3.4. Percentage of women and men on the research council boards and rectors at higher education institutions in the Nordic region in 2010

Country	Board representation (%)		Rectors (%)	
	Women	Men	Women	Men
Denmark	35	65	14	86
Finland	45	55	25	75
Iceland	40	60	20	80
Norway	46	54	32	68
Sweden	49	51	27	73

Source: European Commission (2013), *She Figures 2012. Gender in Research and Innovation*, pp. 115–117 [accessed 10.01.2014].

Firstly, among the factors that the Scandinavians themselves considered to be detrimental to the scientific development of women's careers is the fact that, although the substantive criteria for evaluation of the work of women scientists are not in doubt from the point of view of their formal nature, the recruitment of researchers by higher education institutions has a much smaller range of formalism. Secondly, one of the essential elements of scientific life turns out to be a kind of informal network of social contacts, which may have a decisive influence on who takes the highest positions in the university. Such practices decisively favour men, due to the fact that on the one hand they constitute the majority in these bodies, and on the other hand are more at ease with self-promotion than women. Not without significance is also the socially established role of women as mothers and carers, which due to the specific nature of the work of researcher inclines women to choose another career (NordForsk, 2013).

Conclusions

In conclusion, it is worth referring to the recommendations that have been formulated by the Norwegian Committee for Gender Balance in Research. These relate to instruments which, according to the Committee's experts, are necessary in order to achieve gender balance in scientific research. These instruments can be divided into two basic groups: structural and specific.

The first group includes: An appropriate personnel policy, affirmative action (positive discrimination), the establishment of day care centres for the children of women scientists, appropriate distribution of administrative tasks (including participation in decision-making), creating databases of women experts in particular areas, to promote the expertise and scientific experience of women, to prevent forms of sexual harassment, and consulting (Committee for Gender Balance in Research Norway, 2014). In turn specific actions might be: financial support for research projects or participation in international scientific exchange, training in the management of scientific and research institutions so that a greater number of women would consider this kind of activity, mentoring projects, campaigns encouraging women students to take up scientific careers (Committee for Gender Balance in Research Norway, 2014).

In the magazine *Nature* (Nature, 2013), we find the suggestion that one possible way to balance representation of women and men in the scientific sector is the introduction of quotas. This would be a good way to ensure young women starting a career in the world of academia had appropriate female role models and authority figures. Some believe, however, that this would lead to a situation where average or even less capable women would be promoted. However, this reasoning contains a certain inaccuracy. Women and men are equally talented. So, if men occupy most senior positions, how many "less capable" must be among them? Is the lack of talent in men more acceptable than in women? In turn, parity in decision-making committees brings the problem of imposing an excessive burden on those women who already work in them. The solution would be, at least for the moment, low parity.

Promoting gender equality in research and innovation is a serious commitment from the European Commission and is one of the basic principles defining the core of the Horizon 2020 Programme. One innovation in the Horizon 2020 programme is the inclusion of equality training to the eligible costs of a given activity. However, the most important goals should be, first, to ensure gender balance in research teams. In line with the European Commission Fact sheet issued in December 2013: Gender Equality in the Horizon 2020 (https://ec.europa.eu/programmes/horizon2020/sites/horizon2020/files/FactSheet_Gender_2.pdf), when signing a grant agreement, the beneficiaries are committed to promoting equal opportunities for men and women in the project. They will also be required, if possible, to ensure gender balance at all levels of employment in the project, including the supervision and management level. Secondly, care should be taken to ensure gender balance in decision-making processes. The European Commission requires the achievement of 40% representation of previously under-represented genders in each group, e.g. expert groups and evaluation panels. In advisory groups and committees gender parity (50/50) is required. In addition, each of the decision-making and advisory bodies in its composition must include a gender expert. Thirdly, an important recommendation for the R&D sector is the inclusion of gender/sex perspectives in the analysis and content of research and innovation. This means that each person applying for funding is required to describe how analysis related to gender and biological sex will be included in the proposed project. Subjects with a strong emphasis on gender/sex issues will be a priority.

It also seems reasonable to highlight, in accordance with the recommendation of the European Organization for Nuclear Research (CERN) for the United Nations (Izlar, 2013), three problems that need to be addressed in the process of equal opportunities for men and women in the field of science and research. The first issue relates to encouraging young women to take up careers in academia. Here it is extremely important to combat stereotypes at all levels: social, economic, and political. It is also important to increase the visibility of women scientists in the media, and make efforts to promote outreach in science careers, and thus to provide role models and mentors for young women.

Another issue is to increase the number of women employed in academia. In this respect, it is proposed to implement anonymous recruitment process, as studies show that in many cases the committees examining the application forms subconsciously favour male candidates, despite there being women candidates with similar or higher qualifications. It is also important to introduce fair rules for parental leave.

The last, very difficult, problem, is to keep women in academia and research. Here we can once again bring up mentoring programs and the promotion of the scientific career path, which can be served by the organization of scientific and networking meetings for women. Furthermore, broad discussion on gender issues is necessary at the numerous scientific meetings. This would help both men and women to realize the essence of the problem of gender imbalance and make a joint effort to solve the aforementioned problems.

Literature

Academy of Finland (2014), *Equality*, http://www.aka.fi/en-GB/A/Funding-and-guidance/The-research-careeer/Equality/ [accessed 12.01.2014].

Bergman, S., Rustad, L.M. (2013), *The Nordic Region – A Step Closer to Gender Balance in Research? Joint Nordic Strategies and Measures to Promote Gender Balance among Researchers in Academia*, Copenhagen: Norden.

Central Statistical Office (2007), *Women in Poland*, Warsaw.

Committee for Gender Balance in Research Norway (2014), http://eng.kifinfo.no/c62414/seksjon.html?tid=62429 [accessed 2.01.2014].

European Commission (2013), *She Figures 2012. Gender in Research and Innovation* [accessed 10.01.2014].

Eurostat (2013), http://epp.eurostat.ec.europa.eu/statistics_explained/index.php/Education_statistics_a_regional_level/pl#Studenci_szk.C3.B3.C5.82_wy.C5.BCszych0 [accessed 10.01.2014].

Fact Sheet: Gender Equality in Horizon 2020 https://ec.europa.eu/programmes/horizon2020/sites/horizon2020/files/FactSheet_Gender_2.pdf [accessed 20.12.2013].

Gender Equality Index (2013), http://eige.europa.eu/content/gender-equalityindex#/domain/knowledge [accessed 9.01.2014].

Geoghegan-Quinn, M. (2012), "Byggesten for ERA," *NordForsk Magasin*.

Government Institutions in Sweden (2014), *Higher institutions in Sweden*, http://www.government.se/sb/d/6943 [accessed 17.01.2014].

Grove, J. (2013), *Gender Equality Index 2013*, http://www.timeshighereducation.co.uk/features/the-global-genderindex/2003517.article [accessed 19.12.2013].

GUS (2007), *Raport „Kobiety w Polsce,"* http://www.stat.gov.pl/cps/rde/xbcr/gus/Kobiety_w_Polsce.pdf [accessed 29.07.2014].

Izlar, K. (2013), http://www.symmetrymagazine.org/article/april-2013/cern-offers-unrecommendations-on-bringing-women-into-science [accessed 20.12.2013].

Ministry of Education, Science and Culture Iceland, http://eng.menntamalaraduneyti.is/publications/ [accessed 20.01.2014].

Ministry of Social Affairs and Health Finland, http://www.stm.fi/en/gender_equality [accessed 20.01.2014).

Nature (2013), http://www.nature.com/news/specials/women/index.html [accessed 5.12.2013].

NordForsk (2013), *Nordic fields of higher education. Structures and transformations of organisation and recruitment*, http://www.nordforsk.org/en/programs/prosjekter/nordic-fields--of-higher-education-structures-and-transformations-of-organisation-and-recruitment [accessed 18.01.2014].

NordForsk (2014), *Apply for FUNDING*, http://www.nordforsk.org/en/funding [accessed 18.01.2014].

Pedersen, L. (2005), *Bringing all talent into play – more women in science*, http://fivu.dk/en/publications/2005/files-2005/bringing-all-talent-into-play-more-women-in-science.pdf [accessed 18.01.2014].

Ruest-Archambault, E. (2008), *Benchmarking Policy Measures for Gender Equality in Science*, Brussels: European Commission.

Swedish Council for Higher Education (2013), *The Swedish Higher Education Act*, http://www.uhr.se/sv/Information-in-English/Laws-and-regulations/The-SwedishHigher-Education--Act/ [accessed 20.01.2014].

The Centre for Gender Equality Iceland (2011), *Gender Equality Action Plan*, http://jafnretti.is/D10/_Files/Gender%20Equality%20Action%20Programme%202011-14.pdf [accessed 19.01.2014[.

The Danish Act on Universities (2011), http://www.science.ku.dk/english/research/phd/student/filer/UniversityAct.pdf/ [accessed 20.01.2014].

UNESCO (2012), uis.unesco.org [accessed 15.01.2014].

du Vall, M., Majorek, M. (2013), "Naukowczynie w polskim systemie szkolnictwa wyższego – trudności i perspektywy," *Aequalitas,* Vol. 2, No. 1, http://aequalitas.ka.edu.pl/2013_v2/A_2013_vol_2_02_Majorek.pdf [accessed 5.12.2013].

Chapter 4

Gender in politics.
Prospects and recommendations

Marta Du Vall, Marta Majorek

Abstract

This study focuses on the issue of participation of women in politics, particularly in the area of gender equality in governance and access to the resources associated with it. The results available show an increase in women's participation in political life. There are definitely more women applying for offices and many of them achieve success. Indubitably, the easily discernible progress is overshadowed by the continuing gender gap, manifested in persistent, lower participation of women. In this chapter, it is primarily quantitative data and reports that have been considered, and analysis of the results available enables us to present the changes in the representation of women in political decision-making circles both at the national and supra-national levels. We have analysed the data describing the situation in Poland, the Nordic countries, and the European Union. In the context of initiatives for equal representation of women in representative bodies exercising functions and decision-making, it is worth noting that, even in countries which have achieved a satisfactory level in terms of numbers, this is not fully reflected in the implementation of gender equality in the area of politics. This is because the practice, often used, is to limit access to certain areas of political activism. There is still a well--established social, stereotypical division into areas traditionally "reserved" for representatives of both sexes, such as social affairs or education.

Key words: women, politics, European Union, Poland, the Nordic countries

Introduction

Empirical studies show a variety of motives for engaging in politics, which may indicate that for various individuals political activity may be valuable for various reasons. Here we can identify motivational factors such as: the need for influence, control or power, the need for affiliation, loyalty to specific groups of people, the search for strong incentives, new experiences, or the need to undertake specific tasks. As you can see, the motivation for political participation is multifactorial, so you can show various types of typologies of the dominant motivation. For example, in studies conducted in the years 1964–1990 on the activists of the

Democratic Party and the Republican Party, it has pointed out that there are four basic factors of motivation: ambition, sociability (affiliation), task orientation, and loyalty (Constantini and Valenty, 1996, pp. 498–524).

The motive referred to as ambitious (achievements, power) is combined with a strong ideological centrism; task-oriented people are more ideological extremists than activists seeking opportunities in politics for influence over policy, promotion, or public offices. The motives of affiliation and loyalty are in turn related with ideological centrism. Participation in political life, however, need not be exclusively instrumental to psychological needs, it can be an end in itself. If in the course of socialization the norm of activity will be produced and internalized, the impact on political life becomes an individual value for the person.

A prerequisite for activity motivated by the value of political influence is a sense of connection with the political system, in conjunction with a lack of sense of alienation, or in other words, political alienation. It is not clear, however, whether alienation leads rather to a withdrawal from participation in politics, or towards active forms of protest against the system. Political participation is thus linked to the level of confidence in the political system, the existing parties, and state institutions. Political distrust is a predictor of contestational activity, and political trust restrains people from participating in acts of protest and unconventional attempts to influence policy.

A low level of political trust characterises people who are passive, alienated, not interested in politics, and poorly educated. Many studies support the idea that the value of politics for the individual and their relation to the political system is largely related to their place in the social system. The higher the socioeconomic status (education, occupation, income), the more active is the participation in politics, especially in conventional forms. Who, therefore, participates in political life? The data acquired in the course of research show broadly that those who will actively participate are: men rather than women, people with higher education, people with high professional status (managers), working professionals and students, people from big cities, and people with high financial status. No interest in political activity, however, is shown by: people with lower education (primary), the unemployed, people from smaller towns, and people with low professional status (Lewicka, 2004, pp. 65–82).

Although we continue to see lower participation of women in politics, gender equality in the exercise of power and access to resources has begun to play an important role. The increase in the participation of women in political life may be referred to as unusual. There are definitely more women applying for offices and many of them achieve success in this race, which is observable on a daily basis, but this applies rather to developed Western democracies (Coffé and Bolzendahl, 2010, pp. 318–333).This points to the growing number of women receiving a social mandate to sit in national parliaments, but also those performing important functions in the executive (Waring et al., 2000, pp. 7–8).

Indubitably, the easily discernible progress is overshadowed by the continuing gender gap, manifested in persistent, lower participation of women. This also applies to the developed democratic countries, which served above as examples of countries with a high number of political positions held by women (Dalton, 2008, pp. 76–98). This raises the idea that if we consider political participation as the main value of a mature democracy, we should look carefully at gender equality in this regard. Aiming to reduce gender inequality in the area of political participation is crucial, because the lack of reflection and suppression of any discussion of this topic may lead to serious repercussions in the form of deepening stratification between men and women in modern societies.

Participation in public life is seen by many researchers as a key factor and is referred to as a basic democratic right. Thus, the persistent unequal participation patterns observed in the political sphere represents a significant threat to political equality and the function of democracy. While in recent decades women have made noticeable progress, demonstrated by the deepening impact on political decisions, a more informal involvement is still clearly visible than that which would translate into a direct effect on real impact in terms of key decisions. Even in countries with a high degree of economic development and well-established democratic institutions (UK, USA), an adverse division conditioned by gender is still observable. It is true that this element is not determinant of the share of power to such an extent as is the case with race or wealth, but it is still identified as limiting participation in political decision-making bodies (Burns, 2007, pp. 104–124).

Many factors are indicated as those which are supposed to be an explanation for this, in particular, reference is often made to women's lower access to socioeconomic resources. For example, men more often hold full-time jobs, and as is evident from the previously mentioned results (Lewicka, 2004), employment and its form translates into political participation, available information resources, and effectiveness (Schlozman et al., 1999, pp. 29–53).

This is, however, not the only explanation for the problem identified. The low level of knowledge in the field of politics, interest, and effectiveness in this area may also be caused by other factors. It is believed that the lack of political resources in the hands of women may also be conditioned by the underlying factors of socialization processes. Socialization is not abstracted from sexuality, because girls are taught to adopt a more passive attitude, focused on privacy, empathy and a reinforced sense of attachment to specific gender roles in society. Boys are rewarded in the educational process with leadership, autonomy and a strengthened conviction of the necessity of independence and reliance on themselves (Wojniak, 2012, pp. 2–18). This type of socialization pattern can not only cause, but also preserve the low level of political involvement observed among women.

Most of the above ideas also in terms of the insufficient participation of women in political life and in relation to their slender impact on the decision-making process are reflected in the data collected by American sociologists (Verba, 1997, pp. 1051–1072). This gives us a global view of the situation; however, it is worth referring to the data that is available to us closer to home, i.e. the European Union. Analysis of the results available enables us to present the changes in the representation of women in political decision-making circles both at the national and supra-national levels. The methodology applied involves quantitative analysis of the available data and their development, consisting of the statement of the results of research conducted by both national and international institutions and included in the available scientific publications. The structure is based on the development of separate parts covering the subject on the basis of geography, including the European Union as a whole, then in terms of the particular, on the example of Poland. For comparative purposes, the situation will be outlined in the Nordic region, which is perceived as a kind of benchmark for pro-equality initiatives. The descriptive approach to the statistics cited has been supplemented with tables and charts, which aim to make the study transparent.

4.1. The European Union

The countries included in the European Union are generally considered to be those that had to meet certain standards in order to become a member of the Community. But it cannot be expected that we will be dealing with an equal dimension of participation of women in politics among all Member States. It is no surprise that in terms of the number of women serving in decision-making bodies, the lead is taken by the Scandinavian countries, which will be presented in more detail later in this paper. First, however, we will look at the more holistic participation by gender, based on data for Members of the European Parliament.

The European Union is home to approximately 495 million people of which over 51% are women, but in the penultimate European elections, only 35% of seats were won by women (elections to the Europarliament, 2009). It is not, however, to judge on this basis the underrepresentation of women in EU decision-making bodies, these indicate only the constant lack of equal distribution of instruments of authority between women and men, which may result, generally speaking, in a democratic deficit. EU institutions do not promote the idea that it is a women's right to be selected, but to have the opportunity.

One of the basic manifest problems is believed to be the infrequency of elections, which in itself is not contested, but has a crucial impact on the changes expected in terms of equal gender representation. Over the last few years, we can mention just a few of the possibilities for the reconstruction of the composition of this body. In addition, there is no doubt that the decision to become a politician is often a defined career choice, thus it is not surprising that many candidates will try again, applying for re-election. Thus, the fluctuation of MEPs is limited and leads to a reduction in the inflow of new politicians, in this case women (European Commission, 2009, p. 18).

The data show a much greater representation of women in the European Parliament than is the case in parliaments at national level. This applies both to the seats in the lower and higher houses. A particularly high disparity, reaching up to 25%, is observed in countries such as: Estonia, Ireland, Hungary, and Slovenia.

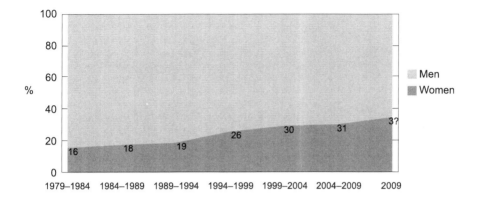

Figure 4.1. Distribution of seats by gender in the European Parliament
Source: European Parliament, http://www.europarl.europa.eu/ [accessed March 2014].

It is hard to pinpoint one reason for this state of things, but we can try to base it on a number of factors, which in turn will not be a uniform set, specific to each country. The first factor is the electoral system. Although each country has their own way of regulating the selection of MEPs, it is necessary to comply with the requirement of proportionality. It has been proved that, where we have a system that allows several candidates to win, more often there is a chance to elect a woman. However, in the situation of an electoral majority, which exists in some countries in the elections at the national level and where the winner takes all, women are statistically less likely to be selected. Moreover, we have to deal with the different types of pre-selection of candidates and how they are situated on the lists of candidates for local elections, and those at the European level (European Commission, 2009, p. 20). Table 4.1 and Figure 4.2 illustrate the disparity discussed. It is worth noting in particular the previously cited countries.

Yet another important factor that cannot be overlooked is the question of the importance that the voter attaches to the body that it is appointing. Although there is no doubt that the EU policy and decisions taken in the European Parliament are becoming increasingly crucial, and we have to deal with the increase in the competence of this body, most Europeans still have little interest in the elections at this level, treating them as less important (Special Eurobarometer, 2008).

This may also lead to the situation that women's representation will increase. Also important here is the informal pressure on the EU itself, that the issue of equal opportunities for women and men should be seen as a key. Perhaps this is also one of the reasons why the authorities of the party groups are willing to put women on electoral lists. Thanks to this, we can expect that their representatives will more often be included in the work of committees and parliamentary groups, under the premise of equal participation of women and men, which will translate into participation in power and influence over the shape of EU policy.

Table 4.1. Number of seats won by women in the European Parliament, taking into account the data from individual EU member states

Country	Seats	Women	Percentage
Finland	13	8	61.5
Sweden	18	10	55.6
Estonia	6	3	50.0
Netherlands	25	12	48.0
Bulgaria	17	8	47.1
Denmark	13	6	46.2
France	72	32	44.4
Austria	17	7	41.2
Slovakia	13	5	38.5
Latvia	8	3	37.5
Germany	99	37	37.4
Belgium	22	8	36.4
Hungary	22	8	36.4
Portugal	22	8	36.4
Romania	33	12	36.4
Spain	50	18	36.0
Cyprus	6	2	33.3
Luxembourg	6	2	33.3
United Kingdom	72	24	33.3
Greece	22	7	31.8
Slovenia	7	2	28.6
Ireland	12	3	25.0
Lithuania	12	3	25.0
Italy	72	16	22.2
Poland	50	11	22.0
Czech Republic	22	4	18.2
Malta	5	0	0.0
TOTAL	736	259	35.2

Source: Interparliamentary Union (the state after the elections to the European Parliament in 2009, http://www.ipu.org/pdf/publications/womeninsight_en.pdf) [accessed March 2014].

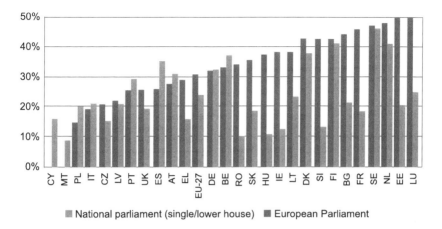

■ National parliament (single/lower house) ■ European Parliament

Figure 4.2. The difference between the percentage of women serving in the national parliaments and the European Parliament
Source: European Parliament, http://www.europarl.europa.eu/ [accessed March 2014].

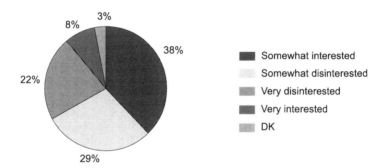

■ Somewhat interested
■ Somewhat disinterested
■ Very disinterested
■ Very interested
■ DK

Figure 4.3. The results of studies identifying the level of interest in the elections to the European Parliament
Source: Eurobarometer, http://ec.europa.eu/public_opinion/archives/ebs/ebs_299_en.pdf [accessed March 2014].

Table 4.2. Participation of women in parliaments by region of the world (as of 2013)

	Single House or Lower House	Upper House or Senate	Both Houses combined
Nordic countries	42%	–	–
Europe – OSCE member countries including Nordic countries	24.6%	22.6%	24.2%
Americas	24.2%	23.8%	24.1%
Europe – OSCE member countries excluding Nordic countries	23%	22.6%	22.9%
Sub-Saharan Africa	21.1%	18.7%	21.7%
Asia	19.1%	13.8%	18.5%
Arab States	17.8%	7.7%	15.9%
Pacific	13.1%	38.6%	15.9%

Source: Interparliamentary Union, http://www.ipu.org/wmn-e/world.htm (data from 2013).

In national parliaments progress in increasing the number of women parliamentarians can also be observed. The change that has taken place since the
mid-1990s is significant. At this time, the number of women present in parliamentary chambers was a few percent, and up to now this has increased significantly achieving an average value varying from 23–24% (The Party of European
Socialists, 2007).

The data presented are global, but were grouped depending on the region. It is
worth comparing these results with the data that were collected 10 years earlier.
This will show the aforementioned change. Summary of these results gives us a picture of the transformation, which can be seen in the European countries. While
the Nordic countries, which have been deliberately separated out, did not record
significant progress in this area, in ten years, when it comes to general European
countries belonging to the OSCE, there is a marked change. The difference is lit-
erally spectacular and reaches almost 10%, which over ten years gives an average
of a 1% increase in the presence of women in parliaments per year.

Table 4.3. Participation of women in parliaments by region of the world (as of 2003)

	Single House or Lower House	Upper House or Senate	Both Houses combined
Nordic countries	39.7%	–	39.7%
Europe – OSCE member countries including Nordic countries	18.2%	17.5%	18.1%
Americas	17.6%	15.5%	17.2%
Europe – OSCE member countries excluding Nordic countries	15.4%	15.5%	15.4%
Sub-Saharan Africa	14.5%	14.3%	14.5%
Asia	14.9%	17.4%	15.2%
Arab States	11.6%	25.9%	13.1%
Pacific	6.0%	7.5%	6.2%

Source: Interparliamentary Union, http://www.ipu.org/wmn-e/world.htm (data from 2003) [accessed
March 2014].

The change is not just in the national issue of sitting in legislative bodies, but
we can also see another important dimension, which is women occupying key
positions. Let us, therefore look at the function of Marshal, a responsible and
prestigious office. For the first time a woman had the opportunity to perform this
office in Austria, and this took place before the Second World War. By 1997 only
in 42 countries of 186 had a woman been chosen to lead the legislative branch,
and in total it took place only 78 times. It can be seen that somewhat more frequently a woman became the head of the upper house of parliament, and this may
be related to the usually limited powers of this body. The situation in November
2013 developed only a little differently from what we have seen before. Namely,
only 38 currently serve as the leader (Marshal) of any of the chambers, of which
there are 188. It is therefore a negligible percentage of just 13.9% of the positions
available (Inter-Parliamentary Union, 2013).

In addition to the supranational and national levels, we should also take into account the level of participation by women in local and regional bodies. Skipping these would result in inaccuracy in the analysis, which would then be incomplete and thus less authoritative. Today, however, we are looking at ever fuller implementation of the principle of subsidiarity, and this could not be performed outside the decentralized regional units.

It is no surprise that a correlation may be observed between the increased representation of women in parliaments at the national level, and their presence in gatherings at regional and local levels. A commonly occurring phenomenon should also be noted, greater representation of women in regional bodies in relation to the national. This is especially when we have a proportional system at lower levels, and a majority system at the national level. For example, in France we have a situation where at the national level there are only 19% of women, compared with 49% at the local level and 35% at the regional level (European Commission, 2009, pp. 23–24). This confirms the earlier thesis about the key influence of the electoral system on the chances of a woman gaining a seat.

In the attempt to assess the data and indicators previously presented, we should pay particular heed to percentage changes in the rate of participation of women in law- and decision-making bodies that have been observed over the space of just over a decade. At the Fourth World Conference on Women, held in Beijing in 1995, the Beijing Declaration and Platform for Action for Equality, Development and Peace was adopted. This document sets out the strategic objectives and actions that the international community, national governments, and civil society should take in order to promote and protect the human rights of women and girls, as an inalienable, inherent and indivisible part of universal human rights and the fundamental freedoms of all women during their entire lifetimes (European Institute for Equality between Women and Men, 2012, p. 6).

The creation of the Platform for Action and the adoption of specific goals is an excellent starting point for assessing developments since that time in the representation of women in decision-making bodies. In 1995, only 10% of women sat in parliaments around the world, now it is estimated that this percentage has doubled. European Union countries are leaders in this regard, for the parliaments of the Member States are nearly a quarter women. In addition, in the twenty countries where the proportion of women is 30% or more, eight of them belong to the EU, and they are: Sweden, Finland, the Netherlands, Denmark, Spain, Belgium, Germany, and Austria. On the other hand, in the EU we still have to deal with the countries in which the number of women sitting in legislative bodies is negligible and has remained at the same low level. In particular, this refers to Cyprus, Slovenia, Romania, and Malta, where the percentage of women parliamentarians has remained at 9%.

In the period indicated the most progress was recorded in Belgium, which increased the percentage of women elected to parliament by more than 20%. On the basis of analyses, the Institute for Democracy and Electoral Assistance (IDEA) found that in countries where there was an increase to over 30% of women MPs, firstly there is a proportional representation system, and secondly, there is some form of quota system. According to IDEA, these two factors are essential for the reduction of obstacles in the area of women's opportunities to participate in power at the national level (IDEA, 2013, pp. 14–15). At the local and regional levels, women have a much stronger voice, emphasizing their presence in legislative gatherings. The percentage of women elected to these bodies sometimes reaches almost 50%, although the average hovers around 30%.

For women in the composition of the governments of EU countries, men are the vast majority, taking a total of about 75% of ministerial positions. We do not have this type of situation in all Member States, for in the Nordic countries women are on average half of the government. In Sweden, this is on average 46%, in Finland 60%, and Norway 53%. Against this backdrop, Spain looks very positive, where the government is made up of 40% women. Unfortunately, only 8 of the EU countries can boast of having a woman as prime minister within their entire history. This refers to the UK, Portugal, Lithuania, France, Bulgaria, Finland, Germany, and Poland (PES, 2007).

4.2. Poland

The Polish struggle for equal rights for women was associated with the process of raising their level of education started in the second half of the 19th century and, in 1918, obtaining political rights. These circumstances, however, were insufficient in the face of men's competition in the public sphere. Girls with higher social status did indeed participate in the educational process, but their upbringing was wholly impractical, and their education did not compare with that obtained by men. In turn, the girls of the lower classes rarely had access to the education obtained in the school system, and also had no material options. Given these relationships, women from the very beginning were condemned to occupy a lower position (Polkowska, 2012). In the interwar period there were few women MPs and senators – in total throughout the period 1919–1939, women in Poland occupied 41 parliamentary and 20 senatorial seats, which accounted for 1.9% of the Sejm and 3.8% of the Senate of the period (Fuszara, 2009, p. 187).

This situation changed in the post-war period, where in the first term women's representation in parliament was 17%, and then fell sharply to 4%, and in successive terms gradually increased and reach the highest point in 1980–1985 (Muchowiecka, 2011). As Małgorzata Fuszara (2009, p. 189) says, "it is a myth that there was a greater proportion of women in power in the period 1945–1989, and so when the official ideology appealed to slogan of equality between women and men." Until 1989, the proportion of women in Parliament never exceeded a quarter of the total number of deputies. In the first term of the Sejm (1952–1956), women accounted for 17%, in the second term (1956–1961) – 4%, in the third term (1961–1965) – 13%, in the fourth term (1965–1969) – 12%, in the fifth term (1969–1972) – 13%, in the sixth term of office (1972–1976) – 16%, in the seventh term (1976–1980) – 20%, in the eighth term (1980–1985) – 23%, and in the ninth term of office (1985–1989) – 20% (Polkowska, 2012).

Table 4.4. The number of women deputies to the Polish Sejm in the years 1991–2005

Specification	Sejm terms				
	I	II	III	IV	V
TOTAL	44	60	60	93	94
In % of total deputies	9.6	13.0	13.0	20.2	20.4

Source: CSO report *Women in Poland*, http://www.stat.gov.pl/cps/rde/xbcr/gus/Kobiety_w_Polsce.pdf [accessed March 2014].

Currently, the share of Polish women in political structures is increasing from year to year, but it is still low. The most common barrier to women's public activities, in addition to historical reasons, are institutional, social and cultural determinants. The barriers to the access to the power structure are a series of stereotypes that impose marked gender roles, in which there is no room for political involvement by women. An important opinion-forming element are the media, giving rise to the stereotypical image of women as a housewives. Equally important impact on the participation of women in public life is a religion that sees women as the guardian of the household. A significant factor to women's political activeness is their social and economic status, a lack of sufficient financial resources, difficulties in the labour market, unemployment, and a double burden: professional work and housework (Lesiewicz, 2011).

Table 4.5. The participation of women in the Senate of the Republic of Poland in the years 1991–2005

Specification	Sejm terms				
	I	II	III	IV	V
TOTAL	8	13	12	23	13
In % of total deputies	8.0	13.0	12.0	23.0	13.0

Source: CSO report *Women in Poland*, http://www.stat.gov.pl/cps/rde/xbcr/gus/Kobiety_w_Polsce.pdf [accessed March 2014].

Also at the local government level there are significant disparities in the participation of men and women. Research shows that women are far less likely to occupy the top positions on electoral lists, which is known to have a large impact on the number of votes gained, which are most frequently given to those in first place. This helps to reduce their chance of getting a seat as a councillor and may partially explain why the number of women taking part in local elections is higher than the number of those that get into the council (Muchowiecka, 2011).

Table 4.6. The number of women councillors in municipalities and cities with county rights in 1990–2006

Specification	Gmina counsils				Councils of city in cities with powiat status
	total	urban	rural	urban-rural	
27 V 1990					
Total	5652	1378	2754	1520	x
In % of total councillors	10.9	16.5	9.2	11.1	x
19 VI 1994					
Total	6913	1651	3672	1590	x
In % of total councillors	13.3	17.1	12.3	12.7	x
11 X 1998					
Total	7797	1374	4348	2075	580
In % of total councillors	15.7	19.9	14.5	16.1	19.9
27 X 2002					
Total	6725	926	4163	1636	494
In % of total councillors	17.8	21.0	17.3	17.4	23.0
12 XI 2006					
Total	8051	1031	4968	2052	490
In % of total councillors	21.3	23.3	20.8	21.6	23.2

Source: CSO report *Women in Poland*, http://www.stat.gov.pl/cps/rde/xbcr/gus/Kobiety_w_Polsce.pdf [accessed March 2014].

Table 4.7. Number of women councillors in district councils and regional assemblies in the years 1998–2006

Specification	11 X 1998		27 X 2002		12 XI 2006	
	councils of powiat	voivodship regional councils	councils of powiat	voivodship regional councils	councils of powiat	voivodship regional councils
Total	1531	93	1000	80	1045	99
In % of total councillors	14.9	10.9	15.9	14.3	16.6	17.6

Source: CSO report *Women in Poland*, http://www.stat.gov.pl/cps/rde/xbcr/gus/Kobiety_w_Polsce.pdf [accessed March 2014].

The quota mechanism for electoral lists introduced into the Polish electoral law in 2011 was an important step towards equal opportunities for men and women in the electoral process. The elections in 2011 were the first in Poland where a quota system was in force, which guaranteed at least 35% of women on electoral lists. The Quota Act was introduced on the initiative of the Women's Congress (it was a civil bill that originally required parity, i.e. half the places on the list). Electoral lists to the Sejm included 42% women, but many of these were placed such that there was no chance of a seat; only 21% of women candidates made first place. As a result of the elections to the Sejm of the current term, women account for nearly 23% of the total number of deputies. This is 3 percentage points more than in the previous term (2007–2011). The experience of other countries that have introduced quotas shows that it takes time to make this legal mechanism result in an increase in the number of women in parliament.

In the Global Gender Gap ranking in 2011, Poland was in 42nd place among 135 countries. It was weakest precisely in politics, defined as the degree of representation of women in parliament, the number of women in positions as ministers, and women holding the office of prime minister. In the five fully democratic presidential elections which have taken place in Poland since the Second World War, women candidates have run only twice – Hanna Gronkiewicz-Waltz in 1995 and Henryka Bochniarz in 2005. None of them, however, reached the second round of elections. Unlike the office of the president, Poland has already had woman prime minister – on 10 July 1992 Hanna Suchocka, a representative of the Democratic Union, was appointed Prime Minister. However, she only held the post for a little over a year.

Up to 2005, the share of women in subsequent governments was minimal, except for the cabinet of Jerzy Buzek (1997–2001), in which women accounted for over 16% of the government. Most frequently there was only one woman among the ministers, and in the government of Jan Olszewski there were none at all. Only in the middle of the first decade of the 21st century, with the formation of the government of Kazimierz Marcinkiewicz (Law and Justice) on 31 October 2005, did the share of women in the Council of Ministers reach 20%, and the following cabinets remained consistently at the same level (Druciarek et al., 2012).

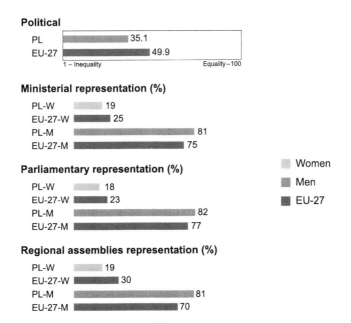

Figure 4.4. The participation of women and men in power structures and decision-making bodies in Poland in comparison with the EU average

Source: European Institute of Gender Equality, *Gender Equality Index*, http://eige.europa.eu/content/gender-equality-index#/domain/power/1?country=PL [accessed March 2014].

Currently in the composition of the government (January 2014) of 18 minis-
terial portfolios 3 are in the hands of women: The Ministry of Education – Joanna
Kluzik-Rostowska, Ministry of Science and Higher Education – Lena Kolars-
ka-Bobińska, and the Ministry of Infrastructure and Development – Elżbieta
Bieńkowska, who simultaneously acts as deputy leader of the Council of Ministers
(Biuletyn Informacji Publicznej, 2014); this represents less than 17%.

To sum up the issue of gender considerations in Polish public life, we should
refer to the *Gender Equality Index* report, presented in June 2013 by the European
Institute of Gender Equality. The report examines, inter alia, the participation of
women and men in power structures and decision-making bodies. According to
these statistics, Poland is slightly below the EU average in terms of the involvement
of women in political life.

4.3. Scandinavia

The Nordic region is considered to be the undisputed leader in the promotion and
actual enactment of gender equality in public life. In asking about the source of
this kind of approach, answers should clearly be sought in the Nordic model of democracy, which was formed and successfully developed over the 20th century. The
determinants of this model should include openness, consensus, and pragmatism,
on which in the development process in Scandinavian societies the ruling social
democratic parties placed emphasis as markers of the state's welfare. It is obvious
that in not all of the countries of the region has this model been implemented in
the same way – despite some degree of homogenization it has shown some differences, resulting from the individual conditions in each of the countries in the
region. The most advanced stage of this model has been seen in force in Norway
and Sweden, somewhat less successful in this field is Denmark, and at the end of
the list come Finland and Iceland (Bergquist et al., 1999, p. 5).

In addition to political factors, this strong commitment to respecting the
principle of gender equality has historical roots. The realisation of the goals and
aspirations of women to obtain their rightful position in the social and political
life proceeded in the Nordic countries according to a schema similar to other
European countries. The starting point was the traditional division of social roles,
resulting in the dominance of men in prominent positions. A kind of breakthrough
in this system happened, increasing women's access to formal education, and
thus the professional aspirations of women started by the industrial revolution.
These processes were accompanied by the development of emancipation movements whose activists emphasized the need for women to participate socially and
politically.

The result of these changes was to grant women the right to vote, which took
place relatively early in comparison with other European countries. First this

reform was introduced in Finland in 1906, then Norway – 1913, followed by Denmark and Iceland – 1915, and in Sweden in 1921. Although this did not lead to the introduction of a visibly increased representation of women in parliament and local government, it was undoubtedly a step towards the position of equality for both sexes, which we have in the region today. In Finland alone before the Second World War a 10-percent level of representation of women in parliament and local assemblies was achieved, and in the 1960s their participation in these bodies reached around 15%.

Although at the end of the Second World War most of the provisions limiting economic, social and political activity of women had been abolished, this did not mean that the problem of discrimination based on sex was spontaneously resolved. The impetus for a debate on the roles of both sexes raging in the Nordic societies in the 1950s and 1960s was the fact that despite formal equal rights for men and women, and accompanying declarations, these were not visible in the actual situation, and discrimination was still strongly apparent in various aspects of social life.

The demands became more assertive in the early 1970s, when the Scandinavian countries were faced with the "second wave" of feminism. This was a reaction to the disenchantment which appeared in connection with the activities carried out so far in favour of equality, which, as already stated, focused primarily on formal guarantees. The changes in the law, however, did not bear fruit in terms of wage equality and access to leadership positions, and the presence of women in decision-making bodies still remained limited. At the same time they were still burdened with the responsibility for the household and childcare.

An especially dynamic development of initiatives for women's rights was undertaken by a relatively wide range of organizations with varying degrees of formalization in Denmark, Iceland and Norway. Sweden and Finland were characterized by a lower degree of activity in this area, preferring recourse to more traditional methods of action taken by women's political organizations. Common to all the countries in the region was the trend for a significant increase in the mobilization of women in political parties, which was reflected in the statistics on the representation of women in legislatures across the region (Skard, 2007).

Among the key determinants for these processes we should mention crucial elements for the level of participation as such, and so primarily socioeconomic factors. After the Second World War Scandinavian society noted fairly rapid economic development, and in the process of transition from industrial to post-industrial society they were able to achieve a high level of social development. Confirmation of this fact may be found in the high HDI, for which, as shown by data from the United Nations for 2012, almost all countries of the region occupy positions in the top twenty of the ranking (United Nations Development Programme, 2011).

Another important element is the electoral system effective in the Nordic countries. As already stated, the proportional system based on multi-member districts is more conducive to the electoral success of women. Indeed, on the one hand, if you can take a number of seats in a given constituency, political parties will be more willing to accommodate women among their candidates. On the other hand, in the case of single-seat system, there will be a clear dominance of men, who usually occupy prominent positions in the parties and their names are associated with specific groups. As noted by Skard (2007), "In Norway, the nomination and election of women for Parliament was for a long time clearly related to the number of representatives the parties obtained in each constituency."

However, despite the undeniably positive impact the proportional electoral system has had on the growth of women's representation in the parliaments of the Nordic countries, it is not the determining factor. One example is Iceland, where, despite its use, the number of women parliamentarians over several decades of the 20th century was low. This was affected by such factors as: the small size of the Icelandic parliament and local councils, and the organizing of parliamentary primaries in which men were favoured. No lesser importance can be attributed to cultural factors and the structure of the economy based on agriculture and fishing, and so on sectors in which the leading role is traditionally played by men.

Table 4.8. The presence of women in the Nordic parliaments in the years 1945–1990 (%)

Year	Denmark	Finland	Iceland	Norway	Sweden
1945	5	9	2	5	8
1950	8	15	0	5	10
1955	9	14	2	7	12
1960	10	14	4	9	13
1965	11	17	2	8	14
1970	11	21	5	9	15
1975	16	24	5	16	21
1980	16	26	5	24	26
1985	24	29	15	26	28
1990	31	32	21	36	38

Source: J.M. Bystydzienski (1995), *Women in Electoral Politics. Lessons from Norway*, Westport CT: Praeger, p. 14.

The scope of the voters to decide on the shape of the party electoral lists may be important. The Scandinavian systems in varying degrees allow for the possibility of personalizing the vote in such a way that in addition to those proposed by the parties, voters can place the name or names of other people preferred on the ballot.

These instruments, however, would not yield results in the form of an increase in the number of women in the Nordic parliaments and local governments, if not accompanied by a range of strategies for involving them in the process of obtaining political support. Examples include the various types of campaigns, meetings, demonstrations, networking with NGOs, and inspiring public debate through the media.

Particularly noteworthy is an institution practiced from the beginning of the twentieth century in Iceland, "the female list," which was to serve as a tool to implement the political aspirations of women from the moment they obtained their full electoral rights. It first appeared in 1908 on the initiative of women's organizations whose activists were running for places in Reykjavik city council. In 1922, the first Icelandic woman parliamentarian was elected from a separate list. The spokesperson for the functioning of the female list was the Women's Alliance active in the years 1983–1998 (Styrkársdóttir, 1999, pp. 88–92).

The result of these aforementioned trends were significant changes in legislation which, combined with consistently implemented activities in the field of gender mainstreaming, made the Scandinavian countries the leader when it comes to the position of both sexes in social and public life. Among the legislative changes were primarily legal solutions to combat gender discrimination in the labour market and on equality issues in the area of wages. The first country to introduce an Equal Pay Law was Iceland (1973). In 1976, this act was replaced by a larger regulation under the name of the Equal Rights Act. Similar solutions were used in Denmark (Equal Treatment Act – 1978), Sweden (1978) and Norway (1978).

It is worth noting that the Scandinavian legislative initiatives are essentially aimed in two directions (Borchorst, 1999, pp. 191–195). Firstly, there are the provisions concerning equal treatment and neutrality of gender. In each of the countries the constitutions provide for prohibition against discrimination on the basis of sex, and ordinary legislation includes provisions to exclude differences in treatment of the sexes. In this context, the Norwegian legislature defined differential treatment as "treatment which de facto results in an unreasonable disadvantage for one sex compared to the other" (Act no. 45 of June 9th 1978 on Gender Equality). In the light of the provisions of section 3 of The Act Relating to Gender Equality 2005, "Direct or indirect differential treatment of women and men is not permitted." The phrase "direct differential treatment" means in this case, on the one hand, discrimination against women or men due to biological gender (sex), and on the other deterioration of women's situation because of motherhood. In turn, "indirect differential treatment" shall mean any apparently gender-neutral action that in fact has the effect of placing one of the sexes in a worse position than the other (The Act Relating to Gender Equality, 2005). Similar solutions have appeared in Finnish legislation, where the concept of discrimination is defined as that which has "de facto resulted in differential treatment" (Ministry of Social Affairs and Health Finland, 1989).

The second trend of anti-discrimination measures taken by the regulators and governments of the Nordic countries are initiatives that can be characterized as positive discrimination. These include all types of manifestations of preferential treatment of women as the under-represented sex. This type of instrument in the fight against discrimination on grounds of sex raises some doubts and has its strong opponents. They point to the fact that positive discrimination leads to the violation of the rights of the individual, and biological sex should not be a criterion for the allocation of jobs or places at universities.

The preferential treatment of women or representatives of disadvantaged groups isolated because of criteria other than gender is also recognized as a factor negatively affecting the result of the selection process of candidates for a particular position, as a person with lower qualifications may be selected. The proponents of the mechanism of positive discrimination indicates that stereotypes and prejudices against women deeply rooted in the social consciousness can only be effectively eliminated by taking radical or controversial steps. The removal of structural barriers to women's access to high political, leadership, and scientific positions is recognized at the same time as a priority that is worth pursuing, even if part of the public expresses their scepticism towards these actions.

The scope of positive discrimination in each of the Scandinavian countries in the region is diverse. For example, in Norway, the aforementioned Act Relating to Gender Equality concerning affirmative action in favour of one of the sexes says that:

> Different treatment that promotes gender equality in conformity with the purpose of this Act is not a contravention of section 3. The same applies to special rights and rules are regarding measures that are intended to protect women in connection with pregnancy, childbirth and breastfeeding. The King may prescribe provisions as to which types of different treatment are permitted in pursuance of this Act, including provisions regarding affirmative action in favour of men in connection with the education and care of children.

The solution, whose introduction in the 1970s was decided on by party authorities in the Nordic countries in order to increase the representation of women in top positions, was the quota system. The initiators of the introduction of at least 40 percent representation of the sexes in all party boards and committees were the Swedish liberals, and the socialists in Norway followed their example. In 1975, this resulted in making Berit Ås party leader, and in 1979 – the election of Liss Schanke as Secretary General of this organization. Subsequently, the quota system was introduced by the Labour Party, the Centre and the Christian People's Party.

It should be emphasized that the quota system has found its application not only in internal party politics associated with their management, but also in the general elections to representative bodies. Initially (1975) in Norway a quota of 1/3 was adopted, and then it was increased to 40%. The Norwegian Labour Party went the furthest, when in 2005 it adopted a quota of 50% (Arbeiderpartiet, 2005).

It should be noted that in all the Nordic countries, the quotas are voluntary, as there are no legal instruments which would impose on political parties a requirement ensure a minimum representation of women in decision-making bodies, either at parliamentary or local government levels. Among the Nordic countries, Finland has not adopted the quota system in their party system. However, thanks to the activity of women's movements, women's representation in the representative bodies in the country has clearly risen. Also interesting is the case of Denmark, where after some time two of the parties deviated from the quota system due to the fact that it did not give significant results.

On the other hand, in the case of public bodies quotas were legally sanctioned during the 1980s. This practice was initiated in Norway, where in 1973 this system came into force in state committees, councils and boards of institutions whose members were appointed by nomination. Each of them was obliged to put forward a male and female candidates for the vacant post, and the final selection was the

Table 4.9. Vertical political segregation: Proportion of women in a number of key political positions in the Nordic countries in the 1990s and 2005–2009

Positions	Denmark		Finland		Iceland		Norway		Sweden	
Parliament and government/year	1994	2007	1995	2009	1995	2009	1993	2005	1994	2006
MPs	34	38	34	42	25	43	39	38	40	47
Speakers (or equivalent)	40	0	67	0	0	100	17	17	50	50
Committees	38	38	31	39	29	34	–	36	44	47
Committee chairpersons	31	38	20	41	25	50	33	31	47	44
Ministers	35	42	41	60	10	42	42	47	50	41
Municipalities/year	1997	2005	1996	2008	1994	2006	1995	2007	1994	2006
Municipal assemblies	27	27	31	37	25	36	33	38	41	42
Diplomatic service/year	1995	2009	1997	2008	1995	2008	1995	2008	1995	2007
Ambassadors	3	15	7	27	5	14	9	28	10*	32*

* Both heads of missions and ambassadors to international bodies.

Source: K. Niskanen (ed.) (2011), *Gender and Power in the Nordic Countries*, Oslo: Norden, p. 23.

choice of the relevant minister, taking care that proportional representation of women was preserved. Rules determining the participation of representatives of both sexes in Norwegian public life defined by the provisions of Section 21 of The Act Relating to Gender Equality, referring to the representation of both sexes in all public committees:

> When a public body appoints or elects committees, governing boards, councils, boards, etc. each sex shall be represented as follows: 1. If the committee has two or three members, both sexes shall be represented. 2. If the committee has four or five members, each sex shall be represented by at least two members. 3. If the committee has six to eight members, each sex shall be represented by at least three members. 4. If the committee has nine members, each sex shall be represented by at least four members, and if the committee has a greater number of members, each sex shall be represented by at least 40 per cent of the members. 5. The provisions of nos. 1–4 shall apply correspondingly to the election of deputy members. Exceptions may be made from the provisions of the first paragraph if there are special circumstances that make it obviously unreasonable to demand that the requirements be fulfilled. The provisions of this section shall not apply to committees, etc. which pursuant to statute shall consist only of members from directly elected assemblies (The Act relating to Gender Equality, 2005).

Conclusions

Based on the above considerations, the conclusion seems justified that a group of complex factors decide on increased presence of women in political life in modern societies. Undoubtedly, the solution in the form of the application of a quota system would provide a clear answer to the question of the success of the

Scandinavian countries in balancing the sex ratio in politics. However, it should be noted that the fact that the representation of women in parliaments in some of the Nordic countries was already noticeable before the political parties began to use this instrument. Thus, as a factor for achieving this state of affairs the fact should be recognized that it was largely the activity of women themselves and their organizations, also in the historical perspective, associated with their struggle for the right to vote. Also, the type of political system, so that the chances of finding women on the electoral lists of each party have become larger, is not irrelevant here. However, the introduction of quotas only strengthened this trend, paving the way for women party candidates to seats in parliaments or to posts related to the exercise of decision-making functions.

For comparison, it is worth referring to the statistics showing the effects of quotas, and therefore the degree of parliamentary representation of women in other regions of the world (Table 4.9). Based on these data, the conclusion can be drawn that the application of the quota system in electoral processes is becoming a global trend, and not limited to the developed countries of Western democracies and societies that have a historically established tradition of women's emancipation. However, this solution should not be treated as an unfailing instrument, which will have the desired effect in every case. It may be only a formal solution, devoid of factual reflection in the political reality, if it is not accompanied by a broader context.

Table 4.10. World ranking list of female representation in parliament

Country	Women in parliament (%)	Type of quota system	Electoral system
1. Rwanda	56.3 (2008)	Quota law	PR*
2. Sweden	47.3 (2006)	Party quotas	PR
3. South Africa	44.5 (2009)	Party quotas	PR
4. Cuba	43.2 (2008)	Non-democratic election	SM**
5. Iceland	42.9 (2009)	Party quotas	PR
6. Finland	42.0 (2007)	–	PR
7. Argentina	40.0 (2007)	Quota law	PR
8. Norway	39.6 (2009)	Party quotas	PR
9. Costa Rica	38.6 (2006)	Quota law	PR
10. Denmark	37.4 (2007)	–	PR
11. Angola	37.3 (2008)	Quota law	PR
12. Belgium	36.7 (2007)	Quota law	PR
13. The Netherlands	36.7 (2006)	Party quotas	PR
14. Spain	36.3 (2008)	Quota law	PR
15. Mozambique	34.8 (2004)	Party quotas	PR
16. New Zealand	33.6 (2008)	–	Mix***

*PR – proportional representation (party lists with multiple candidates),
**SM – single mandate constituencies (each party nominates candidate who received the majority of the votes,
***Mix of proportional representation and single-mandate constituencies.

Source: Interparliamentary Union, www.ipu.org; International IDEA, Stockholm University, www.quotaproject.org [accessed March 2014].

First of all, the type of quota system used should be consistent with the relevant national electoral system. Second, the system should be implemented in such a way that the electoral lists use a mechanism for placing the names of male and female candidates alternately. This is justified to the extent that even if a 40% of quota is introduced, the names of the women candidates may be at the end of the electoral lists, and so the likelihood of their winning a seat will be much smaller. Another requirement associated with the quota system should be the existence of a sanction mechanism if the parties fail to comply with the regulation, for example in the form of refusal to register an electoral list so constructed (Dahlerup, 1999, p. 65).

Table 4.11. Women and men in the selected parliamentary committees (%) and total number of members/committees in the selected years

Committee	Denmark			Finland			Iceland			Norway			Sweden		
	F. %	M. %	Tot.	F. %	M. %	Tot.	F. %	M. %	Tot.	F. %	M. %	Tot.	F. %	M. %	Tot.
Labour Market and Equality	29	71	17	65	35	17	–	–	–	42	58	12	59	41	17
Civil	–	–	–	–	–	–	–	–	–	–	–	–	41	59	17
Finance	24	76	17	29	71	21	18	82	11	11	89	18	41	59	17
Defence	0	100	17	29	71	17	–	–	–	13	87	8	47	53	17
Justice	41	59	17	47	53	17	–	–	–	50	50	10	53	47	17
Constitutional Affairs (Judicial and Consti- tutional Review)	–	–	–	41	59	17	44	56	9	22	78	9	41	59	17
Culture and Edu- cation; Family and Culture	47	53	17	–	–	–	–	–	–	64	36	11	53	47	17
Environment and Agriculture; Environ- ment and Energy	–	–	–	59	41	17	56	44	9	33	67	15	41	59	17
Agriculture and Forestry; Agriculture and Fisheries	24	76	17	24	76	17	11	89	9	–	–	–	–	–	–
Industry (Trade)	35	65	17	41	59	17	33	67	9	21	79	14	47	53	17
Taxation	29	71	17	–	–	–	–	–	–	–	–	–	41	59	17
Social Insurance	–	–	–	–	–	–	–	–	–	–	–	–	35	65	17
Social Issues	71	29	17	65	35	17	56	44	9	–	–	–	53	47	17
Transport and Communications	12	88	17	29	71	17	33	67	9	27	73	15	47	53	17
Education	59	41	17	53	47	17	67	33	9	47	53	15	53	47	17
Foreign Affairs	35	65	17	35	65	17	56	44	9	50	50	17	47	53	17
EU and Europe	47	53	17	–	–	–	–	–	–	–	–	–	41	59	17

* The data relates to the following years: Denmark, 2003–04 (total number of parliamentary committees, 23); Finland, 2008 (total number of committees, 16); Iceland, 2009 (total number of committees, 12); Norway, 2005 (total number of committees, 13); and Sweden, 2006 (total number of committees, 16).

Source: K. Niskanen (ed.) (2011), *Gender and Power in the Nordic Countries*, Oslo: Norden, p. 53.

In the context of initiatives for equal representation of women in representative bodies exercising functions and decision-making, it is worth noting that, even in countries which have achieved a satisfactory level in terms of numbers, this is not fully reflected in the implementation of gender equality in the area of politics. This is because the practice, often used, is to limit access to certain areas of political activity. There is still a well-established social, stereotypical division into areas traditionally "reserved" for representatives of both sexes, such as social affairs or education.

Literature

Act no. 45 of June 9th 1978 on Gender Equality, http://www.regjeringen.no/en/doc/laws/acts/the-act-relating-to-gender-equality-the-.html?id=454568 [accessed 30.12.2013].

Arbeiderpartiet (2005), http://www.arbeiderpartiet.no/ [accessed 15.01.2014].

Bergquist, Ch. et al. (1999), *Gender and Politics in the Nordic Countries*, Oslo.

Biuletyn Informacji Publicznej (2014), http://bip.kprm.gov.pl/kpr/bip-rady-ministrow/sklad-rady-ministrow/1635,Sklad-Rady-Ministrow.html [accessed 15.01.2014].

Borchorst, A. (1999), "Gender equality law," [in:] Ch. Bergqvist (ed.), *Equal Democracies? Gender and Politics in the Nordic Countries*, Oslo: Scandinavian University Press.

Burns, N. (2007), "Gender in the aggregate, gender in the individual, gender and political action," *Politics & Gender*, no. 3.

Bystydzienski, J.M. (1995), *Women in Electoral Politics. Lessons from Norway*, Westport CT: Praeger.

Coffé, H., Bolzendahl, C. (2010), "Same Game, Different Rules? Gender Differences in Political Participation," *Sex Roles*, No. 62(5–6), March.

Constantini, E., Valenty, L.O. (1996), "The motives-ideology connection among political party activists," *Political Psychology*, No. 17.

Dahlerup, D. (2011), "Women in Nordic politics – a continuing success story?," [in:] K. Niskanen (ed.), *Gender and Power in the Nordic Countries*, Oslo: Norden.

Dalton, R. J. (2008), "Citizenship norms and the expansion of political participation", *Political Studies*, No. 56.

Druciarek, M., Fuszara, M. et al. (2012), *Kobiety na polskiej scenie politycznej*, Raport Instytutu Spraw Publicznych http://isp.org.pl/uploads/filemanager/Program%20Prawa%20i%20Instytucji%20Demokratycznych/aa338207000.pdf [accessed 16.01.2014].

European Commission (2009), *Women in politics – time for action*, Luxembourg.

European Institute for Gender Equality, *Gender Equality Index*, http://eige.europa.eu/content/gender-equality-index#/domain/power/1?country=PL [accessed 15.01.2014].

European Institute for Equality between Women and Men (2012), *Przegląd realizacji Pekińskiej Platformy, 2012, Działania: kobiety i gospodarka. Główne wnioski*, Bruksela, http://eige.europa.eu/sites/default/files/Women%20and%20the%20Economy%20-%20Reconciliation%20of%20Work%20&%20Family%20-%20Main%20findings_PL.pdf [accessed 29.07.2014].

Fuszara, M. (2009), *Raport Kongresu Kobiet "20 lat transformacji 1989–2009,"* http://pokl.up.gov.pl/efs/download/raport_KKP.pdf, pp. 187–202.

GUS (2007), *Raport „Kobiety w Polsce,"* http://www.stat.gov.pl/cps/rde/xbcr/gus/Kobiety_w_Polsce.pdf [accessed 29.07.2014].

International Institute for Democracy and Electoral Assistance (2013), *Democracy and Gender Equality. The Role of the UN, United Nations*.

International Institute for Democracy and Electoral Assistance (IDEA) (2013), *Global overview of women's political participation and implementation of the quota system – Draft Speaking*

Notes, http://www.idea.int; International IDEA, Stockholm University, www.quotaproject. org [accessed 12.12.2013].

Interparliamentary Union (2013), *Women speakers of national parliaments. History and present*, http://www.ipu.org/wmn-e/speakers.htm [accessed March 2014].

Lesiewicz, E. (2011), *Droga polskich kobiet do Parlamentu Europejskiego*, https://repozytorium. amu.edu.pl/jspui/bitstream/10593/6175/1/055-066.pdf http://www.ipu.org/wmn-e/speakers. htm [accessed March 2014].

Lewicka, M. (2004), "Kup Pan książkę... Mechanizmy aktywności obywatelskiej Polaków," *Studia Psychologiczne*, nr 4.

Ministry of Social Affairs and Health Finland (1989), http://www.stm.fi/en/gender_equality [accessed 14.12.2013].

Muchowiecka, L. (2011), *Kobieta i władza – bolesny proces integracji. Kwestia równouprawnienia kobiet w polityce*, http://socjogender.blox.pl/2011/02/Kobieta-i-wladza-bolesny-proces--integracji.html [accessed 15.12.2013].

Niskanen, K. (ed.) (2011), *Gender and Power in the Nordic Countries*, Oslo: Norden.

Parlament Europejski (2009), http://www.europarl.europa.eu/aboutparliament/en/00082fcd21/ Results-by-country-(2009).html [accessed 14.12.2013].

Polkowska, D. (2012), *Droga kobiet do polityki – porównanie międzynarodowe*, http://www. kulturaihistoria.umcs.lublin.pl/archives/4198 [accessed 15.01.2014].

Schlozman K.L, Burns N., Verba S. (1999), "What happened at work today? A multistage model of gender, employment, and political participation," *The Journal of Politics*, no. 61.

Skard, T. (2007), *Women in politics: Nordic experience*, http://aa.ecn.cz/img_upload/666f7275 6d35302d6669313030313139/Rev._Women_Nordic_Politics___version_2_18.1.2007.doc [accessed 18.12.2013].

Special Eurobarometer (2008), *The European elections 2009*, http://ec.europa.eu/public_opinion/ archives/ebs/ebs_299_en.pdf, pp. 1–43 [accessed 18.12.2013].

Styrkársdóttir, A. (1999), "Women's lists in Iceland – A response to political lethargy," [in:] Ch. Bergqvist (ed.), Equal *Democracies? Gender and Politics in the Nordic Countries*, Oslo: Norden.

The Act relating to Gender Equality (2005), http://www.regjeringen.no/en/doc/laws/acts/the--act-relating-to-gender-equality-the-.html?id=454568 [accessed 16.12.2013].

The Party of European Socialists (2007), *Women's participation in politics in Europe. Figures and data*, http://www.pes.eu/fr/system/files/Women_in_politics-data_figures.pdf [accessed 16.12.2013].

United Nations Development Programme (2011), https://data.undp.org/dataset/Table-Human--Development-Index-and-its-components/wxub-qc5k [accessed 15.12.2013].

Verba, S. (1997), "Knowing and caring about politics. Gender and political engagement," *Journal of Politics*, no. 59.

Waring, M., Greenwood, G., Pintat, C. (2000), *Inter-Parliamentary Union's Report "Politics: Women Speakers of National Parliaments. History and Present,"* http://www.ipu.org/wmn-e/ speakers.htm [accessed March 2014].

Wojniak, J. (2012), "Podręcznikowa wizja świata a społeczna rzeczywistość. Kreowanie wizerunków płci w ramach kształcenia literacko-kulturowego w szkole podstawowej," *Aequalitas*, Vol. 1.

Chapter 5

The professional situation of women and men in Poland – declarations and realities

Danuta Kopycińska

Abstract

The existing legislation in Poland, both national and international, provides equal professional rights to women and men. The declared professional equality, however, is not synonymous with equality in practice, since the impact on the realities are, admittedly regulations, but also tradition or socio-cultural norms. The aim of this study is to assess the situation of women and men in Poland and the research covers the years 2000–2012. The study justifies the statement that during the period considered the professional situation of women compared unfavourably to that of men. The realities were therefore different from the declarations of equality. The causes of this state of affairs did not stem from economic factors or legislation – it must be assumed that the worse situation of women in Poland resulted primarily from existing traditions and socio-cultural norms.

Key words: professional equality, regulation, labour market, Poland

Introduction

In Poland, equal rights for men and women in the workplace – as in other spheres of life – are covered by laws both domestic and international.[1] The most important domestic legislation is undoubtedly the Constitution of the Republic of Poland of 2 April 1997, providing men and women with equal rights to employment and promotion, and to equal pay for work of equal value (Constitution of RP 1997 art. 33 para 2). In terms of international regulation the Convention on the Elimination of Discrimination against Women dated 18.12.1979 passed by the General Assembly of the United Nations is noteworthy, where in the field of work the following rights are guaranteed: the right to permanent work and equal working

---

1 In this paper we will present only selected regulations on the equality of women and men.

conditions, equal employment opportunities and equal criteria for selection, the right to choose an occupation and employment, promotion and access to training, equal pay for work of equal value and to social security (art. 11).

Poland's integration with the European Union resulted in the need to adapt national legislation to EU legislation, which resulted in both the amendment of existing legislation and the introduction of a number of new solutions. From the point of view of the subject of discussion in this study – the most important rules in this field **before accession** include amendments made to the Labour Code of 1974 and the establishment of an institution with the task of equalising professional opportunities for women. The main changes in the Labour Code, made in 2001–2004, consisted of terms in the provisions relating to "Equal treatment in employment," a definition of direct discrimination, detailing the concept of indirect and positive discrimination and the introduction of penalties for violation of the principle of equal treatment for men and women.[2] At the same time, in 2001 a Plenipotentiary for Family Affairs and Equal Status of Women and Men was appointed, and in 2002 converted to the Government Plenipotentiary for Equal Status of Women and Men (Regulation of the Council of Ministers dated October 20, 2001, and the Regulation of the Council of Ministers dated 26 June 2002).[3]

After integration with the European Union – the implementation of certain EU provisions (directives) took place in Poland on equality of opportunity and equal treatment of men and women in employment and work (Directive 2006/54/EU of 2009).[4] This resulted in a further amendment to the Polish Labour Code (Act dated 25 November 2010, Act dated 3 December, 2010) and the establishment in 2008 of the Government Plenipotentiary for Equal Treatment (Regulation of the Council of Ministers dated 22 August 2008) and from 1 January 2011 – the Ombudsman for Citizen's Rights and the Government Plenipotentiary for Equal Treatment. It should be emphasized that while the previous authorities acting for equal treatment for men and women were appointed by the Council of Ministers – the Government Plenipotentiary for Equal Treatment was appointed at the rank of Secretary of State in the Office of the Prime Minister and was appointed through an Act, which greatly enhances its institutional significance (Act dated 3 December 2010).

The view in the legal regulations covering professional equality between men and women, however, is not equivalent to the existence of such equality in practice. This is because the realities in the country are affected by both law and tradition, socio-cultural norms, and the strength of the existing gender stereotypes (Mandel, 2004).

---

2   A detailed discussion of the changes in the Labour Code of 1974 is included, among others, in the papers: Boruta, 2004, pp. 2–8; Strusińska-Żukowska, 2004, pp. 3–5; Suzdorf, 2004, pp. 336–342; Kalinowska-Sufinowicz, 2013, pp. 163–166; and others.

3   The Office of the Government Plenipotentiary for Equal Status of Women and Men was abolished in Poland in 2005 (Regulation of the Council of Ministers dated 3 November 2005)

4   This directive dated 15.08.2009 repealed 7 earlier directives relating to, inter alia, equal pay for men and women, or equal access to employment, promotion and vocational training, and working conditions.

The aim of this study is to assess the situation of women and men in Poland and the research covers:
- potential resources for jobs by gender,
- labour force participation of women and men,
- evolution of employment and unemployment rates among men and women,
- and, the men and women inactivity in the labour market.[5]

The basic research period is the years 2000–2012 during which numerous EU regulations and institutions working for equal rights for women and men were introduced.[6]

5.1. Potential labour resources in Poland by gender in the years 2000–2012

From the point of view of the analysis of potential labour resources in Poland, it is important to present both the number of the population structure in general and of the potential labour force – age 15 years and older. The data on population by these criteria have been included in the Tables 5.1 and 5.2.

Table 5.1. The population of Poland in the years 2000–2012 (individuals)

Years	Total	Men	Women	Women's share (%)
2000	38 253 955	18 537 339	19 716 616	51.5
2001	38 242 197	18 525 163	19 717 034	51.6
2002	38 218 531	18 506 749	19 711 782	51.6
2003	38 190 608	18 486 430	19 704 178	51.6
2004	38 173 835	18 470 253	19 703 582	51.6
2005	38 157 055	18 453 855	19 703 200	51.6
2006	38 125 479	18 426 775	19 698 704	51.6
2007	38 115 641	18 411 501	19 704 140	51.7
2008	38 135 876	18 414 926	19 720 950	51.7
2009	38 167 329	18 n428 742	19 738 587	51.7
2010	38 529 866	18 653 125	19 876 741	51.6
2011	38 538 447	18 654 577	19 883 870	51.6
2012	38 533 299	18 649 334	19 883 965	51.6

Source: own study based on CSO Labour Force Survey, 2001–2013.

---

5   Due to the limited scope, the study presents only the basic issues concerning the professional situation – which is part of the economic situation – of women and men in Poland.
6   The analysis has been performed based on statistical data.

Table 5.2. Potential labour force in Poland – age 15 and older (individuals)

Years	Total	Men	Women	Women's share (%)
2000	30 959 504	14 802 587	16 156 917	52.2
2001	31 202 973	14 920 707	16 282 266	52.2
2002	31 414 267	15 022 477	16 391 790	52.2
2003	31 610 437	15 115 835	16 494 602	52.2
2004	31 796 598	15 202 968	16 593 630	51.9
2005	31 967 880	15 282 034	16 685 846	53.6
2006	32 103 119	15 339 965	16 763 154	52.2
2007	32 214 763	15 385 793	16 828 970	52.2
2008	32 306 436	15 424 931	16 881 505	52.3
2009	32 384 552	15 460 694	16 923 858	52.3
2010	32 674 100	15 649 812	17 024 288	52.1
2011	32 719 470	15 669 618	17 049 852	52.1
2012	32 736 685	15 675 128	17 061 557	52.1

Source: own study based on CSO Labour Force Survey, 2001–2013.

Analysis of the statistical data contained in Tables 5.1 and 5.2 shows that throughout the period considered there was predominance of women over men both in the total population and at the age of 15 and over. The share of women in the total population in each year was from 51.5% to 51.7% and at the age of 15 and over – 52.1% to 53.6%. The potential labour resources of women of working age were therefore higher than the potential labour resources of men. As the number of people aged 15 and over is not sufficient for a more precise definition of the labour force in a given country in this group, the working age population constituting a potential labour supply has been extracted. The number of working-age population by gender in Poland is presented in Table 5.3.

Table 5.3. The working age population of Poland in the years 2000–2012 (individuals)

Years	Total	Men	Women	Women's share (%)
2000	23 361 003	11 973 901	11 287 102	48.5
2001	23 526 497	12 099 304	11 427 193	48.6
2002	23 789 827	12 220519	11 569 288	48.6
2003	24 038 777	12 336 704	11 702 073	48.7
2004	24 239 587	12 429 287	11 810 300	48.7
2005	24 405 034	12 506 049	11 898 985	48.8
2006	24 481 670	12 567 550	11 914 120	48.7
2007	24 545 254	12 637 643	11 907 611	48.5
2008	24 590 475	12 707 283	11 883 192	48.3
2009	24 624 443	12 776 715	11 847 728	48.1
2010	24 830 001	12 982 094	11 848 907	47.7
2011	24 738 527	12 970 846	11 767 681	47.6
2012	24 605 558	12 929 780	11 675 778	47.5

Source: own report based on CSO Labour Force Survey, 2001–2013.

In contrast to the data in Tables 5.1 and 5.2, the number of women of working age was lower than that of men, and from 2006 showed a downward trend, while at the same time the number of men increased. The share of women of working age in the total population in this age group decreased from 48.8% in 2005 to 47.5% in 2012. Still, women accounted for almost half of the population of this group, too, so it can be concluded that both quantitative demographic structure and the structure of the supply-side potential of women and men were equivalent.

On the margins of labour resource considerations by sex – it is worth recalling that both occurring and projected demographic changes in Poland will have a negative impact on the labour market. The decreasing total population and the decreasing number of people of working and pre-workingage, while the population of post-working age increases, will constitute a serious threat to the socioeconomic development of the country. Making full use of the existing labour force of both men and women is therefore a necessity (Kopycińska, 2012, 2013).

5.2. Professional participation of women and men in Poland in the years 2000–2012

The data on the size of the labour force in Poland presented in the previous section are not equivalent to the full use of these resources in the labour market, since they only constitute potential labour force. Included in the labour force (including working age) are both people employed or actively seeking employment, as well as inactive in the labour market – not working and not looking for work. From the point of view of efficient use of the labour force and human capital in a given country primarily significant is the size of the labour force, and in that – people who are working. Among people not in the labour force, however, the reasons for this inactivity are important. The number of people actively working and labour force participation rate in Poland by gender in the years 2000–2012 are presented in Tables 5.4 and 5.5.

The data given in Table 5.6 on women of working age show a greater participation than men in this population group. The analysis of the data in the tables 5.4 and 5.5 showed that the numerical superiority of women over men aged 15 and over is not equivalent to their predominance in employment. Throughout the period considered, the number of working women was lower than the number of men, and the difference in percentage points to the disadvantage of women in the final year was more than 16 points.

Here it is also worth pointing out that the unfavourable difference in labour force participation of women and men in Poland occurred regardless of the level

Table 5.4. Labour force in Poland in the years 2000–2012 (thous. people)

Years	Total	Men	Women
2000	17 311	9348	7962
2001	17 376	9379	7997
2002	17 213	9308	7905
2003	16 946	9173	7773
2004	17 025	9246	7780
2005	17 161	9362	7799
2006	16 938	9283	7655
2007	16 859	9234	7626
2008	17 011	9317	7694
2009	17 279	9455	7824
2010	17 123	9446	7677
2011	17 221	9504	7717
2012	17 340	9551	7789

Source: own report based on CSO Labour Force Survey, 2001–2013.

Table 5.5. Labour force participation rates – people aged 15 and older in Poland

Years	Total	Men	Women
2000	56,6	64,1	49,7
2001	56,3	63,8	49,5
2002	55,4	62,9	48,6
2003	54,7	62,2	48,0
2004	54,7	62,3	47,8
2005	54,9	62,8	47,7
2006	54,0	62,1	46,6
2007	53,7	61,9	46,3
2008	54,2	62,7	46,6
2009	54,9	63,4	47,3
2010	55,3	63,7	47,6
2011	55,5	64,0	47,8
2012	55,9	64,3	48,1

Source: own report based on CSO Labour Force Survey, 2001–2013.

of education, which is illustrated by Table 5.6. Analysis of the data contained in the table below shows that the labour force participation rates for women throughout the whole period and for all levels of education were lower than the activity rates of men. From the point of view of the quality of human capital, particularly important to the formation of this factor is the group of people with higher, post-secondary vocational or secondary vocational education. The difference in these rates to the disadvantage of women in the final year of research was as follows: 5.1 percentage points, 21.5 percentage points, and 17.9 percentage points. Similarly, there is a disadvantage when comparing the labour force participation rates of men and women in Poland of working age which is shown in Table 5.7.

Table 5.6. Labour force participation rates of people in Poland aged 15 and older in the years 2003 to 2012* by gender and level of education (%)

Years	Gender	Education					
		Tertiary	Post--secondary education	Secondary vocational	Secondary general	Vocational	Secondary Schools Basic and incomplete basic
2003	M	81.0	77.2	73.2	52.0	74.7	31.5
	W	78.8	72.4	63.3	45.1	58.7	18.6
2004	M	81.4	77.1	72.8	50.7	74.9	31.6
	W	78.2	71.0	62.0	43.2	58.8	18.0
2005	M	81.0	79.9	73.5	51.1	75.1	31.2
	W	79.9	68.8	61.5	43.4	57.4	16.1
2006	M	79.8	87.9	73.0	50.1	73.7	29.4
	W	78.8	65.5	60.0	43.3	53.8	14.3
2007	M	80.8	83.7	73.5	49.4	72.5	29.4
	W	79.7	66.6	58.7	41.4	52.8	14.9
2008	M	82.3	75.9	74.2	56.1	72.5	28.6
	W	79.7	69.3	58.2	42.1	52.7	13.7
2009	M	83.3	81.9	74.2	58.1	71.3	27.4
	W	78.9	69.1	57.4	41.0	52.5	12.8

* No data for the years 2000–2002.

Source: own report based on CSO Labour Force Survey, 2001–2013.

Table 5.7. Labour force participation rates of people of working age in Poland by gender in the years 2000–2012 (%)

Years	Total	Men	Women
2000	72.0	76.3	67.5
2001	71.7	75.9	67.2
2002	70.5	74.9	65.8
2003	69.8	74.3	65.0
2004	69.6	74.3	64.6
2005	69.8	74.8	64.6
2006	69.2	74.5	63.7
2007	69.1	74.4	63.5
2008	69.9	75.3	64.4
2009	70.9	76.0	65.6
2010	71.6	76.0	66.8
2011	72.1	76.4	67.4
2012	72.9	76.9	68.5

Source: own study based on CSO Labour Force Survey, 2001–2013.

As with the labour force participation rates at the age of 15 years and up – rates for women of working age were lower than the activity rates of men of this age. This statement applies to the entire study period, and in the last year the difference at the expense of women was 8.4 percentage points.

5.3. Employment of women and men in Poland

This working population – as mentioned earlier – includes the population at work, the most important from the point of view of socioeconomic development of the country. The data on the employment of women and men in Poland is given in Tables 5.8 and 5.9.

Analysis of the employed population in Poland clearly demonstrates that the situation of women in the entire study period was worse than that of men. The number of working women in each year was lower than the number of working men and this difference was more than 1,370 thousand in the base year to more than 1,550 thousand in the final year of the period. The growth rate of female employment rate in the final study year compared to the base year was lower than the growth rate of male employment and the difference in percentage points during this period increased from 11.9 to 13.2 percentage points.

Table 5.8. People working in Poland in the years 2000–2012 by gender (thous. people)

Years	Total	Women	Men
2000	14526	6522	8004
2001	14207	6410	7797
2002	13782	6253	7529
2003	13617	6185	7432
2004	13795	6230	7565
2005	14115	6306	7809
2006	14594	6513	8081
2007	15241	6838	8403
2008	15800	7082	8718
2009	15868	7146	8722
2010	15747	6908	8566
2011	15562	6914	8648
2012	15591	6940	8651

Source: own report based on CSO Labour Force Survey, 2001–2013.

Table 5.9. Employment rate in Poland in the years 2000–2012 by gender (%) (LFS)

Years	Total	Men	Women	Difference in percentage points (M–W)
2000	55.1	61.2	49.3	11.9
2001	53.7	59.2	48.3	10.9
2002	51.7	57.0	46.7	10.3
2003	51.4	56.4	46.4	10.0
2004	51.4	56.8	46.1	10.7
2005	52.8	58.9	46.8	12.1
2006	54.5	60.9	48.2	12.7
2007	57.0	63.6	50.6	13.0
2008	59.2	66.3	52.4	13.9
2009	59.3	66.1	52.8	13.3
2010	59.3	65.6	53.0	12.6
2011	59.7	66.3	53.1	13.2
2012	59.7	66.3	53.1	13.2

Source: own report based on CSO Labour Force Survey, 2001–2013.

As can be seen from the data presented in Table 5.10 regardless of the level of education – employment rates for women were lower than the rates for men in every year studied. With higher education the difference in 2012 at the expense of women was 5.8 percentage points, to 21.1 percentage points. At post-secondary education, and at secondary vocational local – 18.1 percentage points.

Table 5.10. Employment rate in Poland in the years 2003–2012 by gender and education (%)

Years	Gender	Education					
		Tertiary	Post--secondary education	Secondary vocational	Secondary general	Vocational	Secondary Schools primary and incomplete primary
2003	M	75.1	64.8	62.1	41.5	58.8	23.2
	W	72.5	60.1	51.3	34.2	42.3	13.8
2004	M	76.7	65.2	63.0	41.6	59.7	23.9
	W	72.2	59.3	50.0	33.8	43.1	13.4
2005	M	75.6	73.1	64.2	43.1	61.4	23.1
	W	73.6	56.9	51.1	33.3	42.7	12.0
2006	M	75.8	77.7	66.6	44.0	64.4	24.1
	W	73.7	58.1	52.0	35.3	44.0	11.4
2007	M	78.0	77.6	68.7	45.0	65.9	25.9
	W	75.5	60.4	53.8	36.1	46.5	12.7
2008	M	79.9	70.7	70.0	51.1	68.4	25.4
	W	76.3	63.5	54.0	37.9	47.6	12.1
2009	M	79.9	73.8	68.8	51.7	65.2	23.0
	W	74.5	64.2	52.2	36.9	46.8	10.8
2010	M	80.0	74.6	68.5	52.2	64.6	23.2
	W	74.7	58.7	52.1	36.2	45.3	11.1
2011	M	79.2	77.5	69.5	53.3	63.6	23.3
	W	73.9	54.5	52.0	34.8	44.3	11.0
2012	M	78.9	75.2	68.7	54.3	61.8	23.2
	W	73.1	54.1	50.6	34.0	43.1	10.3

Source: own report based on CSO Labour Force Survey, 2001–2013.

Given that the proportion of women with higher education is greater than that of men in the population aged 15–64 in Poland, it can be said that investment in women as human capital did not translate into effective use of that capital in the labour market. Employment according to gender in the NACE sections is presented in Table 5.11.

From the point of view of employment structure, the analysis of the number of employed women and men in such areas as education, health care and other activities is interesting. **These sections are clearly feminized and women's employment there is several times higher than the employment of men. Similar considerations apply to the analysis of the structure of employment by major**

occupational groups. Here, the largest share of employed women (36%) is in the group of specialists in occupations dominated by those typically "feminine" such as: midwives, nurses, etc. Women also have a higher share than men in the following groups: office workers, unskilled workers and in the group: technicians and associate professionals. Men dominate the competition in the group: representatives of public authorities, senior officials and managers, industrial workers and craftsmen, and in the group: operators and assemblers of machinery and equipment (GUS, 2011, Form 2–12, p. 2).

Table 5.11. Employment in Poland in NACE sections by gender in 2008–2011 (thous. people)

NACE sections	2008		2010		2010	
	M	W	M	W	M	W
Agriculture, Fishing, Forestry	1226	980	1150	900	1173	870
Mining and quarrying	206	28	210	20	226	29
Manufacturing	2129	1099	1975	986	2017	1008
Production and distribution of electricity, gas, water	139	35	145	37	143	35
Construction	1164	71	1205	80	1232	86
Trade and repairs	1059	1267	1075	1300	1069	1308
Hotels and restaurants	97	210	111	239	117	238
Transportation storage	710	187	700	187	723	177
Financial intermediation	115	225	128	243	132	257
Property and business, science	59	85	77	97	69	101
Public administration, Defence, Insurance, Social and health insurance	495	490	523	526	529	535
Education	263	921	277	977	278	950
Health and social care	156	701	170	765	169	755
Other services, social community	88	137	90	157	88	156
TOTAL	**7906**	**6436**	**7836**	**6514**	**7967**	**6505**

Source: own study based on CSO Labour Force Survey, 2001–2013.

To conclude the discussion in this section it is worth presenting the employment of women and men in Poland in managerial positions, as illustrated in Table 5.12.

As can be seen from the data in Table 5.12 women in Poland, although having completed higher education, were not frequently employed in managerial positions. The share of men in leadership positions in all organizational units over the entire study period was much higher than women, and almost everywhere grew. It is worth noting that, except for the heads of other internal organizational units, the share of women in other leadership positions decreased in 2010 compared to the base period. And so, as leaders of large and medium-sized organizations their share decreased from 39% to 27%, and Directors-General from 32% to 25%. The largest decrease was in small business managers, where the participation of women in 2004 amounting to 27%, decreased to 8% in 2010.

Table 5.12. Workers employed in managerial positions by gender in Poland in 2004–2010* (%)

Years/Gender	Including:				
	Managers of large and medium-sized organizations	Directors--General, Executive presidents and their deputies	Managers of internal organizational units of core business	Managers of other internal organizational units	Managers of small enter-prises
2004 Total	100.0	100.0	100.0	100.0	100.0
Men	61.0	68.0	61.0	55.0	73.0
Women	39.0	–	–	–	–
2006 Total	100.0	100.0	100.0	100.0	100.0
Men	59.0	67.0	57.0	48.0	60.0
Women	41.0	33.0	43.0	53.0	40.0
2008 Total	100.0	100.0	100.0	100.0	100.0
Men	59.0	68.0	56.0	55.0	72.0
Women	41.0	32.0	44.0	45.0	28.0
2010 Total	100.0	100.0	100.0	100.0	100.0
Men	73.0	75.0	62.0	32.0	92.0
Women	27.0	25.0	38.0	68.0	8.0

* No data, published every two years.
Source: own study based on CSO Labour Force Survey, 2006–2012.

5.4. Unemployment among women and men in Poland

When assessing the situation of women and men in Poland – alongside the analysis of employment – it is vitally important to analyse unemployment including job seekers. These people because they are both worse off than working people and undergoing the process of rapid decrease in the level of possessed and utilized human capital. The number of unemployed and the unemployment rate in Poland by gender are shown in Tables 5.13 and 5.14.

Analysis of the data showed that the number of unemployed women in the entire study period was higher than the number of men and the difference in each year ranged from more than 40 thousand (2009) to over 300 thousand people (2007). The situation for women is similarly unfavourable based on the analysis of data on the unemployment rate. Indeed, this rate was higher for women than men, both aged 15–64, and individuals aged 25–74 years. The long-term unemployment rate was also higher for women. It is worth mentioning that in the latter case, the difference to the disadvantage of women in 2012 was 2.8 percentage points.

The unemployed are characterized by different levels of human capital, re-sulting partially from the already discussed level of formal education. Hence, it is extremely important to analyse unemployment in terms of the level of education of the unemployed. Statistics on the number of unemployed men and women in Poland by level of education is presented in Table 5.15.

Table 5.13. The number of unemployed in Poland in the years 2004–2012 (thous. people)[7]

Years	Total	M	W	Difference M-W
2004	2 999,6	1 431,1	1 568,5	137,5
2005	2 773,0	1 286,6	1 486,4	199,9
2006	2 309,4	1 003,7	1 305,7	302,0
2007	1 746,6	729,2	1 017,3	288,1
2008	1 473,8	640,3	833,4	193,1
2009	1 892,7	926,3	966,4	40,2
2010	1 954,7	939,9	1 014,8	74,9
2011	1 982,7	922,5	1 060,2	137,7
2012	2 136,8	1 037,6	1 099,2	61,6

Source: own report based on CSO Labour Force Survey, 2001–2013.

Table 5.14. The unemployment rate in Poland in the years 2004–2012 by gender (%)

Years	Unemployment rate					Long-term in the unemployed population	
		At the age of 15–64		At the age of 25–74			
	Total	M	W	M	W	M	W
2004	19.4	18.8	20.0	15.4	17.0	52.7	55.5
2005	18.0	16.8	19.4	13.9	16.8	56.1	59.3
2006	14.0	13.1	15.1	10.9	12.9	54.7	57.7
2007	9.7	9.1	10.4	7.6	8.7	50.8	51.8
2008	7.2	6.5	8.0	5.3	6.5	31.8	35.1
2209	8.3	7.9	8.8	6.3	7.2	27.9	33.0
2010	9.7	9.4	10.1	7.8	8.4	30.8	31.5
2011	9.8	9.1	10.5	7.4	8.7	36.2	38.2
2012	10.2	9.5	11.0	7.9	9.2	39.0	41.8

Source: own study based on CSO Labour Force Survey, 2001–2013.

Table 5.15. Number of unemployed men and women in Poland by education in the years 2004–2012

Years	Education									
	Tertiary		Post-secondary education – secondary vocational		Secondary general		Basic		Primary	
	M	W	M	W	M	W	M	W	M	W
2004	52 380	97 036	246 320	409 486	55 423	153 973	557 757	456 663	519 185	451 378
2005	51 536	100 814	223 665	383 064	57 366	154 154	482 184	421 425	471 808	426 984
2006	45 892	94 826	175 826	332 936	50 803	144 063	356 097	357 820	375 088	376 059
2007	38 938	81 294	128 339	257 893	41277	117 700	248 200	268 363	272 471	292 098
2008	41 705	83 143	116 311	212 174	42 335	107 771	214 764	207 293	225 202	223 054
2009	63 065	115 263	175 700	242 681	69 874	133 926	313 876	233 849	303 744	240 702
2010	67 809	136 870	175 233	254 634	70 499	142 649	317 168	239 025	309 205	241 614
2011	70 585	155 247	172 843	267 850	69 125	145 338	308 332	247 494	296 807	244 275
2012	80 475	170 514	195 957	276 503	78 420	147 780	348 578	255 334	334 129	249 055

Source: own study based on CSO Labour Force Survey, 2004–2013 – unemployment by level of education and gender.

---

7   Polish integration with the European Union allowed an influx of workforce, and therefore presents data since 2004.

By analysing the data on the number of unemployed by level of education in general it can be said that with higher and secondary education levels the situation of women was worse – and much worse – than their male counterparts. A particularly unfavourable situation for women occurred in the group of unemployed with higher education, and so thus formally characterized by a high level of human capital. The number of unemployed women at this level of education was not only more than three times higher than the number of unemployed men,[8] but the figure was higher than the number of unemployed women with a secondary education.

Compared to men – the worse situation for women also occurred among unemployed people with post-secondary and secondary vocational and secondary education. In the last level of education, the number of unemployed women in each year was 2 or 3 times higher than the number of unemployed men. And while unemployment in this group is caused to a large extent by the lack of any occupation for graduates of general secondary schools – this does not explain the situation of women. The lack of a specific occupation applies after all to both women and men. It should also be noted here that the number of unemployed women at this level of education was the highest number of women at all levels of education and thus also those with basic and primary education.

Analysing the statistical data on unemployed people with the lowest levels of education it can be stated that the "main" unemployed in these groups were men, and the number of unemployed men with basic and primary education greatly exceeded the number of unemployed men who hold higher levels of education. Against the background of unemployed men – the situation of unemployed women with vocational and primary education were in better shape because the number of unemployed women throughout the study period was lower than the number of unemployed men.

Table 5.16. Number of people not included in the labour force in Poland by gender in the years 2004–2012 (thous. people)

Years	Total	M	W	Women's share of the total
2004	14 098	5 586	8 512	60.4
2005	14 097	5 540	8 557	60.7
2006	14 427	5 655	8 773	60.8
2007	14 533	5 675	8 858	61.0
2008	14 362	5 549	8 777	61.1
2009	14 181	5 454	8 727	61.5
2010	13 832	5 376	8 456	61.1
2011	13 782	5 339	8 443	61.3
2012	13 698	5 307	8 391	61.3

Source: own report based on CSO Labour Force Survey, 2005–2013.

---

8   In 2012, the unemployment rate for women in higher education was 6.3% and the unemployment rate for men – 4.8%.

The analysis of the professional situation of women and men in Poland based on statistical data on the supply and demand for labour should be complemented by an analysis of career inactivity. The number of people inactive in Poland are presented in Table 5.16. As can be seen from the data in Table 5.16 – the number of inactive people in Poland was very high – not much lower than the number of employed (see Table 5.8) – and over 60% in the group of people inactive in the labour market were women. The number of inactive women was in all the years studied much higher than the number of men, and the difference to the disadvantage of women was approx. 300 thousand people.

The basic reasons for inactivity are: retirement, education, difficulties in finding a job, health problems, childcare, and housework (Strzelecki et al., 2013, p. 142). Inactivity due to studies, health problems, or difficulties finding a job is almost the same among both men and women. Larger differences occur at the expense of women in inactivity due to retirement and inappropriate age, where the share of women is almost twice as large as men. While taking into account two additional reasons for inactivity, we can say that they only concern women, as the share of women in housework in 2011–2013 amounted to approx. 94% and the share in the care of children – 97%.

It must be added that even in the care of the disabled or the elderly – women's participation in the period discussed amounted to approx. 76%. Inactivity for these reasons was therefore almost "assigned" to women, which has an adverse impact on their situation in the labour market. It is also extremely important here to emphasize that over the entire study period the number of inactive women was higher than the number of working women and the difference in individual years ranged from 2300 thousand. people in 2004 to approx. 1500 thousand in 2012. The number of inactive men, however, was lower than the number of men working and the difference amounted to: from more than 1500 thousand (2004) to 3300 thousand people (2012).

Conclusion

The analysis of the employment situation of women and men in Poland on the basis of statistical data enables the following conclusions to be drawn:
  – both the overall population structure and the structure of the population of working age 15 and older, and in the age 18–64 gives an equivalent position to women and men in the potential labour force in Poland,
  – both the number of people in the labour force and labour force participation rates of women – with all of the criteria – were lower than those for men,
  – employment – which is the basic measure of the assessment of professional situation – over the whole study period was negative for women as compared to men, regardless of the level of education. The total em-

ployment rate of women was from 46.1% of the volume (2004) to 53.1% (2012) and the employment rate for men at the same time ranged from 56.8% to 66.3%.[9] The difference to the disadvantage of women in 2012 was 13.2 percentage points. Similarly adverse was the employment of women in relation to men taking into account levels of education. In the last year of the study – the difference to the disadvantage of women with higher education was 5.8 percentage points and with post-secondary education 21.1 points, and with secondary general education 20.3 percentage points,

– compared to men the number of unemployed women and the unemployment rate for all criteria was higher. Particularly unfavourable compared to men was the unemployment of women with higher and secondary levels of education. The number of unemployed women was approx. three times the number of unemployed men,

– during the whole period the number of inactive women was higher by approx. 3000 thousand people, with the number of inactive men and (unlike men) approx. 2000 thousand from the number of working women. Some of the reasons for inactivity, such as looking after the home, caring for children, or care for the disabled or elderly related only to women.

Given the above conclusions (defined) in relation to the main purpose of the paper, which was to assess the professional situation of women and men in Poland it can generally be stated that during the period considered the employment situation for women compared unfavourably to that of men. The realities were therefore different from the declarations of equality. Because the causes of this state of affairs did not stem from economic factors or legislation – it must be assumed that the worse situation of women in Poland resulted primarily from existing traditions and socio-cultural norms.[10]

Literature

Borowska, M., Branka, M. (ed.) (2010), *Równość szans kobiet i mężczyzn a rynek pracy*, Warszawa: Centrum Rozwoju Zasobów Ludzkich.

Boruta, I. (2004), "Zakaz dyskryminacji w zatrudnieniu – nowa regulacja prawna," *Praca i Zabezpieczenie Społeczne*, nr 2.

Gawrycka, M., Wasilczuk, J., Zwiech, P. (2007), Szklany *sufit i ruchome schody – kobiety na rynku pracy*, Warszawa: CeDeWu.

GUS (2014), *Rocznik statystyczny Rzeczpospolitej Polskiej 2001–2013*, Warszawa.

Jarmołowicz, W., Kalinowska, B. (2007), "Równouprawnienie płci i dyskryminacja na rynku pracy – postęp czy regres?," [in]: M. Staniszewski (ed.), *Miasto postępu*, Poznań: Forum Naukowe.

---

9 These were the minimum and maximum sizes.

10 The impact of socio-cultural norms on the economic situation (including professional) of women is emphasized in many Polish publications, see for example: Kalinowska-Nawrotek, 2005; Gawrycka et al., 2007; Kotowska et al., 2009; Borowska and Branka, 2010; Kalinowska--Sufinowicz, 2013; and others.

Kalinowska-Nawrotek, B. (2005), *Dyskryminacja kobiet na polskim rynku pracy*, Poznań: Akademia Ekonomiczna w Poznaniu.

Kalinowska-Sufinowicz, B. (2013), "Polityka społeczno-gospodarcza państwa wobec pracy kobiet," Poznań: Wydawnictwo Uniwersytetu Ekonomicznego w Poznaniu.

Kopycińska, D. (2012), "Determinants of raising retirement age in Poland," *Actual Problems of Economics*, Vol. 2, No. 10.

Kopycińska, D. (2013), "Demographic transformation in Poland and its effect on the labour market," *Transformation in Business & Economies*, Vol. 12, No. 28.

Kotowska, J.E., Sztanderska, U., Wójcicka, I. (2009), "Diagnoza kulturowych i strukturalnych uwarunkowań łączenia pracy zawodowej i aktywności rodzinnej przez kobiety w Polsce," [in:] J.E. Kotowska (ed.), *Strukturalne i kulturowe uwarunkowania aktywności zawodowej kobiet w Polsce*, Warszawa: Wydawnictwo Naukowe Scholar.

Mandel, E. (2004), "Stereotypowe postrzeganie ról kobiet i mężczyzn jako wyznacznika karier zawodowych i funkcjonowania na rynku pracy," [in:] *Płeć a możliwości ekonomiczne w Polsce*, Warszawa: Biuro Banku Światowego, Gender and Economic Opportunities in Poland.

Rozporządzenie Rady Ministrów z 20 dnia października w sprawie ustanowienia Pełnomocnika Rządu do spraw Rodziny oraz Równego Statusu Kobiet i Mężczyzn, Dz. U. Nr 122, poz. 1331.

Rozporządzenie Rady Ministrów z dnia 26 czerwca 2002 r. w sprawie Pełnomocnika Rządu do Spraw Równego Statusu Kobiet i Mężczyzn, Dz. U. Nr 96, poz. 849.

Rozporządzenie Rady Ministrów z dnia 3 listopada 2005 r. w sprawie zniesienia Pełnomocnika Rządu do Spraw Równego Statusu Kobiet i Mężczyzn, Dz. U. Nr 222, poz. 1913.

Rozporządzenie Rady Ministrów z dnia 22 sierpnia w sprawie Pełnomocnika Rządu do spraw Równego Traktowania, Dz. U. Nr 75, poz. 450.

Strusińska-Żukowska, J. (2004), "Kodeks Pracy po 1.01.2004 r.," *Prawo Pracy*, No. 1.

Strzelecki, P., Saczuk, K., Grabowska, J., Kotowska, J.E. (2013), *Warunki życia gospodarstw domowych. Rynek pracy. Diagnoza Społeczna 2013. Warunki i Jakość Życia Polaków – Raport*, Warszawa: Ministerstwo Pracy i Polityki Społecznej.

Suzdrof, J. (2004), "Najnowsze zmiany w przepisach kodeksu pracy," *Służba Pracownicza*, No. 1.

Ustawa z dnia 3 grudnia 2010 r. o wdrożeniu niektórych przepisów Unii Europejskiej w zakresie równego traktowania, Dz. U. Nr 254, poz. 1700.

Chapter 6

Entrepreneurship of women and man in Poland – a comparative analysis

Katarzyna Białek

Abstract

Women entrepreneurs are in a minority among entrepreneurs in most developed countries. Previous studies have shown a negative relationship between the probability of becoming an entrepreneur and gender. Entrepreneurship is dependent on many different factors. Some affect the entrepreneurship of women and men in similar ways, but others seem to have a different impact on each of the sexes. In this chapter a comparative analysis of entrepreneurship in Poland is broken down by gender. Among the entrepreneurs we can also see signs of occupational segregation.

Key words: gender, entrepreneurship, segregation, Poland

Introduction

Women entrepreneurs are in a minority among entrepreneurs in most developed countries. Previous studies have shown a negative relationship between the probability of becoming an entrepreneur and gender (der van Peter et al., 2012; Parker, 2009). Bonte and Piegeler (2012), and Estrin and Mickiewicz (2011) showed that women were less willing to compete and risk than men, and in countries where the public sector is larger, they were less willing to start companies. In turn, others perceive the source of this negative relationship in the differences between the sexes in education, family conditions and motivation to establish a company (Cowling and Taylor, 2001; Blanchflower, 2004; Minniti and Naudé, 2010).

In the literature, on the one hand (Gardawski, 2013; Goedhuys and Sleuwaegen, 2000; Minniti and Naudé, 2010) the importance of education for entrepreneurship is emphasised. Among others, Shim and Eastlick (1998), using data on Spanish business owners, showed that entrepreneurs have a higher education level compared to other respondents. However, at the same time the educational differences between men and women entrepreneurs were not significant in their view. On the other hand, some scholars suggest that the lack of formal education can be compensated by the experience of the individual (Nafziger and Terrell, 1996; Langowitz and Minniti, 2007; Davidsson and Honig, 2003; Oberschacht-siek, 2012). Additionally, Lazear (2004, 2005; Wagner, 2006) draws attention to the fact that entrepreneurs have very varied experience and skills. It is worth emphasizing here that most women entrepreneurs are far less experience based on years of work than male entrepreneurs (Lee and Rendall, 2001; Minniti and Naudé, 2010).

Additionally, marital status and number of children seem to affect the involve-ment of women in entrepreneurship (Parker, 2009; Edwards and Field-Hendrey, 2002; van der Peter et al., 2012). Justo and DeTienne (2008) showed that mar-ried women are more likely to become entrepreneurs than unmarried women. Others have noted that the presence of young children can also affect women taking self-employment, especially when their partner supports them in childcare (Caputo and Dolinský, 1998). Maloney (2004) showed that women with young children decide to engage in self-employment rather than paid employment in the countries of South America.

Kepler and Shane (2007) found that male entrepreneurs more often believe that the company they run is more important than time spent with their families. In addition, men are more likely than women entrepreneurs to set up a business due to financial reasons. In contrast, women decide to start a business mainly because of the flexible working hours (Justo and DeTienne, 2008). In the case of Poland, among the reasons for founding a company women listed the money, the threat of unemployment, and the need to be independent (Rollnik-Sadowska, 2010).

In addition, it is worth mentioning that the differences in entrepreneurship exist not only between countries, but also between regions (Wach, 2008). Garcia (2012) showed that the number of new firms is positively correlated with the size of a city. Gardawski (2013), in turn, suggests that in the case of Poland the size of a city has no direct impact on entrepreneurship.

In summary, we can conclude that entrepreneurship is dependent on many different factors. Some affect the entrepreneurship of women and men in similar ways, but others seem to have a different impact on each of the sexes. In this chapter a comparative analysis of entrepreneurship is broken down by gender in Poland.

The paper is divided into seven parts. The first part contains a brief description of the data and the methodology used in the analysis. The second part is devoted to the analysis of statistical data for entrepreneurs disaggregated by gender. In the third part an attempt is made to capture the differences between people working as self-employed and employers. The fourth section is devoted to entrepreneurs operating in agriculture. The fifth part contains a comparison between entrepre-neurs and other respondents. The last part is a brief summary.

6.1. Data and method

In this study we used the combined database collected in the survey of Household Budgets in the years 2010 and 2011. The survey is conducted every year by the Central Statistical Office and is representative of the country (CSO, 2011). For the purposes of this study, it was assumed that entrepreneurs are employers or self-employed outside the agricultural sector. In contrast, farmers were defined as people who run a farm.

Among the respondents those aged 18–75 were selected, and so people who could potentially be employed. These individuals were classified into one of four areas of economic activity: employed persons, entrepreneurs (excluding farmers), farmers, and inactive persons. The breakdown by type of economic activity was made on the basis of two variables: main source of income and an additional source of income. Types of activity were defined according to the criterion of the amount of income from that source of work. For the classification of the respondents to particular types of economic activity both variables were included. The classification began with the self-employed and employers. This group of respondents included those who said this type of work was the main or additional source of income. Those who chose farm use as the main or additional source of income are classified as farmers. A small proportion of respondents (approx. 250) reported as the main or additional source of income running a company and at the same time managing a farm.

Table 6.1. Respondents by economic activity

Employed persons	51%
Inactive persons	38%
Entrepreneurs	6%
Farmers	5%
Total (in thous.)	152.6 = 100%

Source: own calculations based on *Household budgets*, CSO, 2010–2011.

These respondents were counted as entrepreneurs, as leading their own company showed that they have the abilities and characteristics needed in order to conduct this type of economic activity. The remaining participants in the study were divided into employees and the inactive. Among the latter were students and people on social benefits, pensions, or having other income. As shown in Table 6.1, the self-employed and employers account for 6% of the respondents and those running a farm 5% of respondents. The other economically active people were predominant (51%).

To test the significance of differences between groups in the study we used Pearson's chi-square tests and column proportions tests. The results of the chi-square test have been given in the text where it was possible to carry it out. The column proportion test assay based on the "z" test with a significance level of 0.05 (Bonferroni correction taken into account). For each significant pair, the category with the significantly higher proportion column has been marked with the letter indicating the group which dominates a given proportion. For example, in Table 6.3 the group of men has been assigned the letter "A" and the group of women the letter "B." At the intersection of the column "Men" and the row "Full-time" next to this share in the group of men appears the letter B. This means that the proportion of men working full-time is significantly higher than the proportion of women working full-time.

6.2. Entrepreneurship and sex

From the cross table (Table 6.2) we can see that about 90% of entrepreneurs declared this work to be the main source of income, including about a quarter of employers. Among those who declared their status to be self-employed or employer as an additional source of income, the majority of respondents reported domestic fixed non-wage labour, an occupational pension, or wage labour in the country as the main source of income.

Respondents who declared running a company as the main source of income reported that their additional source of income was from running a farm (9%), workers' fixed non-wage labour (8%) and occupational pension (8%). Two-thirds of entrepreneurs (both main and additional source of income) are men. Most of them, as an additional source of income, reported use of a farming (about 13%), fixed non-wage labour (8%) and occupational pension (6%). For women, the most common additional source of income is an occupational pension (about 10%), fixed on-wage labour (about 8%), and other social benefits (about 5%).

Women entrepreneurs are better educated than male business owners (Figure 6.1). More than one-third of women running a company have a university degree, while among male entrepreneurs this proportion is about one quarter. Secondary education characterizes 40% of male (including one third who declared secondary vocational education) and about 45% of female (including one quarter who declared secondary vocational education) entrepreneurs.

Vocational education characterizes one-third of men and one-fifth of women entrepreneurs. For both women and men entrepreneurs, 1% of respondents have a scientific degree. In turn, the proportion of business owners with basic vocational education and primary, lower secondary and without education is significantly higher among men. In testing the dependencies between the variables of education and gender, the Chi-square test could not be used as the numbers for each category were too low. Therefore this variable has been grouped into four more numerous categories. The value of the Chi-square test ($X^2 = 153.57$; $p < 0.001$) for the grouped variable of sex and education allows us to reject H_0 for the independence of these variables. The column proportion test confirms the significance of the dependency described above. Statistics for age of entrepreneurs are similar for both sexes.

Table 6.2. Major and additional source of income for entrepreneurs

	Main source of income			Additional source of income		
	Man	**Woman**	**Total**	**Man**	**Woman**	**Total**
Domestic fixed non-wage labour	3.3%	7.2%	4.6%	8.0%	8.4%	8.1%
Domestic fixed wage labour	1.8%	1.2%	1.6%	1.8%	0.6%	1.3%
Casual wage labour	0.1%	0.1%	0.1%	0.8%	0.5%	0.6%
Permanent – domestic self-employed	61.0%	58.3%	60.1%	30.8%	32.5%	31.5%
Permanent – self-employed abroad	1.2%	0.5%	1.0%	0.1%	0.0%	0.1%
Casual – domestic self-employed	3.1%	3.8%	3.3%	15.3%	19.0%	16.8%
Casual – self-employed abroad	0.2%	0.1%	0.1%	0.1%	0.0%	0.0%
Domestic employer	24.9%	22.0%	23.9%	4.2%	6.1%	5.0%
Employer abroad	0.3%	0.1%	0.2%	0.0%	0.0%	0.0%
Runs a farm	0.6%	0.3%	0.5%	12.7%	3.0%	8.7%
Assists on a farm	0.0%	0.6%	0.2%	5.7%	2.9%	4.5%
Unemployment benefits	0.1%	0.3%	0.2%	0.4%	0.3%	0.3%
Occupational pension	2.2%	3.6%	2.6%	6.0%	10.1%	7.6%
Other pension	0.0%	0.1%	0.0%	0.2%	0.7%	0.4%
Benefits	0.7%	0.6%	0.6%	5.9%	4.7%	5.4%
Other income	0.1%	0.2%	0.1%	3.6%	2.0%	2.9%
Other income and benefits	0.4%	1.0%	0.9%	4.4%	9.2%	6.8%
Total persons (in thous.) = 100%	5.9	2.9	8.8	1.1	0.8	1.9

Source: own calculations based on *Household budgets*, CSO, 2010–2011.

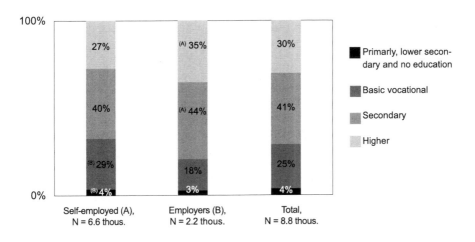

Figure 6.1. Businesses by gender and education groups
Source: own calculations based on *Household budgets*, CSO, 2010–2011.

Table 6.3. Entrepreneurs by sex and working time

	Man (A)	Woman (B)	Total
Full-time	(B) 93%	88%	91%
Part-time	6%	(A) 11%	8%
Not applicable	1%	(A) 2%	1%
Total persons (in thous.) = 100%	5.9	2.9	8.8

Source: own calculations based on *Household budgets*, CSO, 2010–2011.

Full-time work was declared by 93% of the men, and 88% of women entrepreneurs (Table 6.3). The value for the Pearson Chi-square test ($X^2 = 58.73$; $p < 0.001$) allows for the rejection of H_0 which states that the variables of working time and gender are independent. In contrast, based on the column proportion test we can conclude that the proportion of women working part-time is significantly higher than the percentage of men working part-time. One tenth of the female respondents declared this type of work and about 5% of the male respondents.

Table 6.4. Entrepreneurs by gender and income* (PLN)

	Man	Women	Total
1 quartile	1 500	1 000	1 300
Average	2 650	2 175	2 501
Median	2 100	1 800	2 000
3 quartile	3 000	2 700	3 000
Standard deviation	2 405	2 192	2 350

* Income calculated only for respondents who said they work full-time.
Source: own calculations based on *Household budgets*, CSO, 2010–2011.

Table 6.4 shows the amount of income from self-employment by gender. Average income for women running a business constitutes about 82% of the average income for men. In the case of the median this proportion is about 86%.

Looking at the data on the sector of activity and gender, we can see some signs of occupational segregation among entrepreneurs. Women dominate the service sectors (with the exception of the motor trade), while men predominate in sectors related to construction, transport and vehicles. One-third of the female respondents (and only one in eight respondents) owning a company operates in the retail trade sector (excluding vehicles). However, almost one fifth of companies founded by men operate in the specialized construction sector. Within the healthcare and other personal service sectors activities one fifth of company managers are women, and about 3% men. About 10% of companies founded by women and about 5% of companies founded by men operate in the legal, accounting, and education sectors. About one-tenth of companies founded by men and 2% of companies founded by women operate in the land transport sector. While in the wholesale and retail trade sectors and construction of buildings, vehicles, companies are run by 12% of men and 2% of women.

Table 6.5. Entrepreneurs by sex and marital status

	Man (A)	Woman (B)	Total
Single	14%	13%	13%
Married	(B) 81%	72%	78%
Widower/Widow	1%	(A) 6%	3%
Divorced (a)	4%	(A) 9%	5%
Separated	0%	(A) 1%	1%
Total persons (in thous.)	5.9	2.9	8.8

Source: own calculations based on *Household budgets*, CSO, 2010–2011.

Most entrepreneurs are married. The value for the Chi-square test ($X^2 = 243.13$; $p < 0.001$) enables us the reject H_0 which states the independence of the variables of gender and marital status. The table above shows the column proportion test results for the variables gender and marital status. The proportion of married men is significantly higher than the proportion of married women (Table 6.5). In turn, the percentage of widows, divorced and separated women is significantly higher than the percentage of such people among male entrepreneurs. A similar relationship can be found considering the responses to the question about life in a relationship. Respondents who said they did not live in a relationship with a person from a given household accounted for 14% of men, and among women as high as 25%. The value for the Pearson Chi-square test ($X^2 = 243.13$; $p < 0.001$) enables us to reject H_0 which states the independence of the variables of relationship and company size. In contrast, the column proportion test confirms that the difference between the proportions of men and women who are not in a relationship is significant.

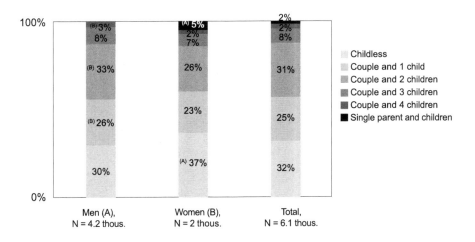

Figure 6.2. Businesses by sex and number of children[*]
[*] The numbers are lower than the number of business owners because of the lack of data.
Source: own calculations based on *Household budgets*, CSO, 2010–2011.

The percentage of male entrepreneurs with one, two or four children is significantly higher than the percentage of female entrepreneurs with one, two or four children. Almost a quarter of male entrepreneurs and about one fifth of female entrepreneurs have two children. Also, the Pearson Chi-square test ($X^2 = 231.61$; $p < 0.001$) enables us to reject the hypothesis that there is no association between the variables of sex and having children.

From Figure 6.3 we can see that the percentage of women entrepreneurs is slightly, but significantly, higher (9%), in relation to the proportion of male entrepreneurs (7%) in cities of between 100 and 200 thousand inhabitants. In turn, in rural areas the proportion of men in enterprises is significantly higher than the proportion of female entrepreneurs (respectively 29% and 26%). The Chi-square test ($X^2 = 13.38$; $p < 0.05$) confirms that it is possible to reject the hypothesis of no dependency between the variables of the size of city and gender.

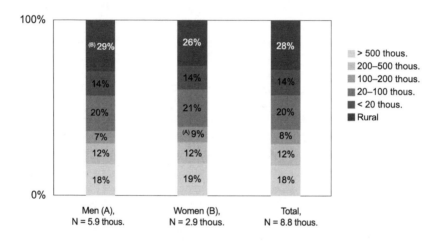

Figure 6.3. Businesses by sex and size of town/city
Source: own calculations based on *Household budgets*, CSO, 2010–2011.

The percentage of men and women entrepreneurs is similar in each of the provinces. The biggest difference (about 2%) occurs in Western Pomerania. The value for the Chi-square test ($X^2 = 27.78$; $p < 0.05$), however, allows for the rejection of H_0 which states the independence of the variables. According to the column proportion test, the percentage of women entrepreneurs in Western Pomerania is significantly greater. In the Wielkopolska province, however, there is a significantly greater percentage of male entrepreneurs.

6.3. Self-employed and employers

In the Household Budget study information on the size of the company has not been collected. In contrast, it distinguishes the self-employed people from employers. Employers are only a quarter of the respondents running a company. The percentage of employers among company owners is similar for men and women and accounts for 24% and 26% respectively (Table 6.6). Despite such a small percentage difference, the Pearson's Chi-square test ($X^2 = 4.95$; $p < 0.05$) enables us to reject the hypothesis H_0 that the variables of sex and size of the company are independent. The percentage of men employers is significantly higher than the proportion of women employers. In the case of the self-employed, the proportion of women is significantly higher compared to the proportion of men.

Employers are slightly older than the self-employed. The average age for employers is 43, while for owners of sole proprietorships it is 41. The oldest respondent who has employees is 74, and the youngest 18.

Table 6.6. Businesses by sex and size of company

	Man (A)	Woman (B)	Total
Self-employed	74%	(A)76%	75%
Employers	(B)26%	24%	25%
Total persons (in thous.)	5.9	2.9	8.8

Source: own calculations based on *Household budgets*, CSO, 2010–2011.

About half of the employers and almost 40% of self-employed declared that their highest completed education is secondary education. From Figure 6.4 we can see that the proportion of employers who have a secondary education is significantly higher than the proportion of respondents who are self-employed with this level. Among the self-employed almost one-third have a basic vocational education (Figure 6.4). This proportion is significantly higher compared to the proportion of employers with basic vocational education.

The percentage of those with the lowest education (primary) among self-employed respondents is significantly higher than the percentage of people with primary education among employers. The value for the Chi-square test ($X^2 = 106.01$; $p < 0.001$) enables us to reject the hypothesis of independence of the variables of company size and education (Table 6.4).

The percentage of male entrepreneurs with one, two or four children is significantly higher than the percentage of female entrepreneurs with one, two or four children. Almost a quarter of male entrepreneurs and about one fifth of female entrepreneurs have two children. Also, the Pearson Chi-square test ($X^2 = 231.61$; $p < 0.001$) enables us to reject the hypothesis that there is no association between the variables of sex and having children.

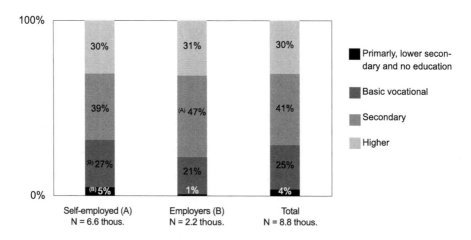

Figure 6.4. Businesses according to company size and level of education
Source: own calculations based on *Household budgets*, CSO, 2010–2011.

Table 6.7. Business owners according to company size and income (PLN)

	Self-employed	Employers	Total
1 quartile	1 200	1 740	1 300
Average	2 301	3 034	2 501
Median	2 000	2 500	2 000
3 quartile	3 000	3 500	3 000
Standard deviation	2 037	2 967	2 350

Source: own calculations based on *Household budgets*, CSO, 2010–2011.

The value for the Pearson Chi-square test (X^2=61.93; p<0.001) enables us to reject the hypothesis which states the independence of the variables of relationship and company size. From Figure 6.5 we can see that the proportion of married (or in a formal relationship) people is significantly lower among the owners of sole proprietorships than for employers. The percentage of people who are not in a relationship (and those who are unmarried) is significantly higher among those with one-person companies in comparison to employers. Table 6.8 shows that about half of those with a company have children. More than one-third of employers

Table 6.8. Entrepreneurs by gender and the number of children

	Self-employed (A)	Employers (B)	Total
No children	(B)34%	28%	32%
Couple and 1 child	25%	25%	25%
Couple and 2 children	29%	(A)35%	31%
Couple and 3 children	8%	8%	8%
Couple and 4 or more children	(B) 3%	2%	2%
Single parent and children	2%	2%	2%
Total persons (in thous.) = 100%	4.6	1.6	6.2

Source: own calculations based on *Household budgets*, CSO, 2010–2011.

and one-third of self-employed workers have two children. The percentage of employers with two children is significantly higher than the percentage of owners of single-person companies with two children. The value for the Pearson Chi-square test, $X^2 = 31.20$; $p < 0.001$, confirms that the variables for having children and company size are not independent.

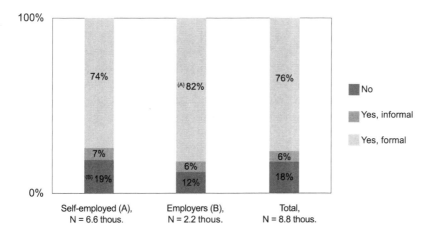

Figure 6.5. Businesses by size of company and personal relationship
Source: own calculations based on *Household budgets*, CSO, 2010–2011.

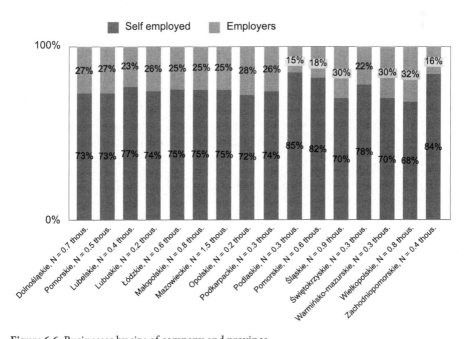

Figure 6.6. Businesses by size of company and province
Source: own calculations based on *Household budgets*, CSO, 2010–2011.

The class of town/city size does not differentiate among firm sizes and the percentage distribution of the two groups is similar. Figure 6.6 shows the share of employers and the self-employed by province. The highest percentage of employers – more than a third – is in Wielkopolska, Silesia, and Warmia and Mazury. The lowest share of employers is in Podlaskie (15%), West Pomerania (16%) and Pomerania(18%). Table 6.11 shows the size distribution of firms by provinces. The value for the Pearson Chi-square test, $X^2 = 87.53$; $p < 0.001$, enables us to reject H_0 which states the absence of a relationship between the variables firm size and province. On the basis of the column proportion test we can conclude that the proportion of employers is significantly higher compared to the proportion of one-person business owners in the provinces of Silesia and Wielkopolska. On the other hand, in Podlaskie, Pomerania and West Pomerania, the proportion of self-employed workers is significantly higher compared to the proportion of employers.

6.4. Farmers and gender

As with company owners who are non-farmers, women account for about one--third of farmers. On the basis of Table 6.9 we can see that women with an income from agriculture are slightly better educated than men. The results of the Pearson Chi-square test ($X^2 = 83.82$; $p < 0.001$) enable us to reject hypothesis H_0 that the variables gender and education are independent of each other. However, according to the column proportion test the percentage of women farmers with secondary and higher education is significantly higher than the proportion of men with this education. In the case of basic vocational education the proportion of men farmers is significantly higher than the proportion of women with this education.

Table 6.9. Farmers by gender and education

	Man (A)	Woman (B)	Total
Primary, lower secondary education, without education	20%	20%	20%
Basic vocational	(B) 54%	43%	50%
Secondary	23%	(A) 31%	25%
Higher	4%	(A) 5%	4%
Total persons (in thous.) = 100%	4.6	2.2	6.8

Source: own calculations based on *Household budgets*, CSO, 2010–2011.

Differences in income from farm labour between the sexes are relatively large (Table 6.10). The average income for women is 47% of the average income for men. In the case of the median, the proportion is only 33%.

As with the rest of the self-employed and employers, most of the respondents are married – in both cases about 80% of those questioned (Table 6.11).

Table 6.10. Farmers by gender and income from agricultural holding (PLN)

	Man	Woman	Total
1 quartile	0	0	0
Average	1 903	896	1 648
Median	800	267	650
3 quartile	2000	1000	1 768
Standard deviation	5 253	1 908	4 659

Source: own calculations based on *Household budgets*, CSO, 2010–2011

Table 6.11. Farmers by gender and marital status

	Man (A)	Woman (B)	Total
Single	(B) 17%	6%	14%
Married	80%	78%	79%
Widower/Widow	1%	(A) 12%	5%
Divorced	1%	(A) 2%	1%
Separated	0%	(A) 1%	1%
Total persons (in thous.) = 100%	4.6	2.2	6.8

Source: own calculations based on *Household budgets*, CSO, 2010–2011.

Among male farmers a fairly high percentage are unmarried – about one-fifth compared to about 5% of women. This ratio is also indicated by the column proportion test as significantly higher in the case of men. The percentage of widows among farmers is 12 times higher compared to the proportion of widowers.

The column proportion test also indicates this ratio as significantly higher for women. In addition, it shows that the proportion of women who are separated and divorced is significantly higher compared to the proportion of men who are separated and divorced. The Pearson Chi-square test ($X^2 = 519.11$; $p < 0.001$) enables us to reject the hypothesis H_0 that there is no association between the variables of gender and marital status.

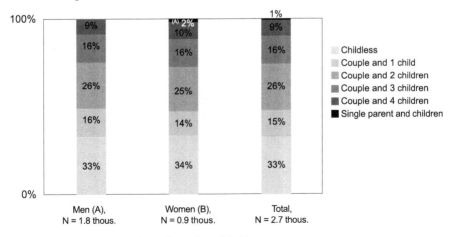

Figure 6.7. Farmers by gender and number of children
Source: own calculations based on *Household budgets*, CSO, 2010–2011.

Most farmers, regardless of gender, have at least one child (Figure 6.7). The proportions of people with children are slightly different between the sexes. However, the value for the Chi-square test ($X^2 = 30.81$; $p < 0.001$) enables us to reject H_0 which states the independence of the variables of gender and number of children. The only exception is the proportion of women farmers bringing up children alone – this proportion is significantly higher compared to the same proportion for men (2% of women farmers and 0% of male farmers).

The highest percentage of women running farms occur in the Podkarpackie and Lesser Poland provinces. The value for the Pearson Chi-square test of, $X^2 = 283.22$; $p < 0.001$, enables us to reject the hypothesis stating independence between the variables of gender and province. According to the column proportion test, the percentages of women farmers in these provinces are significantly higher compared to the proportion of men. And in Kujawy-Pomerania, Lublin, Lodz, Podlasie, Warmia and Mazury, and Wielkopolska the proportion of men farmers is significantly higher compared to the proportion of women. The highest percentage of men farmers are in the Lublin province – 15% of all men farmers, and in Mazowieckie – 14%.

6.5. Business owners and other respondents

Figure 6.8 presents the basic statistics on the age of the respondents. The median age of all respondents is about 44, the 1 quartile is 30 years, and the 3 quartile 57 years. Male respondents are slightly younger than female respondents – the median age is 41 years of age (women 45), the 1 quartile at 29 (women 31), and 3 quartile at 55 years of age (women 59). Farmers are older than other respondents – the median age is 47 years (salaried employees – 38), 1 quartile at 39 years old (salaried employees – 29), while 3 quartile is at 54 years (salaried employees – 49 years). Most entrepreneurs are older than 34 (1 quartile is 34), while the median age of entrepreneurs is similar to the average and is 42 years old. The graph for professionally inactive people is more extended than the others, because this category includes students and retired persons.

The structure of education of entrepreneurs is slightly different from the structure of education of other people (Table 6.12). The group of business owners has the lowest percentage of people with primary education (barely 4%) compared to other types of economic activity. Also, the percentage of people with basic vocational education in the group of respondents engaged in economic activities (25%) is lower than the percentage of those people among wage earners and farmers. Statistics calculated for the Pearson Chi-square ($X^2 = 21\ 126.36$; $p < 0.001$) enables us to reject the hypothesis H_0 that the variables economic activity and education are independent.

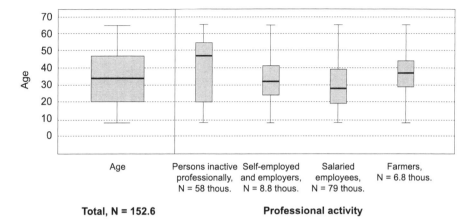

Total, N = 152.6   **Professional activity**

Figure 6.8. Economic activity and age (in years)
Source: own calculations based on *Household budgets*, CSO, 2010–2011.

Table 6.12. Economic activity and education of the respondents

	Inactive persons (A)	Entrepre- neurs (B)	Salaried workers (C)	Farmers (D)	Total
No education	(B C D) 1%	0%	0%	0%	0%
Primary	(B C D) 21%	4%	(B) 7%	(B C) 20%	13%
Lower Secondary	(B C D) 8%	0%	(B D) 1%	0%	4%
Basic vocational	26%	25%	(A B) 31%	(A B C) 50%	30%
General secondary	(B C D) 15%	(D) 10%	(D) 10%	4%	12%
Secondary vocational	18%	(A C D) 28%	(A D) 23%	(A) 20%	21%
Post-secondary	(D) 2%	(A C D) 4%	(A D) 3%	1%	3%
College	(B C D) 0%	0%	0%	0%	0%
Bachelor/Engineer	(D) 3%	(A C D) 7%	(A D) 6%	1%	5%
Master/Doctor	(D) 6%	(A C D) 22%	(A D) 19%	3%	13%
Doctorate	(D) 0%	(A C D) 1%	(A D) 1%	0%	0%
Total persons (in thous.) = 100%	57.9	8.8	79.0	6.8	152.6

Source: own calculations based on *Household budgets*, CSO, 2010–2011.

Farmers are the group with the highest share of people with basic vocational education. Half of the respondents living on agriculture declared this education as their highest level. Also, the column proportion test shows that the percentage of people with basic vocational education is significantly higher among farmers than among other types of economic activity. One fifth of farmers reported that they had completed primary school. The proportion of farmers with primary education, as in the case of basic vocational education, is much higher than for other types of economic activity. A similar proportion of farmers (20%) declared having secondary vocational education. However, this percentage is lower than the percentage of people with secondary vocational education among salaried workers and business owners.

Table 6.13 shows the statistics for income/revenues from particular types of economic activity. Inactive persons have been omitted. The highest average incomes are those respondents who run a company, the lowest – farmers. The median income of farmers is very low, less than half the average income. The third quartile in their case is a little higher than the average. This indicates that most farmers' income is below the average in this group. For the rest of the economically active respondents, these differences are not this large.

Table 6.13. Economic activity and income (PLN)

	Entrepreneurs	Employed persons	Farmers	Total
1 quartile	1 300	1 200	0	1 185
Average	2 501	1 916	1 648	1 959
Median	2 000	1 650	650	1 650
3 quartile	3 000	2 300	1 768	2 400
Standard deviation	2 350	1 385	4 659	1 906

Source: own calculations based on *Household budgets*, CSO, 2010–2011.

On the question of occupation (ISCO-88 classification) entrepreneurs most often answered that they were managers in charge of production and services (19%), retailers (13%) and construction workers (10%). Experts from various fields account for about 15% of business owners. Maids and cleaning people are only 2% of entrepreneurs. For the most part, farmers declared that they are farmers of commodity production (over 60%). One sixth of respondents living from agriculture declared that they are farmers and fishermen working for their own needs. The shares of salaried employees in occupational groups are evenly distributed between the remaining occupations. Salespeople slightly predominate (7%), construction workers and related workers (6%), specialists in teaching and education (5%) and experts in economics and management (5%).

Table 6.14. Economic activity and marital status of the respondents

	Inactive persons (A)	Entrepre- neurs (B)	Salaried workers (C)	Farmers (D)	Total
Single	(B D) 26%	13%	(B D) 26%	14%	25%
Married	53%	(A C) 78%	(A) 66%	(A C) 79%	62%
Widower/Widow	(B C D) 16%	3%	2%	(B C) 5%	8%
Divorced	(D) 4%	(A D) 5%	(A D) 5%	1%	4%
Separated	1%	1%	(A) 1%	1%	1%
Total persons (in thous.) = 100%	57.9	8.8	79.0	6.8	152.6

Source: own calculations based on *Household budgets*, CSO, 2010–2011.

Table 6.14 lists the variables: economic activity and marital status. Based on a Pearson Chi-square test ($X^2 = 11\ 267.26$; $p < 0.001$), we can reject the hypothesis H_0 saying that the variables economic activity and marital status are independent.

Among entrepreneurs only 13% are unmarried, and as many as 78% of people are married. This proportion is higher than the proportion of married both in total for everyone in the sample, as well as for employees and inactive people.

An almost identical structure is shown by the variable of marital status among people who earn their living from agriculture. The exception is the percentage of divorced persons, which is much lower among farmers than in the other groups. These differences are confirmed by the column proportion test. Among the employed and the inactive the percentage of unmarried people is significantly higher than in the case of business owners and farmers.

Table 6.15. Economic activity and relationship of the respondents

	Inactive persons (A)	Entrepre-neurs (B)	Salaried workers (C)	Farmers (D)	Total
Yes, formal	51%	(A C) 76%	(A) 64%	(A B C) 78%	61%
Yes, informal	(D) 3%	(B C D) 6%	(A D) 5%	1%	4%
No	(B C D) 46%	18%	(B D) 30%	(B) 21%	35%
Total persons (in thous.) = 100%	57.9	8.8	79.0	6.8	152.6

Source: own calculations based on *Household budgets*, CSO, 2010–2011.

The proportion of married people is significantly higher for business owners as compared to other people. The percentage of divorced persons among farmers also turns out to be significantly lower compared to the other groups. The variable life in a relationship with a person of a given household has a similar percentage distribution (Table 6.15). Based on a Pearson Chi-square test ($X^2 = 6\ 085.65$; $p < 0.001$), we can reject the hypothesis H_0 saying that the variables economic activity and marital status are independent. The column proportion test leads to the conclusion that the percentage of farmers living in a formal relationship is significantly higher compared to the other groups studied. In addition, there turns out to be a significant difference in the percentages of people living in non-marital relationships – the proportion of entrepreneurs and those living in non-marital relationships is significantly higher compared to the percentage of people living in non-marital relationships in the other groups. Hence the proportion of people not in a relationship in this group is the lowest among all treatment groups. More than half of the farmers have at least two children, and a quarter of farmers have three or more children (Table 6.16). The proportion of farmers with three and four or more children is significantly higher than the percentage of such persons among the other groups.

The proportion of people with their own company (excluding farmers) with two children is significantly higher compared to the proportion of employed persons, farmers and inactive people with two children. The percentage of employees with a family of a couple plus one child or one of the parents and children is significantly higher compared to the other groups. These observations were confirmed by a Pearson Chi-square test of, on the basis of which ($X^2 = 9\ 930.44$; $p < 0.001$), we can reject the hypothesis H_0 that the variables economic activity and having children are independent.

Table 6.16. Economic activity and number of children

	Inactive persons (A)	Entrepre-neurs (B)	Salaried workers (C)	Farmers (D)	Total
No children	(B C D) 65%	32%	32%	33%	45%
Couple and 1 child	12%	(A D) 25%	(A B D) 27%	(A) 15%	21%
Couple and 2 children	13%	(A C D) 31%	(A) 28%	(A) 26%	22%
Couple and 3 children	6%	(A) 8%	(A) 8%	(A B C) 16%	7%
Couple and 4 or more children	3%	2%	3%	(A B C) 9%	3%
Single-parent and children	1%	(A D) 2%	(A B D) 2%	1%	2%
Total persons (in thous.)= 100%	34.4	6.1	43.4	2.7	86.7

Source: own calculations based on *Household budgets*, CSO, 2010–2011.

Table 6.17 presents the data concerning respondents disaggregated by economic activity and place of residence. Based on a Chi-square test ($X^2 = 10\ 192.89$; $p < 0.001$), we can reject the hypothesis H_0 of the independence of the variables place of residence and type of economic activity. One-third of entrepreneurs come from cities over 200 000 inhabitants. The column proportion test shows that the proportion of entrepreneurs living in cities with over 200 000 inhabitants is significantly higher compared to all other types of economic activity. The share of employees is significantly higher in cities from 100 to 200 thousand inhabitants. The percentage of self-employed persons and employers who live in rural areas is significantly lower as compared to other types of economic activity, and the share of farmers significantly higher.

Table 6.17. Economic activity of the respondents by size class of the town/city

	Inactive persons (A)	Entrepre-neurs (B)	Salaried workers (C)	Farmers (D)	Total
Over 500 000	(D) 11%	(A C D) 18%	(A D) 14%	0%	12%
200 000–500 000	(D) 10%	(A C D) 12%	(D) 10%	0%	10%
100 000–20 000	(D) 8%	(D) 8%	(B D) 9%	1%	8%
20 000–100 000	(D) 20%	(D) 20%	(D) 20%	2%	19%
Lower than 20 000	(C D) 15%	(D) 14%	(D) 14%	4%	14%
Village	(B C) 36%	28%	(B) 34%	(A B C) 93%	37%
Total persons (in thous.) = 100%	58.0	8.8	79.0	6.8	152.6

Source: own calculations based on *Household budgets*, CSO, 2010–2011.

Table 6.18 shows the variable of economic activity by province. A Chi-square test was conducted ($X^2 = 3\ 963.69$, $p < 0.001$), the results of which allow for the rejection of H_0 which states the independence of the variables of province and economic activity. The highest percentage of entrepreneurs live in Mazovia – nearly one-fifth of respondents with their own company. This percentage is significantly higher compared to other types of economic activity. This province is also inhabited by a similar percentage of employees (15%). The next province, where the percentage of self-employed workers and employers is higher compared to other provinces, is the Pomerania (about 10% of the self-employed and employers). The percentage of farmers is significantly higher compared to other types of economic activity in the regions: Lublin, Łódź, Lesser Poland, Subcarpathian, Podlaskie and Świętokrzyskie.

Table 6.18. Economic activity of respondents by province

	Inactive persons (A)	Entrepre-neurs (B)	Salaried workers (C)	Farmers (D)	Total
Lower Silesia	(D) 8%	(D) 8%	(D) 8%	4%	8%
Kujawsko-Pomorskie	(D) 5%	(D) 6%	(D) 5%	4%	5%
Lublin	(B) 5%	5%	5%	(A B C) 14%	6%
Lubuskie	(D) 3%	(D) 3%	(D) 3%	1%	3%
Łódzkie	7%	6%	7%	(A B C) 8%	7%
Lesser Poland	(C) 9%	(C) 9%	8%	(A B C) 12%	8%
Mazovia	12%	(A C D) 17%	(A D) 15%	(A) 13%	14%
Opole	(D) 3%	(D) 2%	(A D) 3%	2%	3%
Subcarpathian	(B) 5%	4%	(B) 5%	(A B C) 13%	5%
Podlaskie	(C) 3%	3%	3%	(A B C) 6%	3%
Pomerania	(D) 6%	(A C D) 7%	(D) 6%	2%	6%
Silesia	(B C D) 14%	(D) 10%	(B D) 13%	3%	13%
Świętokrzyskie	(B C) 3%	3%	3%	(A B C) 7%	3%
Warmia and Mazuria	(B D) 4%	3%	(D) 3%	3%	3%
Wielkopolskie	9%	9%	9%	9%	9%
West Pomerania	(D) 4%	(C D) 5%	(D) 4%	2%	4%
Total persons (in thous.) = 100%	57.6	8.8	79.0	6.8	152.6

Source: own calculations based on *Household budgets,* CSO, 2010–2011.

In Subcarpathia the share of respondents that have their own company and employers is significantly lower compared to the proportion for other types of economic activity (4% of the self-employed and employers). In the case of Silesia the percentage of employees is significantly higher than the percentage of people with their own company and farmers.

Conclusions

The article presents a comparative analysis of the characteristics of non-agricultural businesses and farmers by gender. In addition, both groups studied were compared to other types of economic activity.

In the introduction to the article there was mention of the various perceptions of education in the context of entrepreneurship. As demonstrated above, the proportion of people with secondary and higher education among entrepreneurs is significantly higher than in the other groups. In addition, employers are a significantly higher proportion of people with secondary education compared to those who are self-employed. Farmers are the highest proportion of people with basic vocational and primary education. In the case of the entrepreneurs and farmers, women are better educated than men.

Farmers are the oldest group among all the groups that are professionally active. The age of men and women is similar for all types of economic activity studied. However, it is worth emphasizing that employers are slightly older than the self-employed.

Women's income is lower for all types of economic activity. In the case of non-agricultural business women's income is about four-fifths of the income of men, while the income of women in agriculture is about half the income of men farmers. It is worth noting that the income of the self-employed is lower by about one-fifth than the income of employers.

Among the entrepreneurs we can see signs of occupational segregation. Women entrepreneurs run companies mainly in the service sectors, while men dominate in sectors related to construction, transport and vehicles. When asked about profession, entrepreneurs most often responded that they are managers in charge of production and services, specialists in various fields, vendors and construction workers. Most men entrepreneurs as an additional source of income reported use of an agricultural holding, salaried employment, and occupational pension. For women, the most common additional source of income is an occupational pension, fixed waged labour, and other social benefits (about 5%). Farmers most often declared that they are commodity producers.

Most entrepreneurs and farmers live in a relationship (formal or informal), but it is worth noting that the percentage of women who are not in a relationship in this group is much higher than the percentage for men. Farmers have three or more children, which is more than other groups, while entrepreneurs have two children which is also often more than other groups.

Literature

Blanchflower, D.G. (2004), "Self-employment: More may not be better," *Swedish Economic Policy Review*, No. 11, pp. 15–73.

Bonte, W., Piegeler, M. (2012), "Gender gap in latent and nascent entrepreneurship: Driven by competitiveness," *Small Business Economics*, Vol. 41, No. 4, pp. 961–987.

Caputo, R.K., Dolinsky, A. (1998), "Women's choice to pursue self-employment: The role of financial and human capital of household members," *Journal of Small Business Management*, Vol. 36, No. 3, pp. 8–17.

Cowling, M., Taylor, M. (2001), "Entrepreneurial women and men: Two different species?," *Small Business Economics*, Vol. 16, No. 3, pp. 167–176.

CSO (2011), *Household Budget Survey in 2010, Statistical Information and Elaborations*, Warsaw.

Davidsson, P., Honig, B. (2003), "The role of social and human capital among nascent entrepreneurs," *Journal of Business Venturing*, Vol. 18, No. 3, pp. 301–331.

der van Peter, Z., Verheul, I., Thurik, R. A. (2012), "The entrepreneurial ladder, gender, and regional development," *Small Business Economics*, Vol. 39, pp. 627–643.

Dubin, J.A., Rivers, D. (1989), "Selection bias in linear regression, logit and probit models," *Sociological Methods and Research*, Vol. 18, No. 2–3, pp. 360–390.

Edwards, L., Field-Hendrey, E., (2002), "Home-based work and women's labour force decisions," *Journal of Labour Economics*, Vol. 20, No. 1, pp. 170–200.

Estrin, S., Mickiewicz, T. (2011), "Institutions and female entrepreneurship," *Small Business Economics*, No. 37, pp. 397–415.

Garcia, A.B. (2012), "Analysing the determinants of entrepreneurship in European cities," *Small Business Economics*, No. 42, pp. 77–98.

Gardawski, J. (2013), *Rzemieślnicy i biznesmeni właściciele małych i średnich przedsiębiorstw prywatnych*, Warszawa: Wydawnictwo Naukowe Scholar.

Goedhuys, M., Sleuwaegen, L. (2000), "Entrepreneurship and growth of entrepreneurial firms in Cote D'Ivoire," *Journal of Development Studies*, Vol. 36, No. 3, pp. 122–145.

Gruszczyński, M. (ed.), Bazyl M., Książek M., Owczarczuk M., Szulc A., Wiśniowski A., Witkowski B. (2012), *Mikroekonometria. Modele i metody analizy danych indywidualnych*, Warszawa: Wolters Kluwer Polska.

Justo, R., DeTienne, D.R. (2008), "Gender, family situation and the exit event: Reassessing the opportunity-cost of business ownership," *IE Business School Working Paper*, no WP08-26, Madrid.

Kepler, E., Shane, S. (2007), "Are male and female entrepreneurs really that different?," *Small Business Research Summary*, No. 309, pp. 1–59.

King, G., Langche, Z. (2001), "Logistics regression in rare events data," *Political Analysis*, Vol. 9, No. 2, pp. 137–63.

Langowitz, N., Minniti, M., (2007), "The entrepreneurial propensity of women," *Entrepreneurship Theory and Practice*, Vol. 31, No. 3, pp. 341–365.

Lazear, E.P. (2004), "Balanced skills and entrepreneurship," *The American Economic Review*, Vol. 94, No. 2, pp. 208–211.

Lazear, E.P. (2005), "Entrepreneurship," *Journal of Labour Economics*, Vol. 23, No. 4, pp. 649–680.

Lee, M.A., Rendall, M.S. (2001), "Self-employment disadvantage in the working lives of blacks and females," *Population Research and Policy Review*, No. 20, pp. 291–320.

Maddala, G.S. (2001), *Introduction to Econometrics*, Chichester: John Wiley & Sons.

Maloney, W.F. (2004), "Informality revisited," *World Development*, Vol. 32, No. 7, pp. 1159–1178.

Martin, B.C., McNally, J.J., Kay M.J. (2013), "Examining the formation of human capital in entrepreneurship: A meta-analysis of entrepreneurship education outcomes," *Journal of Business Venturing*, Vol. 28, pp. 211–224.

Minniti, M., Naudé, W. (2010), "What Do We Know about the Patterns and Determinants of Female Entrepreneurship across Countries?," *European Journal of Development Research*, No. 22, pp. 277–293.

Nafziger, E.W., Terrell, D., (1996), "Entrepreneurial human capital and the long-run survival of firms in India," *World Development*, Vol. 24, No. 4, pp. 689–696.

Oberschachtsiek, D. (2012), "The experience of the founder and self-employment duration: a comparative advantage approach," *Small Business Economics*, Vol. 39, pp. 1–17.

Parker, S.C. (2009), *The economics of entrepreneurship*, Cambridge: Cambridge University Press.

Rollnik-Sadowska, E. (2010), *Przedsiębiorczość kobiet w Polsce*, Warszawa: Difin.

Shim, S., Eastlick, M.A. (1998), "Characteristics of Hispanic female business owners: An exploratory study," *Journal of Small Business Management*, Vol. 36, No. 3, pp. 18–34.

Wach, K. (2008), http://ideas.repec.org/p/pra/mprapa/31488.html, MPRA Paper 31488, University Library of Munich, Germany.

Wagner, J. (2006), "Are nascent entrepreneurs 'Jacks-of-all-trades'? A test of Lazear's theory of entrepreneurship with German data," *Applied Economics*, No. 38, pp. 2415–2419.

Chapter 7

Analysis of time use data – time allocation between women and men in Poland

Katarzyna Filipowicz, Anna Zachorowska-Mazurkiewicz

Abstract

People spend time on paid work in the market, unpaid work for the household or community, as well as on leisure. In this regard, there is a clear differentiation between the sexes, because women do most of the unpaid work, while men are more involved in paid work. Economic theories explain this distinction in different ways – neoclassical theories point to the rational choice associated with the varying efficiency of women and men both in the labour market and in the household, while heterodox theories point to the influence of norms, social values and traditions, according to which the man is the breadwinner and the woman the caregiver. The following paper presents the allocation of time for men and women between paid and unpaid work. The time use data presented in the paper show that if you treat work extensively as paid work performed in the labour market or unpaid in the household, women work much longer than men. Women's workload, both unpaid and paid, requires some skill in order to combine these duties, which may translate into innovative solutions in this field.

Key words: time budgets, paid work, unpaid work, gender, Poland

Introduction

Time is an important factor affecting people's quality of life. People spend time on paid work in the market, unpaid work for the household or community, as well as on leisure. A crucial element in time allocation is unpaid work. Spending time on household duties does not give the worker monetary income, and it cannot be regarded as rest. In this regard, there is a clear differentiation between the sexes when it comes to the amount of time spent on unpaid work, which translates into the women's and men's opportunities.

This paper presents the allocation of time for men and women between paid and unpaid work, and free time. The paper presents a theoretical approach to the allocation of time between women and men in economic theories, both mainstream and heterodox. Analysis of actual time allocation in Poland is based on data obtained during the survey on time use conducted by the Central Statistical

Office in 2003–2004. This hypothesis tested in the chapter is that women spend more time on unpaid work and total work (paid and unpaid). This burden has negative consequences associated with the possibility to engage in paid work. At the same time it is a stimulus that makes women look for innovative solutions to combine the roles they exercise in the labour market and in the family.

7.1. Theoretical view of time allocation by women and men

7.1.1. The neo-classical approach to the problem of time allocation

In the 1960s within neoclassical economics a new school developed called New Home Economics. Representatives of the new home economics tried to analyse the gender division of labour in the home. This division is largely explained by the comparative advantage model, which argues that marriage provides economic gains to both partners. Households maximize their total bundle of goods and services – those produced in market as well as those produced at home (Becker, 1973). In this way this approach offers an explanation as to why women specialize in home-based goods and services. Family members specialize in the paid labour market or in domestic labour in accordance with their relative productivities in those sectors. In a household of identical individuals no more than one person will contribute time to both paid labour in the market and household work, the dual contributor being equally productive in the two sectors. To maximize household output those who are more productive than the dual contributor in the market sector will specialize there, while those who are more productive in the home will become specialized domestic workers. Constant or increasing returns to scale in the production of household commodities raise the payoff to specialization and each member will specialize in one sector only. To identify who will specialize in the paid labour market, and hence who will be an altruistic head of the household, biological sex must be introduced. Women are defined as having a comparative advantage in household work because of their role in the reproductive process (Hewitson, 2003, p. 269).

Originally in neoclassical theory the time available to an individual of working age is divided into work and leisure time. Jacob Mincer in his paper in 1962 devoted to married women in the labour market subjects this simple division to question. He writes that such a simple dichotomy – work and leisure – is not even true in relation to men, and especially in the case of women. A logical part of the free time in this sense is in fact work, for which no remuneration is received. For actions defined, inter alia, by Becker as leisure we can include investment in oneself, or production for our own household. Mincer writes that as educational activity is an important part of the lives of children in society, like work for the family is an important component of women's lives, and sometimes their only job. Therefore, we cannot analyse the lives of women (married in Mincer's case) only by their demand for leisure time. Projected changes in women's leisure time may be due to changes in working time in the market, which in turn are the result of changes in the burden of housework (Mincer, 1962, p. 213). In the same article Mincer shows that the distribution of free time, work in the labour market and housework take place not only under the influence of tastes and preferences, but are also determined by biological and cultural functions, as well as the relative values of the work of each member of the family (Mincer, 1962, p. 214).[1] Gary S. Becker, in his paper of 1965, also made changes to the model household making a distinction between paid work and other types of work performed at home. In the context of further enlargement of the neoclassical models made in 1980 Gronau distinguished three types of work time allocation: paid work, household work and free time (Wunderink-van Veen, 2003).

Thus, the economic agent on the market has to decide on the amount of time spent on paid work and unpaid work. Remuneration for work is determined by the forces of supply and demand in the labour market, and its amount remains the same regardless of the amount of time spent on the market. However, the marginal product of work for the household due to the operation of the law of diminishing returns, assuming the constancy of capital in the household, will decline. The rational economic agent will allocate time between work in the market and for the household, until the decreasing value of the marginal product of homework is equal to the market rate. In analysing these relationships it is worth remembering that the market wage for men is higher than women, which is illustrated in Graph 7.1.

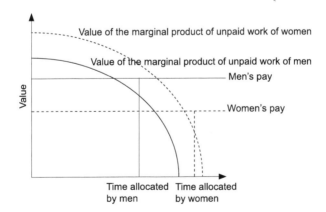

Graph 7.1. The allocation of time between paid and unpaid work by gender
Source: N. Folbre (2004), "The theory of the misallocation of time," [in:] N. Folbre, M. Bittman (eds.), *Family Time. The Social Organization of Care*, London, New York: Routledge, s. 11.

---

1   Interestingly, in a commentary to Mincer's work, Clarence D. Long writes that "... two to three wives are at home, at school, in institutions, or play bingo with the other wives, and therefore do not want to or cannot work"(Mincer, 1962, p. 246), presenting, however, the typical approach in which performing tasks at home is not a job.

As is clear from the above-described model, women are more effective in performing housework than men, and the latter's market wages are in turn higher. Women on the open market can compensate for their lack of productivity by lowering the prices of their work. In other words, women have to accept lower wages, if they want to find a job (Baxter, 2000, p. 60). Thus, rational decision-makers make decisions regarding the traditional division of labour between the sexes, in which women are more involved in the work of the household, and men in employment in the labour market.

Specialization in market work or work for the household is the result of an efficient allocation of time by individual family members, leading to an increase in the total family product. Gary S. Becker (1985) draws attention to the importance of human capital for the division of labour and time allocation between the sexes.[2] Due to the fact that the care of children and doing housework require much more effort than rest, or other activities, married women put less effort into the work carried out on the market. For this reason, women receive lower hourly rates for human capital similar to men and on the labour market they seek jobs requiring less commitment. Thus, according to Becker, women's responsibility for carrying out the work for the household has important implications for the level of remuneration for men and women, as well as explaining the feminization of certain professions or positions. The earnings of women are inversely affected by their household duties, even if they want to participate in the labour market for the same number of hours as men. This is because they are tired, have to stay at home when the children get sick or in the case of other emergencies, and are less likely to work unsocial hours or to take a job that requires travel.

Becker argues that married women invest less in their human capital than men, due to their lower earnings and the occupational segregation they experience. However, this is not the result of lesser involvement in the labour market (which is the traditional assumption), but of the workload at home and childcare. Thus, women earn less due to their lesser involvement in work and lower investment in human capital. Market equilibrium would occur if women started to fully specialize in work for the household, or other non-market activities (Becker, 1985, p. S53).

The models discussed above are based on traditional economic assumptions. However, in neoclassical economics more realistic models were developed to represent intra-household decision making (Humphries, 1998), examples of which could be bargaining models. In these models, such as the one developed by Lundberg and Pollack (1993), the concept of gender replaces biological sex. In this model the bargaining power of each spouse is determined by their wellbeing in their 'separate spheres'. This equilibrium is characterized by spouses undertaking the activities assigned to their socially sanctioned and exogenously determined genders – husbands specialize in earning income and wives specialize in domestic labour (Hewitson, 2003, p. 270–271). Another bargaining model using gender is the one developed by Akerlof and Kranton (2000), in which socially sanctioned gender roles are incorporated into the bargaining framework by inserting 'gender

---

2   More specifically between husbands and wives, see Becker, 1985, p. S33.

identity' into the utility functions of the spouses. The relative hours spent by husbands and wives in the performance of paid and unpaid labour is the result of their utility-maximizing strategies to maintain membership of their gender categories. More specifically, both partners suffer loss of utility when the wife works more than half the couple's total labour market hours or when the husband contributes more than a half the unpaid domestic labour since these situations cause a loss of coherence with the content of their respective gender identities (Akerlof and Kranton, 2000). An interesting observation arises from this model. When wives increase their relative hours in the labour market, causing both partners a utility loss due to the incompatibility of this change with their gender identities, husbands reduce their relative domestic labour contribution, creating an offsetting utility gain for each spouse (Hewitson, 2003, p. 271).

Neoclassical economics uses the rational choice theory in order to clarify choices about engaging in unpaid work by women and men. It assumes that women have a natural inclination to engage in activities for the household, and the division of labour between the sexes, in which the woman specializes in unpaid work, and the man in paid, is considered to be beneficial. Inequalities in the distribution of work in the household and the asymmetry in the division of labour is explained as a consequence of individual choices that maximize utility (Beneria, 1995 after: Barker, 1999, p. 574). However, the inequality occurring in time allocation can also be interpreted differently, which is what heterodox theories do.

7.1.2. Heterodox theories and the question of time allocation between the sexes

In addition to the neoclassical theory of time allocation between paid and unpaid work, there is economics which takes gender relations into account. Papers written from this perspective relate to the impact of reproductive life on economic decisions, through the study of the impact of social norms and legal and political institutions. An important point of discussion is how people (women and men) spend their time. Men and women make choices about how to allocate their time, but their choices are considerably constrained by the various restrictions and social conditions they encounter. Studies of time allocation in married households show that regardless of the methodology applied the wife definitely performs most of the work, even if she formally works full-time (Sirianni and Negrey, 2000, p. 61).[3] It can therefore be assumed that modern women are expected to engage in the work in the formal market, but also to perform duties in the household (see McDowell, 2001). However, this means a huge burden of formal and informal work on women.

---

3   It should also be noted that Robinson and Godbey's study (1997) showed that respondents tend to report more than the actual time spent to perform work for the household. Despite these deviations, Robinson and Godbey's study showed that the ratio of women's work time to men's time, in the case of work for the household, is constant.

According to Sirianni and Negrey (2000, p. 59) time allocation is shaped by social relations and social inequality. Gender relations shape the diverse experiences of women in the context of paid and unpaid work time. Women are more likely than men to do unpaid work for the household, which can take many forms: cleaning, laundry, cooking, gardening, or care for children or adults in need of assistance. Men, in turn, spend more time engaged in paid employment in the labour market. The labour market is not an example of a level playing field where all participants have an equal chance, because women participate in it loaded with the baggage of housework. The unequal distribution of domestic work has long been recognized as a cause of the unfavourable position of women in the labour market (Humphries, 1998, p. 223).

From a historical point of view, household duties meant that women had less time for a series of steps that could strengthen their position in the labour market – training, trade union activities, and full-time work. At the same time housework imposes a negative impact on the earnings of women (see Sirianni and Negrey 2000, p. 64). Sirianni and Negrey (2000) show that the formal working hours of women are shorter than men's, mainly due to the higher share of women in less than full-time or on temporary employment. The involvement of women in work in a manner other than full-time work, and breaks in employment due to maternity and parental leaves influence their careers. The career model adopted requires continuity and full commitment, which is often not possible for women to meet. Many of the most vigorous pressures and key promotion stages occur during childbearing years, thus disadvantaging those who interrupt their careers.

According to Maria Floro (1995), any attempt to assess welfare should take into account the length and intensity of the work done by the person concerned. The unpaid work performed by women affects the level of production in the national economy through the reproduction of labour power which takes place every day in households. This type of work is predominantly done by women, which is reflected in their vulnerable economic position within the system of production for the market, and in particular on the labour market (Beneria, 1979, after: Esquivel, 2011, p. 223). The way in which the division of labour is carried out for paid and unpaid work between men and women within the household and within society has strong implications for gender relations. The unequal division of labour between the sexes explains the limited opportunities that are available to women, and their long hours of work when they decide to be active in the formal labour market (Esquivel, 2011, p. 226).

Decisions relating to women's allocation of time between paid work in the labour market and unpaid in the household have more in common with the beliefs of the society than with rational economic choice. The entrance and participation of women in the labour market and other areas of the economy is dependent on the amount of time spent on unpaid work in the household, including care. Most men do not make such a division of their time. This inequality limits the ability of women to take up paid employment, reduces labour productivity and reduces the future global output of the economy. The constraints experienced by women in terms of taking on full-time, rewarding work arising from the unequal division of labour in the household are due to the norms and values in the labour market (World Bank, 1995, p. 4).

7.2. Analysis of time allocation between women and men based on the time use survey in Poland in 2003–2004

7.2.1. Time use survey

Time allocation can be studied using time use data. Time-use data make it possible to show how work performed outside the marketplace represents an essential and distinctive part of national economies and to highlight how this work is unevenly distributed among women and men (Gálvez-Muñoz et al., 2011, p. 125). Time use surveys are a theoretical construct used to measure the distribution of time between different types of activities. In Poland, the first attempt to study the time use was made by the Institute of Social Economy in 1927. A post-war nationwide analysis of the distribution of the time, by the Central Statistical Office, took place in 1969. However, the sample did not represent the entire Polish population as it mainly covered the urban population. Subsequent studies were conducted periodically by the CSO in 1976, 1984, 1996 and 2003/2004 (Hozer-Koćmiel, 2010, p. 72). In the case of the Polish study conducted every 12 years by the Central Statistical Office, information about activities performed during the day is collected by means of a diary, i.e. an official form for the registration activities performed during the day.

In the analysis of time allocation, the data obtained in the study of time use surveys in Poland in the years 2003–2004, which is based on a representative sample of 10 256 households, was studied. The survey covered people aged 15 years and older. In this study information was provided on the time devoted to various activities. In this analysis, a division was conducted into activities related to performance of paid and unpaid work, and the time spent on these two types of work was disaggregated by sex. In the context of paid work there was a division between main and additional work which qualified – paid employment, self-employed, and work on a farm. In the case of the main job additional activities related to employment were also isolated. In the case of unpaid work there was a division into work for the household, care, and unpaid work for the community. Housework included a number of activities in the home, such as, for example, cooking, cleaning, laundry, construction, and renovation. Care refers to care to both children and dependent adults. Further, in the context of work carried out for the benefit of the local community work for an organization, informal help, or mere participation in organizations and informal groups can be distinguished. A detailed breakdown is available in Appendix 7.1.

7.2.2. The division of time between the sexes

Time allocation between paid and unpaid work for men and women was analysed with a division into working days (Monday–Friday), Saturdays, and Sundays and holidays. Detailed information on hours of work can be found in Appendix 7.2. Both the table and graphs display the average size for all respondents. The study included people over 15 years of age. Thus some people were economically inactive, which affects the average workload of the study group. The detailed structure of the age of the respondents is given in Appendix 7.3. Figure 7.1 and 7.2 represent the length of time the men and women worked on weekdays.

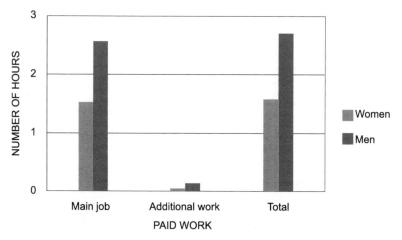

Figure 7.1. Paid work for men and women on weekdays (Monday–Friday)
Source: own calculations.

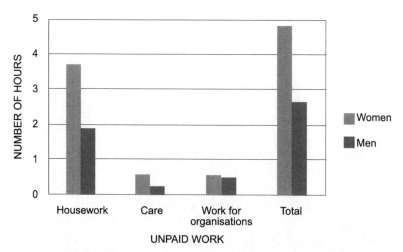

Figure 7.2. Unpaid work for men and women on weekdays (Monday–Friday)
Source: own calculations.

During the weekdays men spend much more time than women on formal work – both the main job, and additional work. A man works an average of 2 hours 43 minutes, while the woman spends on average 1 hour 35 minutes at work. Men spend 11.3% of the day doing paid work, while women spend 6.6%. The proportions are different in the case of unpaid work, as presented in the chart below.

On weekdays, women spend 4 hours 50 minutes on unpaid work, while men almost half – 2 hours and 38 minutes. It is similar with time spent on work in organizations, but significant differences occur in the case of work for the household and care work. Unpaid work occupies more than 20% of a woman's day and 11% of a man's day. For Saturdays, it is extremely interesting that the average time spent on work, both paid and unpaid, increases (Figures 7.3 and 7.4).

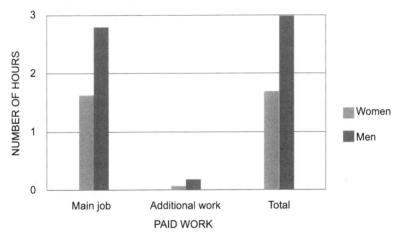

Figure 7.3. Paid work for men and women on Saturdays
Source: own calculations.

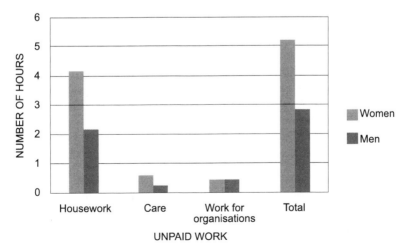

Figure 7.4. Unpaid work for men and women on Saturdays
Source: own calculations.

And so on Saturdays women increase the time spent on paid work by 7 minutes, while on unpaid work as much as 22 minutes, in other words they work an average of almost half an hour longer than on weekdays. For men, paid work is extended by 17 minutes, and unpaid by 12, for a total and almost half an hour, although the structure of this additional work time is different for the different sexes. The workload is reduced only on holidays (Sundays and holidays), which is shown in Figures 7.5 and 7.6.

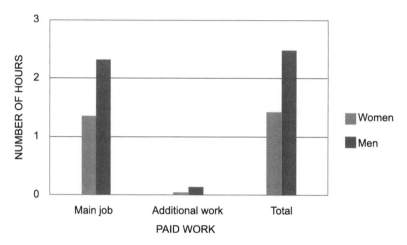

Figure 7.5. Paid work for men and women on Sundays and holidays
Source: own calculations.

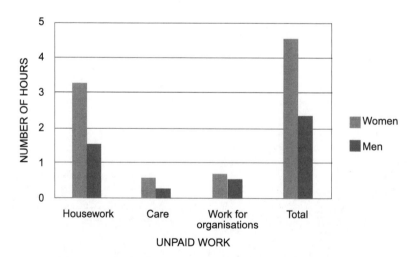

Figure 7.6. Unpaid work for men and women on Sundays and holidays
Source: own calculations.

For women, paid work on Sundays and public holidays is reduced to 1 hour 25 minutes and unpaid to 4 hours and 34 minutes, which in total accounts for nearly 25% of the day. Men spend 2 hours 29 minutes on paid work and 2 hours and 21 minutes on unpaid work, which together accounts for over 20% of the day. Summarizing and totalling the time spent on paid and unpaid work over 7 days a week (5 working days, Saturday and Sunday) men work 37 hours and 25 minutes weekly, of which nearly 51% is paid work. Women spend 44 hours and 58 minutes weekly on working, and paid work is less than 25% of that time.

Conclusions

As in other countries, in Poland the traditional division of labour has been maintained in which men are active in the labour market and women work in the household. Economic theories explain this distinction in different ways – neoclassical theories point to the rational choice associated with the varying efficiency of women and men both in the labour market and in the household, while heterodox theories point to the influence of norms, social values and traditions, according to which the man is the breadwinner and the woman the caregiver. This simple division is a simplification, but also in the context of developments in the labour market after the Second World War and the mass mobilization of women, it does not present a true picture of the division of labour in society. Much more than in the past women engage in formal job market;[4] this has not translated, however, into a more balanced division of labour within the household.

The time use data for men and women presented in the paper show that if you treat work extensively as paid work performed in the labour market or unpaid in the household, women work much longer than men. Women's workload, both unpaid and paid, requires some skill in order to combine these duties, which may translate into innovative solutions in this field. Creativity and innovation in combining paid work and family responsibilities is an area that is worth examining in further studies.

Literature

Akerlof, G.A., Kranton, R.E. (2000), "Economics and Identity," *The Quarterly Journal of Economics*, Vol. 115, No. 3, pp. 715–753.

Barker, D.K. (1999), "Neoclassical economics," [in:] Lewis, M., Peterson, J. (eds.), *The Elgar Companion to Feminist Economics*, Cheltenham: Edward Elgar, pp. 570–577.

Baxter, A. (2000), "The free market, family and gender," [in:] *Market, State and Feminism. The Economics of Feminist Policy*, Cheltenham, Northampton: Edward Elgar, pp. 58–74.

---

4   See Kopycińska's paper in this collection, also Zachorowska-Mazurkiewicz (2006).

Becker, G.S. (1965), "A Theory of the allocation of time," *The Economic Journal*, Vol. 75, September, pp. 493–517.

Becker, G.S. (1973), "A Theory of marriage: Part I," *Journal of Political Economy*, Vol. 81, No. 4, July/August, pp. 813–846.

Becker, G.S. (1985), "Human capital, effort, and the sexual division of labour," *Journal of Labour Economics*, Vol. 3, no. 1, pp. S33–S58.

Benería, L. (1979), "Reproduction, production and the sexual division of labour," *Cambridge Journal of Economics*, Vol. 3(3), pp. 203–225.

Beneria, L. (1995), "Toward a greater integration of gender in economics," *World Development*, 23(11), pp. 1839–1850.

Esquivel, V. (2011), "Sixteen years after Beijing: What are new policy agendas for time-use data collection?" *Feminist Economics*, Vol. 17(4), October, pp. 215–238.

Floro, M. (1995), "Women's Well-Being, Poverty, and Work Intensity," *Feminist Economics*, Vol. 1(3), pp. 1–25.

Folbre, N. (2004), "The theory of the misallocation of time," [in:] N. Folbre, M. Bittman (eds.), *Family Time. The Social Organization of Care*, London, New York: Routledge, pp. 7–24.

Gálvez-Muñoz, L., Rodríguez-Monroño, P., Domínguez-Serrano, M. (2011), "Work and time use by gender: A new clustering of European welfare systems," *Feminist Economics*, Vol. 17(2), October, pp. 125–157.

Gronau, R. (1980), "Home production, a forgotten industry," *The Review of Economics and Statistics*, Vol. 62(3), pp. 408–416.

Hewitson, G.J. (2003), "Domestic labour and gender identity: are all women carers?," [in:] D.K. Barker, E. Kuiper (eds.), *Towards a Feminist Philosophy of Economics*, London, New York: Routledge, pp. 266–284.

Hozer-Koćmiel, M. (2010), „Statystyczna analiza podziału czasu i wartości pracy kobiet," [in:] *Wybrane zagadnienia gospodarowania i zarządzania w pracach doktorskich obronionych na Wydziale Nauk Ekonomicznych i Zarządzania, Studia i Prace Wydziału Nauk Ekonomicznych i Zarządzania*, nr 20, Szczecin: Wydawnictwo Uniwersytetu Szczecińskiego, pp. 69–84.

Humphries, J. (1998), "Towards a family-friendly economics," *New Political Economy*, Vol. 3, No. 2, pp. 223–240.

Lundberg, S., Pollak, R.A. (1996), "Bargaining and Distribution in Marriage," *The Journal of Economic Perspectives*, Vol. 10, No. 4, pp. 139–158.

Mincer, J. (1962), "Labour force participation of married women: A study of labour supply," [in:] H.G. Lewis (red.) *Aspects of Labour Economics*, Princeton: Princeton University Press, pp. 63–105.

Robinson, J., Godbey, G. (1997), *Time for Life: The Surprising Ways the Americans Use Their Time*, University Park, PA: Pennsylvania State University Press.

Sirianni, C., Negrey, C. (2000), "Working time as gendered time," *Feminist Economics* 6(1), pp. 59–76.

World Bank (1995), *Towards Gender Equality. The Role of Public Policy*, Washington, D.C.

Wunderink-van Veen, S. (2003), „Nowa ekonomia gospodarstwa domowego: dzieci a udział kobiet w rynku pracy," [in:] *Ekonomia i płeć*, G.A. Dijkstra, J. Plantega (eds.), Gdańsk: Gdańskie Wydawnictwo Psychologiczne, pp. 27–43.

Zachorowska-Mazurkiewicz, A. (2006), *Kobiety i instytucje. Kobiety na rynku pracy w Stanach Zjednoczonych, Unii Europejskiej i w Polsce*, Katowice: Wydawnictwo Śląsk.

Appendix 7.1. Time allocation – summary of activities

		Activity
PAID WORK	Main job	Unspecified activities related to employment
		Time spent on main job
		Paid main job as an employee
		Paid main job as an employee using a computer
		Paid main job as an employee using the Internet
		Paid main job self-employed
		Paid main job self-employed using a computer
		Paid main job self-employed using the Internet
		Paid main job on a farm
		Paid main job on a farm using a computer
		Paid main job on a farm using the Internet
	Additional work	Time spent on additional work
		Additional work as an employee
		Additional work as an employee using a computer
		Additional work as an employee using the Internet
		Additional work self employed
		Additional work self-employed using a computer
		Additional work self-employed using the Internet
		Additional work on a farm
		Additional work on a farm using a computer
		Additional work on a farm using the Internet
		Help children learning on their parents' (guardians') farm
		Help children learning in a self-employed business run by parents (guardians)
		Other work activities unspecified precisely
		Other specified activities related to work

UNPAID WORK	Working in organizations	Unlisted types of work in organizations and informal groups
		Other work for an organization unspecified precisely
		Work for the organization itself
		Work for people through the organization
		Other specified work for the organization
		Other informal help unspecified exactly
		Food processing
		Janitorial
		Plant growing and caring for pets
		Construction, repair, maintenance of housing and household equipment
		Shopping and use of services
		Help on the farm and non-farm work
		Childcare
		Care for adults
		Other unspecified informal assistance
		Other types of participation in organizations and informal groups unspecified precisely
		Meetings
		Religious practice and activities
		Other specified types of participation in organizations and informal groups

UNPAID WORK	**Working for the household**	Unspecified activities and housework
		Other unspecified precisely activities related to food processing
		Preparing meals, snacks and drinks
		Cooking (all activities associated)
		Washing up
		Making conserves
		Other specified activities related to food processing
		Other activities related to maintaining tidiness unspecified precisely
		Cleaning
		Cleaning the yard, pavement near the house, snow removal
		Activities related to the supply of heating and household water
		Cleaning and tidying activities related to the household
		Other specified activities related to the maintenance of order
		Other activities related to preparing and maintaining clothing unspecified precisely
		Laundry
		Ironing, pressing
		Crafts and clothing production
		Other specified work related to the preparation and maintenance of clothing
		Other activities related to gardening and caring for pets unspecified precisely
		Gardening
		Breeding of domestic animals – livestock intended for consumption in own household or for pleasure
		Other specified precisely activities related to gardening and caring for pets
		Other unspecified precisely activities related to building, renovation, and repair
		Home construction, reconstruction, major repairs
		Repairs, minor repairs to the home
		Producing, repairing, and maintaining home appliances
		Repairs, maintenance of vehicles
		Other specified activities related to construction, renovation and repairs
		Other shopping and services unspecified precisely
		Shopping
		Commercial and administrative services
		Paid personal or insured services
		Other specified activities related to the purchase and use of services
		Household management
		Using the Internet to manage the household
		Other activities unspecified precisely
	Care	Childcare and babysitting
		Study with children
		Reading, playing, and talking with children
		Going out with children
		Other specified activities related to childcare
		Care of adult members of the household

Appendix 7.2. Time allocation between women and men

		Monday–Friday		Saturday		Sunday and holidays		
		M	W	M	W	M	W	
PAID WORK	Main job	10,7%	6,4%	11,7%	6,8%	9,7%	5,7%	% day
	Additional Work	0,6%	0,2%	0,8%	0,3%	0,6%	0,2%	
	TOTAL	11,3%	6,6%	12,5%	7,1%	10,3%	5,9%	
UNPAID WORK	Working for the household	7.8%	15.4%	9.0%	17.4%	6.4%	13.7%	
	Care	1.1%	2.4%	1.0%	2.4%	1.1%	2.4%	
	Working in organizations	2.1%	2.3%	1.8%	1.8%	2.3%	2.9%	
	TOTAL	11.0%	20.1%	11.8%	21.6%	9.8%	19.0%	
TOTAL		22.3%	26.7%	24.3%	28.7%	20.1%	24.9%	
PAID WORK	Main job	154	92	168	98	140	82	minutes
	Additional Work	9	3	12	4	9	3	
	TOTAL	163	95	180	102	149	85	
UNPAID WORK	Working for the household	112	222	130	251	92	197	
	Care	16	35	14	35	16	35	
	Working in organizations	30	33	26	26	33	42	
	TOTAL	158	290	170	312	141	274	
TOTAL		321	385	350	414	290	359	
PAID WORK	Main job	2 h 34 min	1 h 32 min	2 h 48 min	1 h 38 min	2 h 20 min	1 h 22 min	hours and minutes
	Additional Work	9 min	3 min	12 min	4 min	9 min	3 min	
	TOTAL	2 h 43 min	1 h 35 min	3 h 0 min	1 h 42 min	2 h 29 min	1 h 25 min	
UNPAID WORK	Working for the household	1 h 52 min	3 h 42 min	2 h 10 min	4 h 11 min	1 h 32 min	3 h 17 min	
	Care	16 min	35 min	14 min	35 min	16 min	35 min	
	Working in organizations	30 min	33 min	26 min	26 min	33 min	42 min	
	TOTAL	2 h 38 min	4 h 50 min	2 h 50 min	5 h 12 min	2 h 21 min	4 h 34 min	
TOTAL		5 h 21 min	6 h 25 min	5 h 50 min	6 h 54 min	4 h 50 min	5 h 59 min	

Appendix 7.3. Percentage of people in each age group

	Age group	Percent	Cumulative percent
Man	15–25	20.3	20.3
	26–45	34.2	54.5
	46–55	20.3	74.8
	56–65	12.3	87.1
	65+	12.9	100.0
	Total	100.0	
Woman	15–25	19.1	19.1
	26–45	33.8	52.9
	46–55	20.5	73.4
	56–65	12.5	85.9
	65+	14.1	100.0
	Total	100.0	

Source: own report.

Chapter 8

Contemporary value profiles of women and men – Polish pilot survey

Anna Dyląg, Marcin Szafrański

Abstract

This chapter presents the results of a questionnaire survey on value profiles of Polish women and men with special emphasis on creativity. The measurement instrument enabled us to gain some insight into respondents' value content and structure from both the individual and organizational perspectives. The similarities and differences between male and female respondents were analysed according to several research questions: (i) will the survey reflect the value patterns depending on the gender reported by participants? (ii) do Polish men and women differ in terms of their emphasis placed upon specific personal values including creativity? (iii) are there any significant differences between males' and females' perception of values emphasized in the organizations they declared working for? Contrary to other findings on the value profiles of Polish women and men, the current survey did not show any stronger value polarization on the basis of gender as declared by participants. This means that the value profiles were shaped in a similar way no matter whether a respondent was a woman or a man. Interestingly, the results of the survey showed, however, that women placed more emphasis on the vast majority of values compared to men. This tendency was visible both at the individual and organizational levels. This general higher value recognition declared by women is discussed with respect to eudaemonic versus hedonic life orientations. Creativity also appeared among the values on which female respondents significantly placed more emphasis then men, but only in organizational contexts.

Key words: men, women, values, creativity

Introduction

For the needs of this chapter, the value profiles of Polish women and men are analysed with a special respect to creativity treated as a possible psychological correlate of innovativeness. Values are thought of as important entities for many disciplines, including philosophy, economics, psychology, sociology, political science, and related areas. Values have been extensively studied at different levels of analysis - from the cultural/societal (e.g. Inglehart and Welzel, 2005; Hofstede, 1980; Boski, 2010; Czapiński, 2013), through organizational (Hofstede and

Hofstede, 2007; Bugdol, 2006) to the individual (e.g. Rokeach, 1973; Schwartz, 1992). Value surveys reflect ongoing scientific effort in explaining changes in the contemporary cross-cultured world. The common dimensions of values that may help to shed some light on differences among cultures and economies seem one of the most important issues within this field of study. It should be noted, however, that the results obtained at the level of population (global, regional, national, etc.) are always biased toward a central tendency, cutting off the extremes. Also, culture can be seen as a phenomenon which manifests in two higher dimensions and can be measured from two perspectives (Boski, 2010, p. 47–48): objective (environment, economy, social institutions) and subjective – as mental programming that is shared among members of the same group and differentiates from members of other groups (Hofstede and Hofstede, 2007, p. 17). In this typology values fall into the category of subjective entities. In this paper we will concentrate on the values from a psychological perspective.

8.1. Research initiatives on values

8.1.1. World Value Survey (R. Inglehart and C. Welzel)

The importance of values as research topics is reflected in the World Value Survey which is a broad project seeking to help scientists and policy makers understand changes in the beliefs, values and motivations of people throughout the world. It should be noted, however, that the main experts for these studies are political scientists with their sharp focus upon the societal level of analysis and the historical development of the countries studied. The data of the WVS is available to political scientists, sociologists, social psychologists, anthropologists and economists who have used these data to analyse such topics as economic development, democratization, religion, gender equality, social capital, and subjective well-being. These data have also been widely used by government officials, journalists and students, and groups at the World Bank have analysed the linkages between cultural factors and economic development (see: www.worldvaluessurvey.org). The World Values Survey Association is governed by the Executive Committee, the Scientific Advisory Committee, and the General Assembly under the terms of the Constitution. WVS is a global network of social scientists studying changing values and their impact on social and political life since 1981. As written on the website, the WVS is the only scientific study covering the full range of global variation, from very poor to very rich countries, in all of the world's major cultural zones. The WVS is the largest non-commercial, cross-national, time series investigation of human beliefs and values ever executed, currently including interviews with almost 400,000 respondents.

Inglehart-Welzel Cultural Map

The analysis of the WVS data conducted by Ronald Inglehart and Christian Welzel asserts that there are two major dimensions of cross-cultural variation in the world:
1. Traditional values versus Secular-rational values, and
2. Survival values versus Self-expression values.

With help of this theoretical model, the authors can locate societies along these two dimensions in four types (see Table 8.1).

Table 8.1. Value types in Inglehart-Welzel Cultural Map

Opposite types	
1. Traditional values importance of religion, parent-child ties, deference to authority and traditional family values	*2. Secular-rational values* the opposite preferences to the traditional values; less emphasis on religion, traditional family values and authority
3. Survival values emphasis on economic and physical security; it is linked with a relatively ethnocentric outlook, low levels of trust and tolerance	*4. Self-expression values* high priority to environmental protection, growing tolerance of foreigners, sexual minorities and gender equality

Source: based on www.worldvaluessurvey.org [accessed 10.07.2014].

The value types identified by Inglehart and Welzel (2005) may be looked upon as consequences of socioeconomic development in the societies studied. They hypothesize that an increase in standards of living promotes a transit from the development country stage via industrialization to a post-industrial knowledge society. Countries tend to "move" in the direction from poor (survival and traditional values) to rich (secular-rational and self-expression values). In societies where survival values are dominant, general needs and efforts related to self-protection and security are present. Physical and economic survival is a must, thus members of such cultures may seem distant and suspicious. In traditional values national pride is emphasized and a nationalistic outlook is present. People who embrace these values place high importance on hierarchy and formal authority which give little space to individual autonomy; they reject divorce, abortion, euthanasia and suicide. In societies where secular-rational values are present, preferences opposite to traditional values are emphasized. These societies place less emphasis on religion, traditional family values and authority. Divorce, abortion, euthanasia and suicide are seen as relatively acceptable. In countries where self-expression values are present, higher needs arise which are reflected in an emphasis on high individual autonomy and tolerance, care for the environment and a need for participation in decision-making in economic and political life.

With regard to the findings of the WVS experts, Poland represents a region which can be described as traditional. In the European database on innovativeness, the Polish economy is characterized as a very weak inventor (with the only exception being the Warsaw region and Mazovia province – see EUROSTAT;[1]

---

1 Eurostat, www.ec.europa.eu [accessed 10.07.2013].

Nowak, 2012; Dyląg and Łącała, 2015). Despite the steady economic growth of Poland since its transformation, Poles are in the majority pessimists (data from 2005, see Boski, 2010, p. 285), highly dissatisfied with the political situation in the country, and displaying a low level of trust toward political participation. The strongest and most stable source of satisfaction for Poles are family life, children, and friends (Boski, 2010, p. 286). In a world ranking of 177 countries based on such indicators of quality of life as: NGP per cap., HDI (objective well-being), SWLS (subjective well-being measured by the Diener scale), life satisfaction (measured by the Veenhoven scale) and the role of religion (participation in religious events and child raising based on religion in %) – Poland ranked in 37th place. The leaders were Norway, Iceland, Australia, Ireland and Sweden. European countries which ranked lower than Poland were, for instance: Estonia, Lithuania, Slovakia, Latvia, Croatia, Bulgaria, Romania, Russia and Belarus (Boski, 2010, p. 288).

8.1.2. Cultural and organizational values (G. Hofstede)

One of the most widely cited studies on organizational and culture specific values was conducted by G. Hofstede in his pioneer works in the years 1968–72. Hofstede used data collected in 50 resident countries of the IBM corporation (later 53 + 16 added postcommunist countries, see Boski, 2010, p. 92), on 116,000 employers, including management. His typology of value orientations initially included 4 dimensions, with one added later (Hofstede and Hofstede 2007, p. 35–36; see the table below).

Some criticism (from the Polish perspective) of Hofstede's model was raised by Boski (2010, p. 126). His critique is mainly related to the lack of a comprehensive theory underlying the typology. A theory would help to explain the differences observed and predict future trends. Also – as Boski highlights –Hofstede may show some ethnocentrism himself while discriminating between cultures, suggesting that one may be "better" (strong, healthy, or effective) than another ("worse" – weak, unhealthy, or less effective); such interpretations are made in favour of Dutch culture (promoted as the optimum compared, for instance, to the American one, although both profiles show almost the same pattern).[2]

Poland in Culture Compass survey

It is possible to look into Hofstede's profile of a country of interest via the website resources (www.geert-hofstede.com, accessed 15.07.2014). It says that if we explore Polish culture through the lens of the proposed model, we get a good overview of the deep specific drivers "relative to other world cultures" (ibid.). When one clicks "Poland" a description appears which includes a diagram and a detailed written

---

2   It may be important to mention here that G. Hofstede's nationality is Dutch, and P. Boski spent several years in Africa which strongly influenced his view on cultures and values.

characterization of Polish culture. As the model has been improved, the structure of the model has changed. The dimension of LTO is replaced by two new ones: pragmatism and indulgence; hence the model is referred to as the 6-D model (six dimensions). The tool and the website itself have been developed by The Hofstede Centre in collaboration with the *itim international*, a culture consultancy that offers a "new cultural survey" (Culture Compass). It is a tool that helps to describe and better understand hidden patterns of behaviour affecting members of a given culture (meaning country).

Table 8.2. Hofstede's typology of cultural dimensions

Dimension	Description
Power Distance Index (PDI)	Refers to the issue of equality and power distribution in a group or society, it is defined as the extent to which the less powerful members of society expect and accept that power is not distributed equally.
Individualism (IDV)	Addresses the issue of "interdependence" and is described by the degree to which people feel linked and dependent on each other and view the whole society as a cohesive group. In strongly individualistic cultures people are supposed to look after themselves and their direct family exclusively, while in collectivist societies people feel they belong to one group, take care of each other and expect loyalty in exchange.
Masculinity (MAS)	This is described as a strong emphasis on competition, achievement and success, with success being defined by the winner/best in field; this approach is a paradigm of the educational system, and in fact is starts in schools (and continues as organizational behaviour in workplaces or as a set of key values in organizational culture).
Uncertainty Avoidance Index (UAI)	The extent to which the members of a culture feel threatened by ambiguous or unknown situations and have created beliefs and institutions that help them to avoid this feeling; for instance, they tend to take actions that are rational, under control and planned in advance.
Long Term Orientation (LTO)	A dimension added to the initial 4-D model in 1991 as a result of additional international study among students with a survey instrument developed together with Chinese professors (it was also a result of inspiration from Far Eastern countries and their Confucian philosophy); it is described as an ability to work hard long term (emphasize on persistent work engagement), even at the expanse of private life; while consumption, free time, and relax are not valued; it was applied in 23 countries.

Source: G. Hofstede, J. Hofstede (2007), *Kultury i organizacje*, Warszawa: PWE; P. Boski (2010), *Kulturowe ramy zachowań społecznych*, Warszawa: PWN–Scientifica SWP, pp. 91–126.

Poland is described as country characterized by (cited from www.geert-hofstede.com):
- high on PDI – meaning that it is a hierarchical society in which people accept that power is not distributed equally and there is a hierarchical order (everybody accepts his or her place with no further justification). Hierarchy in an organization is seen as reflecting inherent inequalities, centralization is popular, subordinates expect to be told what to do and the ideal boss is a benevolent autocrat,

- high on IDV– Poland is an individualistic society. This means there is a high preference for a loose social framework in which individuals are expected to take care of themselves and their immediate families only. The employer/employee relationship is a contract based on mutual advantage, hiring and promotion decisions are supposed to be based on merit only, management is the management of individuals. The Polish culture however, carries a "contradiction" – although highly individualistic, the Polish need a hierarchy. This combination (high score on power distance and high score on Individualism) creates a specific "tension" in this culture, which makes the relationship delicate but intense and fruitful once you manage it (managers are advised to establish a second "level" of communication, having personal contact with everybody in the structure, enabling the impression that "everybody is important" in the organization, although unequal),
- rather high on MAS – Poland is a masculine society. In masculine countries people "live in order to work," managers are expected to be decisive and assertive, the emphasis is on equity, competition and performance, and conflicts are resolved by fighting them out,
- very high on UAI (the highest score in the entire profile) – in Poland there is a very high preference for avoiding uncertainty. Countries exhibiting high uncertainty avoidance maintain rigid codes of belief and behaviour and are intolerant of unorthodox behaviour and ideas. In these cultures there is an emotional need for rules (even if the rules never seem to work) time is money, people have an inner urge to be busy and work hard, precision and punctuality are the norm, innovation may be resisted,[3] security is an important element in individual motivation,
- pragmatism (PRA) – Poland's (low) score in this dimension means that it is more normative than pragmatic culture. People in such societies have a strong concern with establishing the absolute Truth; they are normative in their thinking. They exhibit great respect for traditions, a relatively small propensity to save for the future, and a focus on achieving quick results,
- indulgence (IND) – with a low score in this dimension Polish culture is one of restraint (the opposite pool). Societies with a low score in indulgence have a tendency to cynicism and pessimism. Also, in contrast to indulgent societies, restrained societies do not put much emphasis on leisure time nor do they control the gratification of their desires. People with this orientation have the perception that their actions are restrained by social norms and feel that indulging themselves is somewhat wrong.

Additionally, as a cross-cultural survey is also available via Culture Compass (ibid.), it may be worthwhile conducting a short analysis of Polish–Norwegian[4]

---

3 This reference is important while keeping in mind the very low innovativeness of the Polish economy.

4 Polish-Norwegian cooperation is one of the key point in the current grant.

comparison with respect to 6-D model (see Table 8.3). Norway was the leader in the mentioned above world ranking of 177 countries with respect to their reported quality of life.

Table 8.3. Polish-Norwegian culture comparison survey based on Hofstede's 6-D Model

Dimension	Poland	Norway
Power Distance Index (PDI)	68	31
Individualism (IDV)	60	69
Masculinity (MAS)	64	8
Uncertainty Avoidance Index (UAI)	93	50
Pragmatism (PRA)	38	35
Indulgence (IND)	29	55

Source: based on www.geert-hofstede.com [accessed 20.07.2014].

There are some clear differences between Polish and Norwegian cultures in such dimensions as MAS, UAI and PDI. The remaining scores seem similar, i.e. individualism or pragmatism. The low score in masculinity in Norway is the most striking result – it has been interestingly interpreted in the Culture Compass report (ibid.)

(...) Norway is the second most feminine society (after Sweden). This means that the softer aspects of culture are valued and encouraged such as levelling with others, consensus, "independent" cooperation, and sympathy for the underdog. Taking care of the environment is important. Trying to be better than others is neither socially nor materially rewarded. Societal solidarity in life is important; work to live and do your best. Incentives such as free time and flexibility are favoured. Interaction through dialogue and "growing insight" is valued and self-development along these terms encouraged. Focus is on well-being, status is not shown. An effective manager is a supportive one, and decision making is achieved through involvement.

Alongside cultural and national values there has been an effort focused upon organizational or corporate values (which are also viewed as collective programming of the mind that distinguishes the members of one organization from others; Hofstede and Hofstede, 2007, p. 47). Hofstede believes that both cultures and organizations share values, which are deeper and more stable elements of life than practices (practices are more tangible than values). Polish researcher M. Bugdol concludes that organizational values are believed to influence economic and social outcomes. "They correspond with income, productiveness and innovativeness. They can strengthen loyalty, social relations and enrich organizational potential. Values ethical in nature are important not only in management (or leadership), but also support the decision making process both on the management side as well as clients: an increasing number of consumers are aware not only of the price of the product and/or its quality, but also the meaning of the ethical values it stands for" (Bugdol, 2006, p. 149).

8.1.3. Values important in Polish society – Social Diagnosis (J. Czapiński)

Values important to Poles have been regularly studied in an ongoing broad national survey called "Social Diagnosis" (Czapiński, 2013). According to the official description of the project (available online at www.diagnoza.com), Social Diagnosis focuses on conditions and quality of life in Poland, both in the economic and psychological senses. A group of researchers studies such issues like income, material wealth, savings and financing as well as education, medical care, problem-solving, stress, psychological well-being, lifestyle, pathologies, engagement in the arts and cultural events, use of new communication technologies and many others. In this sense the project is interdisciplinary, drawing on the work of the main authors of the Social Monitoring Council (Rada Monitoringu Społecznego) and a team of experts appointed by the Council. The Social Diagnosis is based on panel research, the authors return to the same households every few years, with the first sample being taken in the year 2000. The following took place three years later, and since then the data has been collected and reports have been published every two years. The results of the Social Diagnosis reveal both the current state of Polish society and the ways it has changed over the last ten years. In this respect it is a unique and rich source of information that we decided to refer to for the purposes of this paper.

The survey of values is organized by the authors of Social Diagnosis as a panel study conducted with the help of a relatively short list of items. They do not refer to any specific theoretical approach however, neither to underlying concepts (such as value hierarchy or dimensions). The leading criteria for selecting values were brevity, simplicity of questions, and ease of providing answers (Czapiński, 2013, p. 228). For the needs of his study the author uses a questionnaire which combines 13 specific values and one non-specific item. Since all of the 13 values are commonly accepted, the respondents' choices have been limited to three most important to them (described as conditions for a happy life). The instruction for respondents is as follows: [please indicate] "what in your opinion is the most important condition of a successful, happy life (please first read through all the answers and then choose no more than three, by crossing the appropriate boxes)," see Czapiński, 2013, Annex 8.1, Individual questionnaire (p. 446). The list of items is presented in the table below.

Table 8.4. List of values derived from the Social Diagnosis 2013

1. MONEY	8. HONESTY
2. CHILDREN	9. KINDNESS AND BEING RESPECTED
3. SUCCESSFUL MARRIAGE	10. FREEDOM
4. WORK	11. GOOD HEALTH
5. FRIENDS	12. EDUCATION
6. PROVIDENCE, GOD	13. STRONG PERSONALITY
7. CHEERFULNESS, OPTIMISM	14. OTHER

Source: J. Czapiński (2013), "Individual quality of life and lifestyle," [in:] *Social Diagnosis 2013*, Warsaw: The Council for Social Monitoring, p. 446.

As presented above, the list includes a mix of different value types ("commonly accepted," Czapiński, 2013, p. 228), including economic, religious, family and work-related items, as well as those which can serve as an assessment of individual health. There are also items on selected psychological characteristics of an individual and her or his environment. It is not clear however, how respondents interpret the items and how to interpret them at a higher level, for instance using a dimensional approach. The absence of a theoretical framework enables many alternative explanations for the results, leaving space for competing interpretations.

The results of the value section of *Social Diagnosis 2013* show that – compared to earlier periods of analysis – the value system of Poles remains quite stable. Values of increased importance were friends (a percentage of indications more than double the amount of 2000) and education (although their impact on the quality of Poles' life in general seem undervalued). Values placed upon money and God showed decline, which is interpreted as a result or correspondence of the rapid increase in the Poles' affluence on the one hand and the general decline in the frequency of religious practices and prayer on the other. Similarly to all the previous years, the following values are indicated as important conditions of a happy and good life: health, successful marriage (a slight decline was noted in the number of indications), children (also a fall in the number of indications, which had already started in 2011), and work. The values indicated least often are freedom, strong personality, education, kindness and being respected (see Czapiński, 2013, p. 228).

Many alternative interpretations of results are presented, as the author states that personal value systems depend on various factors like culture, social environment, life events and conditions, status, education, age, etc. For instance, the importance of selected values may correspond with their absence or deterioration (e.g. good health), troubles in life (God, money) or the opposite – as desired life events, such as happy marriage or children. For instance, the importance of children in a value system depends above all on such socio-demographic factors as: (a) relationship – whether someone is in a relationship, (b) gender – whether a respondent is a woman, and c) age – is the respondent between 25–44 years old. As the results of a regression analysis showed, those who placed most importance on value of marriage were themselves married, relatively young, better off and better educated, while those choosing friendship more often than others were wealthy, unmarried and better educated.

Comparison of value systems with respect to gender shows that women appreciate family values, health and religion as well as kindness and peer respect, while men value work, money freedom and a strong character. In addition, younger respondents more than the elderly value a successful marriage, friends, education and freedom. Such outcomes may reflect a traditional view on the social roles of women and men – and remain contrary to our findings, where no "typical" gender related pattern of values has been found (see below).

8.2. The Schwartz value model as a theoretical framework for own research

In recent decades the most widely used approaches to study values were these offered by M. Rokeach (1973), G. Hofstede (1980) and S. Schwartz (1992). Schwartz developed his model with the intention of avoiding such limitations of the previous ones as absence of integrated value theory, data driven approach, and cultural bias (see Spini, 2003). Schwartz and Bilsky (1987, p. 551) defined values as "concepts or beliefs, about desirable end states or behaviours, that transcend specific situations, guide selection or evaluation of behaviour and events, and are ordered by relative importance."

Schwartz proposed a universal taxonomy of values that distinguishes among 10 value types. These categories are: Achievement, Benevolence, Conformity, Tradition, Universalism, Power, Security, Hedonism, Stimulation and Self-direction. Each value type contains several common values (see Figure 8.1). These values stem from a need to cope with three universal requirements, thus they can be recognized cross-cultural. These requirements relate to: (1) the needs of the individual as biological organisms, (2) requisites of coordinated social interaction, and (3) requirements for the smooth functioning and survival of groups (see Dyląg et al., 2013).

OPENESS TO CHANGE	SELF-TRANSCENDENCE
Stimulation *(a varied life, an exciting life)* **Self-direction** *(creativity, curiosity, freedom, choosing own goals, independence)* **(some) Hedonism** *(pleasure, enjoying life)*	**Universalism** *(protecting the environment, a world of beauty, unity with nature, broad-minded, social justice, wisdom, equality, a world at peace, inner harmony)* **Benevolence** *(helpful, honest, forgiving, loyal, responsible, true friendship, a spiritual life, mature love, meaning in life)*
(some) Hedonism *(pleasure, enjoying life)* **Power** *(social power, authority, wealth, preserving my public image, social recognition)* **Achievement** *(successful, capable, ambitious, influential, intelligent, self-respect)*	**Conformity** *(politeness, honouring parents and elders, obedient, self-discipline)* **Tradition** *(devout, accepting portion in life, humble, moderate, respect for tradition)* **Security** *(clean, national security, social order, family security, reciprocation of favours, healthy, sense of belonging)*
SELF-ENHANCEMENT	CONSERVATISM

Figure 8.1. Simplified Schwartz model of values – 4 dimensions (capital letters), 10 value types (underlined), and 56 single values
Source: D. Spini (2003), "Measurement equivalence of 10 value types from the Schwartz value survey across 21countries," *Journal of Cross-Cultural Psychology*, Vol. 34(1), p. 6.

According to Schwartz, the 10 value types can be grouped along four higher order (opposed) dimensions, organized along two main axes: I. "openness to change" versus "conservation" and II. "Self-enhancement" and "Self-transcendence." The dimension of "Openness to change" includes stimulation and self-direction, as well as some hedonism. These values motivate people to follow their own emotional and intellectual impulses in a rather unpredictable way; change seems more attractive to them than stability. We believe that this dimension is strongly emphasised in individual and organizational value orientations toward innovativeness – at least at the first or initial stage of the innovative process. According to the NESTA approach (see NESTA, 2008a, p. 6), two main stages to innovation may be recognized: (1) generation – which encompasses the creativity, problem-solving and decision-making involved in the development of an innovation, and (2) adoption – the process of becoming aware of an innovation and implementing it within a market or organisation.

The dimension of "Conservatism" contains values on tradition, conformity and security. Such values direct people towards certainty, maintaining stable relations and preserving the status quo. The dimension of "Self-enhancement" includes values on power, achievement and some hedonism (this value is related to both "Openness to change" and "Self-enhancement"). This set of values motivate people to concentrate on their own personal goals and interests (even at the expense of others). The dimension of "Self-transcendence" contains values on universalism and benevolence and refers to the extent to which values motivate people to transcend selfish concerns and promote the welfare of all humans as well as of nature (Schwartz, 1992, p. 44).

In this model values belong to 10 separate categories, forming a circular continuum (with some values overlapping two dimensions, like hedonism). As stated by Schwartz (1994, p. 25): "the motivational differences between value types are continuous rather than discrete, with more overlap in meaning near the boundaries of adjacent value types." As a result, values that are in opposition in the structure are competing and have consequences that are incompatible with each other (Schwartz, 1994).

In addition, the theory identifies a central motivational goal which is specific for each separate value type. In conclusion, it seems that Schwarz value model might well serve our need for a comprehensive, validated theoretical value structure, also with respect to future research on innovativeness (see Spini et al., 2003).

8.3. Research on values

Main goal of the present research was to identify value profiles of Polish women and men with respect to creativity. Guiding research questions referred to similarities and differences among values recognized by female and male respondents as the most and least important, at the individual and organizational level of analysis. Research questions were formulated as follows: (i) will the survey reflect value patterns depending on the gender reported by participants? (ii) do Polish men and women differ in terms of their emphasis placed upon specific personal values, including creativity? (iii) are there any significant differences between males' and females' perception of values manifested in organizations they declared working for?

8.3.1. Data and sample

The dataset that served for the needs of this paper has already been analysed (see Dyląg et al., 2013). The previous research referred to the perceived value discrepancy in relation to positive and negative work related well-being. Initially empirical data were gathered from a sample of 342 females (69.7%) and 149 males (30.3 %) white-collar workers who participated in the study (total N = 491). All respondents were employed in Polish public and private organizations from various industry sectors including education, healthcare, sales, etc. The mean age of respondents was about 36.5 (SD = 10.3), ranging from a minimum of 21 to a maximum of 64 years old. The response rate was almost 60% (58.6%). During the course of data analyses, ratings from 11 respondents were excluded, leaving 480 results in total.

8.3.2. Measure and results

The data was collected and analysed with the help of questionnaire including 33 value items, based on the original work of Schwartz (1992). The list of items as well as the rating scale were modified by the authors, and all changes have been described in the mentioned above publication (Dylag et al., 2013). The list of values used in the questionnaire is presented in tables below. Respondents were asked to evaluate importance of a given value for themselves (part A of the questionnaire), and for the organization they worked for (part B). The 6-point rating scale gave the possibility to indicate values most important for respondents (max score plus 4 – key values), as well as values opposite to their value system (min score minus 1 – opposite).

The results of our study are presented from two perspectives (or at two levels of analysis): individual and organizational. Individual values refer to items that are reported as important for each person (see Table 8.5). The organizational level of analysis pertains to the values perceived by respondents as widely manifested and important in the organizations they work for (see Table 8.6).

The individual values most important for women were: 1) self-respect, 2) meaning in life, 3) health, and 4) honesty. Female respondents also highly ranked inner harmony, loyalty, equality, wisdom, and responsibility. The values they ranked as least important were social power, authority, and sacrifice. Interestingly these

Table 8.5. Values – individual level, comparison of means with respect to sex

Values	Values important for individual A		Value women	Value men	Sign at least at level of
	M	SD	M (N = 336)	M (N = 144)	p < .05
1. Equality	3.19	.89	3.26	3.01	*
2. Inner harmony	3.29	.79	3.34	3.19	
3. Social power	**1.48**	**1.1**	*1.41*	*1.63*	*
4. Spiritual life	2.24	1.13	2.31	2.04	*
5. Sense of belonging	2.72	.94	2.89	2.53	*
6. An exciting life	2.15	1.1	2.17	2.08	
7. Meaning in life	3.37	.76	3.47	3.12	**
8. Wealth	2.36	.93	2.36	2.35	
9. Self-respect	3.41	.77	3.49	3.22	**
10. Creativity	2.8	.89	2.82	2.72	
11. Respect for tradition	2.49	1.0	2.54	2.35	
12. Self-discipline	2.73	.87	2.77	2.62	
13. Distance	2.47	.90	2.48	2.44	
14. Social recognition	2.78	.88	2.86	2.59	*
15. Wisdom	3.15	.77	3.23	2.97	**
16. Authority	**1.56**	**1.1**	*1.51*	*1.69*	
17. Social justice	2.75	.90	2.84	2.52	**
18. Independence	3.1	.83	3.16	2.98	*
19. Loyalty	3.27	.73	3.34	3.11	*
20. Ambition	2.77	.91	2.9	2.67	
21. Choosing own goals	3.05	.82	3.09	2.96	
22. Health	3.41	.78	3.46	3.29	*
23. Capability	2.93	.77	2.99	2.8	*
24. Honesty	3.36	.78	3.43	3.21	*
25. Preserving one's public image	3.13	.85	3.19	2.99	*
26. Obedience	2.78	.85	2.83	2.34	*
27. Help	2.98	.76	3.01	2.89	
28. Enjoying life	3.1	.92	3.14	2.99	
29. Responsibility	3.17	.74	3.22	3.05	*
30. Curiosity	2.7	.87	2.75	2.6	
31. Forgiving	2.62	.86	2.68	2.49	*
32. Success	2.86	.83	2.92	2.75	*
33. Sacrifice	**1.63**	**1.26**	*1.56*	*1.79*	

Note: 1) scale ranging from –1 (min) to + 4 (max),
2) bold highlights cases in which male respondents scored higher than females.

Table 8.6. Values – organizational level, comparison of means with respect to sex

Values	Values important in organization B		Value women	Value men	Sign at least at level of
	M	SD	M (N = 336)	M (N = 144)	p < ,05
1. Equality	2.56	1.18	2.61	2.43	
2. Inner harmony	2.38	1.1	2.4	2.34	
3. Social power	2.04	1.16	2.06	1.95	
4. Spiritual life	1.45	1.23	1.5	1.33	
5. Sense of belonging	2.16	1.06	2.2	2.07	
6. An exciting life	**1.5**	**1.12**	**1.43**	**1.64**	
7. Meaning in life	2.49	1.07	2.64	2.19	**
8. Wealth	2.34	1.10	2.35	2.31	
9. Self-respect	2.79	1.00	2.88	2.6	**
10. Creativity	2.64	1.02	2.74	2.39	**
11. Respect for tradition	2.16	1.15	2.24	1.98	**
12. Self-discipline	2.69	0.96	2.75	2.52	**
13. Distance	2.16	1.03	2.2	2.07	
14. Social recognition	2.68	0.98	2.78	2.39	
15. Wisdom	2.82	0.96	2.91	2.58	
16. Authority	2.16	1.14	2.21	2.04	
17. Social justice	2.36	1.12	2.37	2.34	
18. Independence	2.65	0.95	2.72	2.53	*
19. Loyalty	2.69	1.10	2.73	2.61	
20. Ambition	2.75	0.97	2.83	2.54	**
21. Choosing own goals	2.29	1.11	2.35	2.19	
22. Health	2.81	1.05	2.87	2.7	
23. Capability	3.11	0.87	3.19	2.88	**
24. Honesty	2.9	1.07	2.96	2.76	
25. Preserving one's public image	2.94	0.97	3.03	2.7	**
26. Obedience	3.06	0.87	3.13	2.84	**
27. Help	2.63	0.95	2.65	2.59	
28. Enjoying life	**2.26**	**1.22**	**2.26**	**2.32**	
29. Responsibility	3.09	0.87	3.17	2.87	**
30. Curiosity	2.33	1.05	2.37	2.23	
31. Forgiving	2.11	1.10	2.14	2.07	
32. Success	2.91	0.96	3	2.69	**
33. Sacrifice	2.17	1.20	2.19	2.06	

Note: 1) scale ranging from −1 (min) to + 4 (max),
2) bold highlights cases in which male respondents scored higher than females.

were the only values reported by male respondents as more important compared to women's ratings (the differences between men and women obtained statistical significance only on social power, but not on authority or sacrifice). In general, women seem to emphasize these values more compared to men, rating the vast majority of values higher as a rule (except 3 items).

The profile of the most important individual values reported by male respondents shows a similar pattern to female rankings. It consists of such items as 1) health, 2) self-respect, 3) honesty and 4) inner harmony. Later they ranked meaning in life, loyalty, responsibility, and equality. The least important values are the only three items men ranked higher then female respondents – social power, authority and sacrifice. In general, men showed less emphasis on the values compared to women.

The value of creativity (individual level), as declared by women, fell into the category of "very important" with an average score of 2.82 (close to point 3 on the rating scale), but has not been indicated as a key value (point 4, maximum on the rating scale). Although it was ranked higher by female respondents than by men, the difference is not statistically significant.

Comparing the overall individual value profiles of men and women, significant differences between the subsamples were found in 19 items out of 33, while non-significant occurred in 14 cases. Interestingly, women declared a significantly higher emphasis on such traditionally males' values as success or independence (plus a non-significant difference on "authority," meaning that both genders evaluated this item similarly). In relation to innovativeness, an absence of statistically significant differences was found not only in creativity, but also in such values as curiosity, enjoying life, or an exciting life. These items belong to two value types called hedonism and stimulation, and together with "choosing own goals" (self-direction type of values), they represent the dimension of "openness to change" (see Figure 8.1). This combination of values may somehow be linked to innovativeness (or at least to the process of idea generation). However, as the organizational context may stimulate or inhibit individual behaviours (including innovativeness), the second part of our research was focused on respondents' perception of values manifested in their work environment.

The organizational values perceived by women as the most important in their workplace were 1) capability, 2) responsibility, 3) obedience, and 4) preserving one's public image. As the least important in the organizations they work for female respondents reported exciting life, spiritual life, social power, and forgiving. In general, it can be noted that –compared to the individual values assessment provided by female respondents –organizational values received lower ratings.

The organizational values perceived by men as most important in their workplace were capability, responsibility, obedience, and honesty. This almost entirely reflects the profile of organizational values provided by female respondents.

Creativity was indicated by women as "very important" in their work environment. The average calculated for female respondents (2.74) was significantly higher than the average obtained for men (2.39). According to this result, from the perspective of female respondents creativity is treated as very important for their workplaces, while male respondents perceived creativity as an important organizational value, but neither highly important nor a key issue for their workplaces.

Interestingly, only two items are seen by male respondents as emphasised higher in organization compared to females. These are an exciting life and enjoying life – both representing the dimension of openness to change (hedonism and stimulation types of values). None of them showed statistical significance, however. The values of the least importance perceived in organization by male respondents were spiritual life, exciting life, social power, and respect for tradition. Considering statistical significance, 14 out of 33 items showed significant differences with regard to gender and values.

8.4. Discussion

The results of our survey are an inspiring starting point towards further studies on gender determined innovativeness. Comparing men's and women's evaluation of values revealed some interesting results, including creativity. First, as a general tendency it appeared that women value values more than men, both at the individual and organizational level. In the vast majority their ratings were higher than those declared by male respondents. Women reported placing more emphasis on personal values and perceiving their work environment as more value-oriented than men did. This may be interpreted in several ways. For instance, it may mean that men remain more critical than women towards themselves as well as while evaluating their workplaces. On the other hand women appeared more "value oriented" in general, which was also noted by Czapiński (2013). Czapiński explains this difference as a eudaemonic attitude (or life orientation) which characterises the majority of women compared to the hedonistic – more "male like" – attitude. While hedonism may be explained as attempts to maximize pleasant events and the positive aspects of life, eudaemonism refers to a "wiser" existence which is led by "real" values (like honesty, relations and forgiveness). Czapiński (2013, p. 185) describes eudaemonists as happier and healthier, more family and relation oriented, less focused on money and excitement; the chance of a woman being a hedonist is 1/3 that of a man. Hedonists, who are oriented towards pleasure turn out more often than eudaemonists to consider money and freedom as conditions for a successful life.

Second, there was no difference found between female and male respondents in reference to creativity, but only at the individual level of analysis. This may be interpreted, as showing that creativity remains equally important to men and women. There was however, significantly higher emphasis perceived by female respondents on creativity in their workplaces , compared to the assessment provided by men. It may be interpreted that women perceive their work environment as more favourable towards creativity than men do. Two alternative mechanisms may be helpful in explaining this observation (and, in general, all findings focused upon values). Following Boski (2010, p. 161), it is worth highlighting that there is always an issue of affirmative versus compensative mechanisms playing a role in evaluating values. Unlike more tangible organizational practices (norms and behaviours), values remain a somewhat idealistic vision of an optimum situation, which is usually far from the reality members of an organization live every day. Hence, a compensation mechanism, which refers to the states or characteristics that are ranked highly while in fact they are missing in an organizational or people's life, is a possible explanation of many value surveys, including the results presented above. Although our study require further analyses, the role of women in innovation processes and policy (including creativity stage) is certainly worth considering.

Third, we have not found any of typical gender related pattern of values, meaning that the value profiles of men and women were similar in shape, which was demonstrated in the case of individual values. While Czapiński showed that women gave more respect to social and family-related aspects of life, and men appeared more work-related and oriented toward strength and goals (2013) our findings do not correspond with these outcomes. Quite the contrary, the profile of the most important individual values reported by male respondents showed many similarities to women's rankings, including such items as health, self-respect, honesty, and inner harmony. Men also highly ranked meaning in life, loyalty, responsibility, and – interestingly - equality. They pointed to such "traditional male values" as social power or authority at the lowest level in their entire profile (this rating, however, was the only exception in which they rated any values higher than women). Interestingly, we would have thought that "sacrifice" is more a "female" than "male" value, although men reported this item as more important for them personally than women did. In general, the results of our studies do not reveal any deeper differences in values with respect to sex. It seems difficult, on the basis of our data, to identify values typical of women that would be contrary to values typical for men.

Finally, it may be worthwhile mentioning the role of the organizational context in relation to individual well-being and innovativeness. This way of thinking represents an empirical approach often referred to as "a person – environment fit." For instance in the NESTA project (2008a, b) the main focus of the project experts is placed upon the relationship (and on causality in the future) between subjective well-being and innovativeness (and creativity). After the literature review they stated that, despite a limited body of evidence and an absence of identified mechanisms, it is highly recommended that such a relationship should be investigated in order to better stimulate innovativeness. In the study by Sagiv and Schwartz (2000) the authors presented several mechanisms that might moderate relationships between value priorities and subjective well-being (which in turn may influence innovativeness, NESTA 2008a, b). Their conclusion is that no particular value type is inherently `healthy' (e.g. self-direction or stimulation) or `unhealthy' (e.g. tradition, conformity or security). "Rather, particular values contribute to positive or negative well-being depending on whether they are congruent with the values emphasized in particular environments" (p. 195). In the previous publication of the first author of this paper and her colleagues (Dyląg et al., 2013) the same theoretical framework has been used (based on Schwartz's value typology). It has been found that the better the fit (in terms of perception) between person and her or his work environment, the higher the chance for positive work-related well-being (as work engagement), and the lower the risk of negative outcomes (as job burnout). Work engagement has been shown to be a crucial characteristic of effective organizations (Bugdol, 2006) and productive teams (Torrente et al., 2012). This means that studies on the psychological determinants of innovativeness (and creativity) may benefit from employing a multilevel and interactional approach, also using values. It is highly recommended to lead such studies at several levels: individual, team, and organization, as well as within the individual – environment congruity paradigm.

8.5. Limitations to the study

The results presented above should be treated with caution for at least two major reasons: (a) this analysis was meant as an exploratory pilot study, and (b) the sample was not equal in terms of percentage of male and female respondents (sample consisted of 2/3 of women while only 1/3 was represented by men). In order to overcome the second limitation of our research, an appropriate statistical analysis was conducted which showed that there was no impact of the sample gender composition on the study outcomes. This means that there is a low probability that the results of this study demonstrate a value profile dominated by "female pattern" values (which in fact has not been found, although the general tendency of female respondents to "value the values" more than men did was visible).

Also, the argument may appear that the two levels of analysis (individual and organizational) have been mixed in one approach, which was given by Boski as a serious limitation in such study design (see Boski, 2010, p. 185). It may be worth considering an interactional perspective while investigating creativity (see Zhou et al., 2009). The authors examined the influence of social networks and conformity values on employees' creativity. The results they obtained showed that a proper match between personal values and network ties may be critical to understanding this phenomenon.

Literature

Boski, P. (2010), *Kulturowe ramy zachowań społecznych*, Warszawa: PWN–Scientifica SWPS.
Bugdol, M. (2006), *Wartości organizacyjne*, Kraków: Wydawnictwo Uniwersytetu Jagiellońskiego.
Czapiński, J. (2013), "Individual quality of life and lifestyle," [in:] *Social Diagnosis 2013*, Warsaw: The Council for Social Monitoring, pp. 166–277.
Dyląg, A., Jaworek, M., Karwowski, W., Kożusznik, M., Marek, T. (2013), "Discrepancy between individual and organizational values: Occupational burnout and work engagement among white-collar workers," *International Journal of Industrial Ergonomics*, Vol. 43, pp. 225–231.

Dyląg, A., Łącała, Z. (2015), „Regionalne zróżnicowanie innowacyjności. Uwarunkowania psychospołeczne," [in:] M. Trojak (ed.), *Zróżnicowanie rozwoju ekonomicznego Polski,* Kraków: Wydawnictwo UJ.

Hofstede, G. (1980), *Culture's Consequences: International Differences in Work-related Values,* Beverly Hills, CA.: Sage.

Hofstede, G., Hofstede, J. (2007), *Kultury i organizacje,* Warszawa: PWE.

Inglehart, R., Welzel, Ch. (2005), *Modernization, Cultural Change and Democracy: The Human Development Sequence,* New York: Cambridge University Press.

NESTA (National Endowment for Science, Technology and the Arts) (2008a), "Innovation and Well-being," Working Paper (September).

NESTA (2008b), *Measuring Innovation: Policy Briefing,* London.

Nowak, P. (2012), „Poziom innowacyjności polskiej gospodarki na tle krajów UE," Prace Komisji Geografii i Przemysłu Nr 19, Warszawa–Kraków.

Rokeach, M. (1973), *The Nature of Human Values,* New York: The Free Press.

Sagiv, L., Schwartz, S.H. (2000), „Value priorities and subjective well-being: Direct relations and congruity effects," *European Journal of Social Psychology,* Vol. 30, pp. 177–198.

Schwartz, S.H., Bilsky, W. (1987), "Toward a universal psychological structure of human values," *Journal of Personality and Social Psychology,* Vol. 53, pp. 550–562.

Schwartz, S.H. (1992), "Universals in the content and structure of values: Theoretical advances and empirical tests in 20 countries," [in:] M. Zanna (ed.), *Advances in Experimental Social Psychology* (Vol. 25), Orlando, FL: Scientific Press, pp. 1–65.

Schwartz, S. H. (1994), "Beyond individualism/collectivism: New cultural dimensions of values," [in:] U. Kim, H.C. Triandis, C. Kagitcibasi, S.C. Choi, & G. Yoon (eds.), *Individualism and Collectivism: Theory, Method and Applications,* Newbury Park, CA: Sage, pp. 85–119.

Spini, D. (2003), "Measurement equivalence of 10 value types from the Schwartz value survey across 21 countries," *Journal of Cross-Cultural Psychology,* Vol. 34 (1), pp. 3–23.

Torrente, P., Salanova, M., Llorens, S., Schaufeli, W.B. (2012), "Teams make it work: How team work engagement mediates between social resources and performance in teams," *Psicothema,* Vol. 24(1), pp. 106–112.

Zhou J., Shin S.J., Brass D.J., Choi Jae P., Zhang, Z.X. (2009), "Social networks, personal values, and creativity: Evidence for curvilinear and interaction effects," *Journal of Applied Psychology,* Vol. 94(6), pp. 1544–1552, Research Collection Lee Kong Chian School of Business.

Chapter 9

Measuring accomplishments in the areas of science, technology, and innovation in terms of gender criterion

Rafał Wisła

Abstract

The chapter gives an overview of the methodological guidelines and recommendations used in the practice of public statistics for gender described in the following areas: science, technology, and innovation activities. Analysis was carried out on the limitations and possibilities of using patent information for the study of gender relations in the context of technological creativity. The chapter also refers to the more important partial research undertaken as part of a large research programme on productivity of scientific and technical men and women. The current development of measuring the effects of scientific, scientific-technical, and innovative activity in terms of the roles ascribed to women and men in society, and that could have a significant impact on the course and nature of that activity, does not aid in its present form in obtaining answers to the question of whether the social roles and relationships men and women affect their creativity and innovation. The transition from the economy of capital, labour and allocation to an economics of innovation and intangible resources has necessitated the development of new methodologies, techniques and tools for data collection and methods of quantification of phenomena and processes related to innovative activity.

Key words: gender, creativity, measurement methods, innovative activities

Introduction

The development of policy and public statistics in the field of science, technology and innovation is a derivative of significant changes in the factors governing economic development. Innovation (technical, process, social) has finally become important characteristics through which we can currently explain the reasons for different levels of economic development. And the concepts of the "knowledge-based economy," "information economy," "creative economy" or "intellectual capital" have permanently entered the catalogue of main categories of economic study. In economic policy they are growing to paradigms for building competitive advantages.

The transition from the economy of capital, labour and allocation to an economics of innovation and intangible resources has necessitated the development of new methodologies, techniques and tools for data collection and methods of quantification of phenomena and processes related to innovative activity. Innovation as a factor of development arises from a complex structure:

- It is the result of cooperation between people with different skills, creativity, interests and capabilities.
- It requires the initiation of interactive and dynamic structures of co-operation in the innovation process.
- It is created by cross-breeding and fusion of a number of areas of expertise far greater than before.
- It arises from the interaction of people with different needs, expectations, social attitudes, and risk appetites.
- In the economic dimension the results of the innovation process are a particularly sought good, becoming the object of market exchange.
- universities, government laboratories, and companies differentiate in time their strategies and programmes for action.

In the context of the growing importance of: multidisciplinary research, the binding of science and industry, commercialization of the results of the innovation process, or the growing scale of public intervention aimed at stimulating attitudes and innovation activity, traditional data collection and development of indicators does not provide rapid responses to the power of the influence of the processes of innovation on economic and social development. When the above set of issues and research problems combine with the process of growing awareness of the obstacles and limitations of the prejudices and stereotypes of gender, often based on the belief of the crucial role of biology in shaping the individual, their behaviours, attitudes, needs, then to design a transparent mental construct about the relationships between sex and the broader concept of gender in conjunction with economic efficiency becomes an intellectually daunting challenge.

This chapter is a synthetic reflection on the methodological achievements in the field of possibilities and limits of quantification of the category of gender in the area of scientific, technological and innovation (A+T+I) activity. It should help in resolving the problem concerning the perspectives that are possible to capture by scientific research, i.e. micro-, meso-, and macro-economic perspectives within the framework of the research task "Innovative Gender" as a New Source of Progress.

9.1. Development of statistics on academia, technology and innovation

Technological changes (in the context of innovation) have become the subject of intense empirical research and data collection in this area since the mid-1950s (Gomulka, 1998). In the 1980s and 90s a wide range of conceptual work was undertaken to develop models and analytical approaches for the study of technological change. But even in the 80s Pavitt (1984) and Pavitt, Robson and Townsend (1989) based the vast majority of their work on their own survey forms and expert opinion in their applied research procedures. Characteristics of contemporary research approaches were:

1) focus on the specific (single) cases,
2) relatively short time horizon for the analysis,
3) the collection under examination was subject to significant changes over time, and
4) the scope of the study did not extend beyond a single sector of the economy,
5) consequently, it was difficult to achieve reliability and time-space comparability.

The need to measure scientific and technical activities was recognized by the OECD as early as the 1960's. The first methodological guide (for official statistics services) was the manual on the measurement of R&D activity of 1963 the *Frascati Manual*. In 2002, the 6th edition of the manual was published under the full title *Frascati Manual: Proposed Standard Practice for Surveys on Research and Experimental Development* (OECD, 2002). This guide is dedicated to the measurement of workload and resources (inputs) engaged in R&D. R&D covers both formal R&D in R&D units and informal or occasional R&D in other units (OECD, 2002, p. 17).

Currently, in order to obtain knowledge on the innovation activities of industrial enterprises in the European Union, within the framework of the international research program *Community Innovation Survey* (CIS) national statistical offices carry out studies to assess the level of innovation in enterprises employing more than 9 employees. The methodological side of the study is inspired by the recommendations of the manual Oslo Manual (2005). The indicators used in the CIS study are aggregated in 12 thematic groups.

The development of methodologies of measurement results in the fields of science, technology and innovation took place simultaneously with the emerging paradigms of development, followed by the development of science and industrial policy, and later innovation policy. The increasing involvement of the state in these areas necessitated the need to evaluate the efficiency and effectiveness of the implementation of these processes. Table 9.1 presents the evolutionary development in terms of measuring the methodical effects of activity S+T+I.

The need for research on the diversity of the participation of women and men in S+T+I activities was raised explicitly in the *Third European Report on Science & Technology Indicators* (European Commission, 2003, p. 257):

... Although female participation in science has increased in recent decades, women are still rarely seen in top scientific positions, such as professorships or other high-level research positions. Career opportunities in science are determined by a number of complex factors, which cannot easily be described using simple statistical indicators. Internal factors – those that depend on the organisation, operation, and structuring of the scientific community itself – form an essential part of the explanation. The internal factors interact with external factors, which are determined and shaped by society at large – such as existing gender roles inside and outside the family, the changing status of women with regard to education and the labour market, and the political frameworks that support equal opportunities.

The report attempted to establish new indicators and review the presence of women in science and technology. It should be emphasized that the data in the area of science and technology with regard to gender have been collected by the European Union at the transnational level since 2001.

Table 9.1. Development of S+T+I indicators

Years	Groups of indicators
2nd decade of the 21st century	expenditure on R&D, patent statistics, balance of payments in technology, high-tech products, bibliometrics, statistics on human resources, surveys of innovative activity in the manufacturing sector, a review of production technologies, innovations described in the technical literature, budgetary support of innovative activities, investments in intangible assets, indicators for ICT, productivity, venture capital, tax incentives, biotechnology and nanotechnology statistics, statistics on commercialization of research, statistics on internationalization and globalization, knowledge-based economy, intellectual capital
1990s	expenditure on R&D, patent statistics, balance of payments in technology, high-tech products, bibliometrics, statistics on human resources, survey of innovative activity in the manufacturing sector, a review of production technologies, innovations described in the technical literature, budgetary support for innovation, investment in intangible assets, indicators in the field of ICT, productivity, venture capital
1980s	expenditure on R&D, patent statistics, balance of payments in technology, high-tech products, bibliometrics, statistics on human resources surveys of innovation activities
1970s	expenditure on R&D, patents statistics, balance of payments in technology
1950s–60s	expenditure on R&D

Source: D. Archibugi, G. Sirilli G. (2001), "The direct measurement of technological innovations in business," [in:] *Innovation and Enterprise Creation: Statistics and indicators*, Luxemburg: European Commission, after: M. Górzyński (2005), *Przegląd wskaźników monitorowania systemów wspierania innowacyjności w krajach UE i wybranych krajach pozaeuropejskich – wnioski i rekomendacje dla Polski*, Warszawa: Polska Agencja Rozwoju Przedsiębiorczości; L. Kozłowski (2009), *Statystyka nauki, techniki i innowacji w krajach UE i OECD. Stan i problemy rozwoju*, Warszawa: Ministerstwo Nauki i Szkolnictwa Wyższego.

The largest research programs in the area of S+T+I in association with gender include:

1) horizontal differences between men and women in sectors and areas of science and technology – *The index of dissimilarity*,

2) vertical inequalities in women's careers and empowerment in the field of science and technology (the percentage of women with a higher scientific degree and in senior positions in academic institutions), the *Equally Distributed Equivalent Percentage,*

3) analysis of the differences in scientific productivity between men and women, through research in patent and bibliometric data.

Jaffé (2006), mentioning the significant participation of women in the development of science and technology, highlights the inadequate level (but also possibility) of quantification of this share. However, the last decade has seen an increase in the proposals for the methodological measurement of scientific and technological achievements within the category of "gender" (Bunker-Whittington and Smith-Doerr, 2005; Naldi et al., 2005; Frietsch et al., 2008; Frietsch et al., 2009). Empirical results of international comparative studies show a clear regularity in the lesser involvement of women in the creation of: scientific knowledge (Larivière et al., 2013), and industrial knowledge (Bunker-Whittington and Smith-Doerr, 2005; Frietsch et al., 2008; Frietsch et al., 2009).

Analysis of bibliometric and patent data is increasingly being used to measure the performance of men and women in the field of science and technology. This is confirmed by the review of previous studies involving gender in science and technology made by Frietsch et al. (2009). The subject of analysis are:

1) staff in research and development institutions, including by gender,
2) representation of women in science and engineering in the United States on the basis of publication data,
3) changes in the careers of women in science and engineering between 1975 and 1995 using mainly publication data,
4) the academic career and interviews with employees of different research units to determine the extent and causes of the differences in patenting between the sexes,
5) differences in the number and quality of publications between women and men,
6) differences in productivity between men and women, through the analysis of publications and citations,
7) the impact of having a family on the productivity of researchers,
8) the impact of motherhood on networking and also indirectly on productivity,
9) the relationship between the degree of an individual's specialization in the research area and productivity,
10) differences in the productivity of researchers of both sexes, through the analysis of publications,
11) the inputs and outputs of the research process as applied to women,
12) productivity and publication habits by gender,
13) differences in co-operation networking and co-authorship by gender,
14) women's participation in the development of science and technology with using analysis of patents and publications,
15) the contribution of women in technological development using patent data.

This list of previous research clearly shows that the data on publications and patent data are widely used to carry out studies on the presence of women in the field of science and technology and gender differentiation in both patent activity and publishing.

Generally, however, it should be emphasized that the changing way of practising science, the nature of R&D and innovation activities do not facilitate good knowledge of the nature of the phenomenon of innovation or the process of innovation. The data and indicators used thus far only allow for an understanding of certain elements of the innovation process, in particular those concerning input. A major limitation is lack of information in the fields of output and impact.

The method of collecting data on innovation and innovative activities widely used in the European Union is surveying companies in various aspects of the innovation process in industry and services and the amount of resources allocated to innovation. This approach enables analysis of innovation in conjunction with other economic variables (such as output, added value, or employment), both at the enterprise and industry levels. (This perspective on data collection is recommended and described by the Oslo Manual[5]).

Currently, the elementary indicators of innovation are:

1) the share of companies in the population studied (enterprises in the industry, or the region), which introduced technological innovations (process, product) and/or non-technological innovations (organizational, marketing) within a defined period of time,

2) the share of companies in the population studied (enterprises in the industry, or the region) that perform R&D in a systematic way,

3) the impact of product innovations on the size/dynamic/return of sales,

4) the impact of process innovations on changes in the cost of the production process and the size/structure of employment,

5) the impact of innovation on productivity,

6) the intensity of cooperation in R&D activity, and the implementation of its results,

7) the share of employees in R&D in the economically active population/in total employment,

8) input on innovation in enterprises per person/in relation to GDP.

In official statistics practice, in studies on innovation, and the recommendations of the OECD methodology, the category of gender is in fact reduced to the category of sex.

The OECD (2006, p. 150), Oslo Manual Guidelines for collecting and interpreting innovation data, Third edition, recommends: "collection of data on human

---

5   Examples of national data collection as part of the European research *Community Innovation Survey* programme are. Report on research and development (PNT-01); Report on research and development (R&D) as well as measures appropriations or outlays on research and development in units of government and local authorities (PNT-01/a); Report on innovation in industry (PNT--02); Report on research and development in nanotechnology research units (PNT-05); Report on activities in the field of nanotechnology in enterprises (PNT-06).

resources from the perspective of both its composition (by qualification, type of work, and sex) and the management of these resources."

The OECD (2002, p. 113), Frascati Manual: Proposed Standard Practice for Surveys on Research and Experimental Development, recommends:

- "data on the number of employees (i.e. headcount data) are also the most appropriate way to collect additional information about the staff working in the field of R&D, such as data on their age and sex,
- to better understand the structure of R&D personnel and its place in the wider resource of scientific and technical personnel, it is recommended to collect data on the number of researchers and – where possible – including those belonging to other categories of R&D personnel, broken down by sex and age,
- the ideal database should cover total national human resources in the field of S&T at certain moments of time, broken down by occupational status and sector and type of employment, it should also include information on inflows (mainly graduates and immigrants) and outflow (mainly retirement and emigration) of S&T personnel. Both the resources and flows should be included in the division into area of science and technology, categories of age and sex, and possibly into categories national or ethnic origin."

Although one of the many socioeconomic objectives of the OECD research on social identity, (gender), including discrimination and related issues, methodological recommendations in the area of measuring innovation to some extent meet the category of sex, but in practice do not take into account gender, i.e. the roles ascribed to women and men in society, and which may have an impact on the course and the nature of creativity and innovation.

Thus, the study of innovation in the current formula does not give the answer to the question of whether gender translates into creativity and innovation. In the author's opinion, patent information still provides more opportunities in this field. It reached maximum depth in such processes as compared with other alternative methodological approaches. Its main advantage is the high flexibility of aggregation and disaggregation of the processes studied. It is not, however, devoid of drawbacks.

9.2. Patent information in the study of creativity and innovation

A patent application is: an economic event; one of the many steps in the process of innovation; and (often) the culmination of research and development work. The right of protection obtained is a potential resource of commercial activities for organizations that can evolve into a production factor. A patent is not an innovation. But its indirect nature means that patent information represents a kind of bridge between the results of R&D activity (i.e. the creativity) and enterprise deployment activities (i.e. the innovation).

Methodological discussion on the scope and methods of use of patent statistics in economic research is not extensive in comparison with the methodological discussions in the areas of innovation or bibliometrics. Nevertheless, a catalogue of several fundamental rules for the design of a survey procedure taking gender into account emerges from it.

The information contained in collections of patent information can be divided into three main pillars:

1) technical specifications and the potential value of the new solution (technical classification, the number of citations in other patents, the number of licences granted, the rhythm of change enabled by the patent as a result of market transactions),

2) the development of the invention (the group structure of the inventors, their affiliations, the structure and nature of the applicants, the development progress of the "triadic family"[6]),

3) the history of the application: the filing date (in a given country, in other modes of protective proceedings, etc.), date of publication, date of refusal or withdrawal, the date of the grant of the patent, and the monopoly expiry date (non-payment or non-extension of the patent).

Patent documentation, called the patent literature, requires a standardized bibliographic description of its content (formal and pragmatic considerations). The standard bibliographic patent document recommended by the World Intellectual Property Organization is Standard ST.9.[7] The main goal of unifying the attributes of patent description is to increase the availability and efficiency of searching the patent literature (calculated in the tens of millions of documents).

Rapid technological development in the field of IT infrastructure for data repositories,[8] including collections of patent information, is a powerful accelerator increasing the quality, intensity and effectiveness of research.[9] An important advantage of patent information collections is their availability in the long term (even counted in decades). This provides great opportunities for their use in research. The content of patent databases and long-time series describing them enable the aggregation of data at any level.

---

6   The "triadic patent family" refers to an invention, which was filed simultaneously in different modes: EPO, JPO and USPTO and obtained a patent in the group of the most economically developed countries in the world. At the core of this concept is the assumption of outstanding significance of technical and economic importance of industrial property rights.

7   http://www.wipo.int/export/sites/www/standards/en/pdf/03-09-01.pdf.

8   There are two basic models of communication and sharing of digital objects (records) in information systems. The first is remote access, in which metadata is introduced to the system repository in the process of harvesting – these resources remain in the provider's repository and can be transferred to the user; the second is a direct placement of the material in the system's repository database.

9   The first to discover the potential were Scherer (1965) and Schmookler (1966) indicating the directions of research. With the advent of technological capabilities (electronic data files), empirical verification of suitability is starting: Griliches (1984, 1990), Griliches, Pakes, and Hall (1987) Schankerman and Pakes (1986) were the first to operate on data from European countries.

One of the most important attributes of patent information is the information on the creator of a new solution. The standard bibliographic record of the description enables a multi-layered analysis of the inventors (women/men) in conjunction with a range of other data. The creator(s) of a technical solution claimed in the patent can be scrutinized in the following dimensions:

1) sex (in the case of a single person indicated as the creator in the patent documentation),
2) structure of the development team by sex (two women, two men, etc.),
3) group structure according to sex and country (region) of origin[10] (Polish woman, a Norwegian woman, a Polish man, a man from Germany),
4) priority of the inventors – the order of inventors in the patent descriptions is not accidental, it is often due to the involvement of individual team members in the development of the new solution,
5) heterogeneity of the development team in terms of patent applications and their success (in the form of patents granted),
6) heterogeneity of the development team in terms of the intensity of citation of the solution in other, subsequent patents,
7) structure of the development team combined with the field of technology which embraces the new solution,
8) heterogeneity and the size of the team in conjunction with the geographical scope of protection (national, regional),
9) heterogeneity of the development team in terms of economic exploitation of the solution (by using information on licences granted for this solution).

For countries where the proportion of individuals acting as operator of an application for patent protection is large (e.g. in Poland), the above analysis schema can be used for individuals (women/men) occurring not in the role of inventors but as applicant and patentee.

Information is provided in different modes; but in practice actual access to the full set of metadata is very difficult. Following are selected barriers identified by the author to access to complete sets of data:

1) part of the collection of patent literature remains on paper media,
2) national patent offices do not provide the functionality and tools to acquire metadata automatically and wholesale,
3) digital repositories of accumulated public patent documents have a fairly simple architecture, and limited functionality available to their users,
4) Patent reporting of national and regional patent organizations transferred to the statistical offices is generic, superficial, and further their visibility in the public statistics does not allow for serious research,
5) against the limitations identified above are commercial distributors; acquisition of patent information in their issue is professional, functional, but also costly for the end user.

---

10 In addition to male and female names, residential addresses are an important component including post codes.

The main international patent databases maintained and provided by various international organizations include:

1) The European Patent Register, European Patent Register and Espacenet – databases run by the European Patent Office,
2) Patentscope – a database maintained by the World Intellectual Property Organization,
3) DEPATISnet – the database and information service of the German patent system,
4) USPTO – full-text database documentation for applications and patents granted in the United States,
5) Thomson Innovation – a commercial database that allows you to explore extensive and structured sets of applications and patents granted.

Others, often of a thematic nature are: Cippix® (chemistry); GenomeQuest (biology); LexisNexis; MicroPatent; and Delphion (integrates USPTO, EPO, and WIPO databases); "JP-Nete;" KPA Search In KIPRIS – Free Services.

From the point of view of the Research Task carried out, taking into account the above considerations, it seems possible to apply the following criteria to looking at gender in terms of creativity as the first phase of the innovation process:

1) terms of applications (divided into successive phases and modes of notification procedures[11]),
2) geographical coverage of protection (international, European, national, regional),
3) technology area (usually using a hierarchical International Patent Classification or other classifications such as Thomson Reuters DWPI^{SM} Classification, or WIPO IPC/TECH Concordance Table),
4) the applicant/co-applicant (if the applicant is not the inventor, the inventor and the basis for the right to obtain a patent is indicated in the application filed),
5) addresses: of applicants and inventors (postal codes enabling precise geographical location in the economic space).

In the years 1994–2013, the Polish Patent Office granted approx. 53 thousand binding patent monopolies in Poland. Working with such a large collection of bibliographical metadata requires the use of automated techniques for grouping objects using: dictionaries of male and female names (separately for the inventors

---

11 Depending on the territorial scope in which you want to protect your invention, a patent may be obtained as follows: (1) nationally, on the basis submitting an invention to the Polish Patent Office, after formally verifying the correctness of the application and on payment of applicable administrative fees charged by the PPO; the patent protection granted nationally (national patent) extends only to a given territory (one country); (2) European, a patent granted on the basis of a single application to the European Patent Office under the provisions of the Convention on the Grant of European Patents; after granting a European patent it protects the invention in the countries mentioned in the application (a bundle of national patents); (3) under the Patent Cooperation Treaty (PCT), on the basis of a single application of "international" lodged in: The Polish Patent Office, the European Patent Office, or directly at the International Bureau of the World Intellectual Property Organisation (IB WIPO). In the latter two cases, the application can be made only if a previous application was filed under the national procedure.

and applicants); post codes (standard recognized separately in the case of inventors and headquarters address/addresses of applicants); typical university abbreviations and common organizational and legal forms of enterprises (University, University of Technology, Ltd., Joint Stock Company, PLC, etc.) and the use of concordance tables for analyzing gender, not only in terms of dynamic, and space, but also from the perspective of the area of technology.

Conclusion

The collection of objects and their further setting in context (i.e. giving them meaning and content) is a key step in the process of cognition. In the scientific layer, the way manner of organizing the data collection process, processing, inference, and presentation determines the approach or departure from the truth. At the application layer (economic policy) this allows you to manage the area of uncertainty associated with the decision-making process; it is intended to support: resource allocation, monitoring of performance, identification and/or indications for social development trends, and forecasting.

The current development of measuring the effects of academic, scientific-technical, and innovative activity in terms of the roles ascribed to women and men in society, and that could have a significant impact on the course and nature of that activity, does not aid in its present form in obtaining answers to the question of whether the social roles and relationships men and women affect their creativity and innovation. In the author's opinion, only the comprehensive collections of patent information allow us to quantify the effects of gender relations in scientific and technical works simultaneously on several levels of economic analysis. The effects of the entire complex process of innovation in terms of gender relations still require a dedicated measurement methodology to be defined which is capable of being performed primarily at the microeconomic level. Subsequent chapters are examples of the approach derived here.

Literature

Archambault, E. (2002), "Methods for using patents in cross-country comparisons," *Scientometrics*, Vol. 54, pp. 15–30.

Archibugi, D., Sirilli, G. (2001), "The direct measurement of technological innovations in business," [w:] *Innovation and enterprise creation: Statistics and indicators*, Luxemburg: European Commission.

Bunker Whittington, K., Smith-Doerr, L. (2005), "Gender and commercial science – women's patenting in the life sciences," *Journal of Technology Transfer*, Vol. 30(4), pp. 355–370.

Ding, W.W., Murray, F., Stuart, T.E. (2006), "Gender differences in patenting in the scientific life sciences," *Science*, Vol. 313(5787), pp. 665–667.

European Commission (2003), *Third European Report on Science & Technology Indicators. Towards a Knowledge-based Economy*, Luxembourg: Directorate-General for Research Information and Communication Unit.

Frietsch, R., Haller, I., Vrohlings, Me., Grupp, H. (2008), "Gender-specific patterns in patenting and publishing," Fraunhofer ISI Discussion Papers Innovation Systems and Policy Analysis, No. 16.

Frietsch, R., Haller, I., Funken-Vrohlings, M., Grupp, H. (2009), "Gender-specific patterns in patenting and publishing," *Research Policy*, Vol. 38, pp. 590–599.

Godin, B. (2002), "Measuring output: When economics drives science and technology measurements," Project on the History and Sociology of S&T Statistics Working Paper No. 14.

Gomułka, S. (1998), *Teoria innowacji i wzrostu gospodarczego*, Warszawa: CASE.

Górzyński M. (2005), *Przegląd wskaźników monitorowania systemów wspierania innowacyjności w krajach UE i wybranych krajach pozaeuropejskich – wnioski i rekomendacje dla Polski*, Warszawa: Polska Agencja Rozwoju Przedsiębiorczości.

Griliches, Z. (1990), "Patent Statistics as Economic Indicators: A Survey," *Journal of Economic Literature*, Vol. 28, pp. 1661–1707.

Jaffé, D. (2006), *Ingenious Women* (Aus dem Engl. von Angelika Beck: Geniale Frauen. Berühmte Erfinderinnen von Melitta Bentz bis Marie Curie), Düsseldorf: Artemis & Winkler.

Kozłowski, J., (2009), *Statystyka nauki, techniki i innowacji w krajach UE i OECD. Stan i problemy rozwoju*, Warszawa: Ministerstwo Nauki i Szkolnictwa Wyższego.

Kuznets, S. (1962), "Inventive activity: Problems of definition and measurement problems of definition," [w:] *The Rate and Direction of Inventive Activity: Economic and Social Factors*, Princeton: Princeton University Press, pp. 19–52.

Larivière, V., Ni, Ch., Gingras, Y., Cronin, B., Sugimoto, C.R. (2013), "Bibliometrics: Global gender disparities in science," *Nature*, Vol. 504, pp. 211–213.

Naldi, F., Luzi, D., Valente A., Parenti, I.V. (2005), "Scientific and technological performance by gender," [in:] H.F. Moed, W. Glänzel, U. Schmoch (eds.), *Handbook of Quantitative Science and Technology Research. The Use of Publication and Patent*, Berlin: Springer Science+Business Media, Inc., pp. 299–314.

OECD (1994), *The measurement of scientific and technological activities using patent data as science and technology indicators. Patent manual*, Paris.

OECD (2001), *Using patent counts for cross-country comparisons of technology output*, Paris.

OECD (2002), *Podręcznik Frascati, Proponowane procedury standardowe dla badań statystycznych w zakresie działalności badawczo-rozwojowej*, Warszawa.

OECD (2005), *Oslo Manual 2005, Guidelines for Collecting and Interpreting Innovation Data*, OECD/European Commission, Paris.

OECD (2006), *Podręcznik Oslo, Zasady gromadzenia i interpretacji danych dotyczących innowacji*, Warszawa.

OECD (2009), *Patent Statistics Manual*, Paris.

Pavitt, K. (1984), "Sectoral patterns of technical change: Towards a taxonomy and a theory," *Research Policy*, No. 13(6), pp. 343–373.

Pavitt, K., Robson, M., Townsend, J. (1989), "Technological accumulation, diversification and organisation in UK companies, 1945–1983," *Management Science*, Vol. 35, No. 1, pp. 81–99.

Stephan, P.E., Gurmu, S., Sumell, A.J., Black G. (2005), "Who's patenting in the university? Evidence from the survey of doctorate recipients. Evidence from a Survey of Doctoral Recipients," *Economics of Innovation and New Technology* (forthcoming).

Verbeek, A., Debackere, K., Luwel, M., Andries, P., Zimmermann, E., Deleus, F. (2001), *Linking Science to Technology: Using Bibliographic References in Patents to Build Linkage Schemes*, Leuven: Katholieke Universiteit Leuven.

Whittington, K.B., Smith-Doerr, L. (2005), "Gender and commercial science: Women's patenting in the life sciences," *Journal of Technology Transfer*, Vol. 30, Issue 4, pp. 355–370.

Chapter 10

Creative patent activity of man and women in Polish economy in the years 1999–2013

Tomasz Sierotowicz

Abstract

Research on the patent activity of men and women should not be limited to an examination of their overall numbers. In this study, there is an indication of the areas of science, technology and the economy in which different patent activity for men and women appears. Data on the inventors is included in the patent description. It can therefore be said that the number of patent inventors is a measure of creative activity. However, patent databases currently do not provide statistics on the types of entities that are inventors of patents, or their membership in a particular geographic area, or gender. It is therefore necessary to mine this kind of information from a rich patent description. Hence, in this paper three research tasks are proposed. The first was to determine the dynamics of change in inventors from Poland and non-Polish for patents granted by the Patent Office of the Republic of Poland (Polish Patent Office). The second aim of the study was to determine the dynamics of changes in the activity of men and women who are the inventors of patents granted by the Polish Patent Office. The third objective of the research was to identify the size and participation of women and men patent activity in industries and areas of technology. Reference to creative patent activity for men and women to the economy and technology is obtained through the use concordance tables. The proposed concept for the measure of creative patent activity in Poland, in conjunction with the various branches of the economy, made it possible to identify the leading areas for men and women in this activity (chemistry), as well as identify joint areas (food), where cooperation between men and women, expressed in common patent activity, reaches its highest level.

Key words: inventions and innovations, research and development, intellectual property, intellectual capital

Introduction

Innovation is associated with the activity of scientific-research, social, and economic agents. It applies to almost all areas of socioeconomic development (Christensen et al., 2004; Davila et al., 2006; DeGraff and Quinn, 2007; Dyer et al., 2011). One of the primary symptoms of innovative activity, including the development of innovation and increase in innovative capacity, is patent activity. In the literature, various proposals have been presented for measuring innovation. It has been pointed out that patent activity is one of the most detailed components of innovation potential (Stern et al., 2000; OECD, 2011). Patent statistics is one of the most important indicators of innovation (Griliches, 1990; OECD, 2005; Schmoch, 2008; European Union, 2014). Patent activity is also a manifestation of the creativity of patent inventors, because an idea is the beginning of an invention, often emerging from creative solutions to a problem (McGowan, 1987; Twiss, 1994; Rothwell, 1994; Sundbo, 1999; DeGraff and Quinn, 2007; Chesbrough, 2011). Hence creative patent activity for men and women can be measured by the number of patents whose inventors are men and women.

In studies of patent activity, patent statistics are often associated with a variety of values describing the economy of the country or region of the European Union, for example the number of inhabitants and the size of the expenditure on R&D (Eurostat, 2014; European Union, 2014). In such references patent statistics are often exhibited from the EPO database (EPO – European Patent Office), which specifies patents obtained internationally. Thus, this kind of statistics is used in the conduct of inter-national or inter-regional comparative analyses in the European Union. The patent description available in the EPO database is based on data obtained from national patent databases. This description is rich and detailed. For example, Thomson Reuters provides more than 300 fields containing a variety of information relating to the application and the legal protection granted (Thomson Reuters, 2007, 2014). One of the ways to describe patents is to assign them to a specific area of science and technology. For this purpose the International Patent Classification is used (IPC – *the International Patent Classification*). The basic information on the patent also includes a list of the inventors. Each patent must have at least one applicant and one creator. At the same time the applicant and the creator may be the same entity. However, patent databases currently do not provide statistics on the types of entities that are inventors of patents, as well as their membership in a particular geographic area, or gender. It is therefore necessary to mine this kind of information from a rich patent description. In this study, three research tasks have been detailed. The first was to determine the dynamics of change in inventors from Poland and non-Polish for patents granted by the Patent Office of the Republic of Poland (Polish Patent Office). The second aim of the study was to determine the dynamics of changes in the activity of men and women who are the inventors of patents granted by the Polish Patent Office. The third objective of the research was to identify the size and share of patent activity of women and men in the various subsections of the Statistical Classification of Economic Activities (NACE – *Nomenclature statistique des Activités économiques dans la Communauté Européenne*) and selected technology groups that describe the sectors of the economy. The patent activity of men and women in the Polish economy will be described in two ways:

– in NACE sections by using the proprietary IPC/NACE concordance table (Okoń-Horodyńska et al., 2012), and

- in 35 technology groups through the use of WIPO IPC/TECH Technology Concordance Table (WIPO 2014b).

Thus, at the methodological level, layer the concordance tables are the tools used in the second research area. However, the first research area uses statistical tools to analyse and evaluate the dynamics of changes in the patent activity of men and women in time.

The content of the cognitive layer of this study is to present new knowledge on the patenting activity of men and women in Poland in the period 1999–2013, in the form of: determining the size of patent activity, determining the dynamics of changes in patent activity, the size of the accumulation of patent activity in NACE subsections and selected technology groups, describing the Polish economy, with an indication of distinctive and common areas for men and women within this activity.

10.1. The assessment method for the creative activity of men and women in the Polish economy

10.1.1. Objectives and scope of the study, the research period and data sources

This chapter lists the following research objectives.

1. Determining the dynamics of change in inventors from Poland and non--Polish for patents granted in the period 1999–2013.
2. Determining the dynamics of change in the activity of men and women who are the inventors of patents obtained in the Polish Patent Office in the period 1999–2013.
3. The third objective of the research was to identify the size and participation of women's and men's patent activity in industries and areas of technology:
   3.1. NACE Subsections;
   3.2. selected technology groups.

The research scope of creative patent activity for men and women in the Polish economy was chosen by the concordance tables used in the study:

- IPC/NACE (Okoń-Horodyńska et al., 2012) and
- WIPO IPC/TECH (WIPO 2014b).

The choice of the research period 1999–2013 was dictated by the availability of the most complete data possible on patent descriptions and the ability to use statistical tools to study changes in patent activity over time. The primary inputs of the study were detailed descriptions of patents, in particular the inventors, in the Polish Patent Office patent database.

10.1.2. Initial assumptions and rationale for selection of concordance tables

The basic assumption adopted in this study was to assess the creative patent activity of men and women in the broadest possible range of industries and the use of the IPC categories. Because the NACE classification is used in the European Union, and also provides a basis for the Polish Classification of Activities (PKD), to achieve the research objectives the IPC/NACE concordance table was adopted. An important complement to the research inquiries, giving a fuller picture of the creative patent activity of men and women, is the use of the WIPO IPC/TECH concordance table, as an example of mapping the activity in a broad area of technology. Further assumptions were adopted:
- the study period 1999–2013 according to the patent grant date available in the patent description,
- the manner of identifying the inventors' country of origin based on their address details given in the patent,
- the manner of identifying the men and women whose country, given in the description of the address data for the inventors of each patent, is Poland,
- non-identification of the remaining entities given in the description of inventors, which include both domestic and foreign: enterprises, universities, research and development units, research institutes, and other entities engaged in social, scientific, research and development, or business activities in the socioeconomic area. They represent a community defined as "other actors and institutions."

To achieve the research objectives appropriately selected research tools were used.

10.1.3. Research tools used

To achieve the first objective of the research, in addition to copular tables liaison statistical device used the average rate of change (Sobczyk, 2002). Its use has enabled the analysis and assessment of the dynamics of changes in patent activity of creative men and women in a given period of research. The calculations of the average rate of change were made based on equations 1 and 2:

$$\bar{y}_z = \sqrt[N_z-1]{\frac{z_2}{z_1} \times \frac{z_3}{z_2} \cdots \times \frac{z_{(i-1)}}{z_{(i-2)}} \times \frac{z_{(i)}}{z_{(i-1)}}} = \sqrt[N_z-1]{\prod_{i=2}^{N_z} \frac{z_{(i)}}{z_{(i-1)}}} \qquad \text{(Equation 1)}$$

where:

$\bar{y}_z$ – the geometric mean of the chain base indexes of the variable analysed over the entire study period,

z_i – the successive annual value of the time series of the variable analysed,

$\dfrac{z_{(i)}}{z_{(i-1)}}$ – the annual value of the chain base index of the variable analysed,

i – the successive values for chain base index,

N_z – number of elements in the time series of the variable analysed.

$$\overline{T}_z = (\overline{y}_z - 1) \times 100 \qquad \text{(Equation 2)}$$

where:

$\overline{T}_z$ – the average rate of change of the variable analysed throughout the study period,

$\overline{y}_z$ – the geometric mean of the chain base indexes of the variable analysed over the entire study period.

This computational procedure for the average rate of change has been applied individually for the variables listed above, which are time series of annual values that describe the creative patent activity of men and women in the Polish economy throughout the study period.

Table 10.1. Summary of the variables analysed, applied separately to equation 1 and 2

Name of the variable analysed in the period 1999–2013	Type designation – z_i for the time series of the variable analysed	Designation of the geometric mean – $\overline{y}_z, \overline{y}_z$ for the variable analysed	Designation of the average rate of change – $\overline{T}_z, \overline{T}_z$ for the variable analysed
Number of patents granted by the Polish Patent Office	z_p	$\overline{y}_p$	$\overline{T}_p$
Number of inventors from Poland	z_{tp}	$\overline{y}_{tp}$	$\overline{T}_{tp}$
Ration of number of inventors from Poland to number of inventors from outside Poland	z_{tpz}	$\overline{y}_{tpz}$	$\overline{T}_{tpz}$
Women from Poland who are inventors of patents awarded by the Polish Patent Office	z_{kt}	$\overline{y}_{kt}$	$\overline{T}_{kt}$
Men from Poland who are inventors of patents awarded by the Polish Patent Office	z_{mt}	$\overline{y}_{mt}$	$\overline{T}_{mt}$
The ratio of women to men who are inventors of patents awarded by the Polish Patent Office	z_{tkp}	$\overline{y}_{tkp}$	$\overline{T}_{tkp}$

Source: own report.

The numbers of women and men were obtained on the basis of the identification of male and female names contained in the Polish Patent Office patent database. The patent also specifies the creator's country. The combination of these data allowed us to identify the men and women who are inventors from Poland as well as other inventors who come from abroad. Thus, it was possible to obtain

the variables in Table 10.1 constituting a time series, whose elements (observations) are quantitative values. Therefore, in the cognitive layer of this study, it was possible to acquire new knowledge concerning the creative patent activity of men and women in Poland in the period 1999-2013, in the form of quantitative determinations of:
- the amount of patent activity,
- dynamics of changes in patent activity,
- the amount of the accumulation of patent activity:
  • for individual NACE sections, and
  • technological groups,

describing the Polish economy, with an indication of areas that are distinctive and joint for men and women in this activity.

The IPC/NACE and WIPO IPC/TECH concordance tables are the research tools used to achieve the second objective of the research. The IPC/TECH concordance table representation of industries covers 19 NACE Subsection 1.1 (Appendix 10.1), described by the groups and subgroups of the IPC (Okoń-Horodyńska et al., 2012). The NACE subsections are described in the concordance table by IPC designation.[1]

Another solution is partial concordance tables. These rely on the description of selected industries or sectors of the economy by a specific group of IPC designations. Examples of such solutions are the proposals: OECD IPC/ICT (IPC/ICT – Information and Communications Technology), developed by the OECD, which uses the methodology of measuring the Information Society (OECD, 2009) and the WIPO IPC/TECH (IPC/TECH – Technology Concordance Table) (WIPO, 2014b). The OECD IPC/ICT concordance table consists of 5 areas that form the ICT sector, described by the selected ICT designation (OECD, 2009):
- telecommunications,
- consumer electronics,
- computers and office equipment,
- semiconductor devices,
- other.

The WIPO IPC/TECH table, on the other hand, contains 35 technology areas described by a broad IPC range (Appendix 10.2). The WIPO IPC/TECH concordance table includes technology areas beyond the scope of ICT. Thus it is a table describing the significantly broader area of the economy than the OECD IPC/ICT table. The summary of IPC designations assigned to specific technology areas is presented in Appendix 10.3. All areas listed in the OECD IPC/ICT concordance table are included in the WIPO IPC/TECH table. For this reason, its application to the analysis and evaluation of creative patent activity of men and women gives significantly greater research capabilities.

---

1   The detailed description of the concordance table in this study with IPC designations is located at: Okoń-Horodyńska et al., 2012, pp. 31-39, 118-212.

10.1.4. Limitations of the method

The numbers of women and men who are inventors are calculated on the basis of male and female names, because the currently available resources of patent databases do not contain separate information on the subject. Obviously, some names may have an identical male and female form. This problem, however, refers to foreign names of those from foreign languages. For example, "Nikola," "Tracy," "Vivian," "Alex," and so on. Another limitation of the methodology is the quality of the mapping of the IPC designations in industries and technology areas. We should keep in mind that these classifications were created for and serve different purposes. There are classifications that cover the same range of the economy or science and technology. Hence there are still new proposals for tables, and those currently used are modified and improved. For the purposes of the research objectives in this study the latest concordance tables were used that describe the broadest possible spectrum both in terms of IPC designations as well as industries. The concordance tables were thus applicable to the acquisition of knowledge about the accumulation of creative patent activity between men and women for the entire period of the study.

10.2. Creative patent activity of men and women in Poland in the period 1999–2013

In the period 1999–2013 the Polish Patent Office granted a total of 39 869 patents (Figure 10.1). In the years 2003 and 2004 and the fewest patents were granted, respectively 1715 and 1770. The highest number of patents were granted in 2007, 2008 and 2009, respectively 3649, 3624 and 3809 (Figure 10.1).

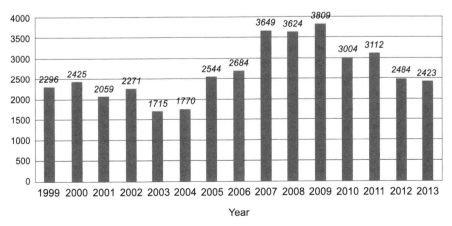

Figure 10.1. Number of patents granted by the Polish Patent Office during the period 1999–2013
Source: own calculations.

Table 10.2. Dynamic of change in the number of patents granted by the Polish Patent Office during the period 1999–2013

Name of the variable analysed in the period 1999–2013	Value of the geometric mean – $\bar{y}_p\bar{y}_p$	Value of the average rate of change – $\bar{T}_p\bar{T}_p$ (%)
Number of patents granted by the PPO (z_p)	1.004	0.39 %

Source: own calculations.

On the basis of this analysis, it was found that the value of the average rate of change in the number of patents granted by the Polish Patent Office was 0.39%. This means that the number of patents granted by the PPO increased over the study period by an average of 0.39% year on year. The description of each patent, in addition to details of its content, contains information about the inventors. Table 10.3 provides a summary of the number of inventors from Poland, from outside Poland, and the ratio of the number of inventors from Poland to the number of inventors from abroad.

The total number of inventors of patents granted by the Polish Patent Office throughout the study period was 116 657, of which 57 379 were from Poland, and 59 278 inventors came from countries outside Poland (Table 10.3).

Table 10.3. Number of inventors of patents granted by the Polish Patent Office

Year/ variable	Number of inventors from Poland – z_{tp}	Number of inventors from abroad	Number of inventors – total	Ratio of number of inventors from Poland to number of inventors from abroad – z_{tpz}
1999	3 422	3 112	6 534	1.100
2000	3 118	3 986	7 104	0.782
2001	2 767	3 146	5 913	0.880
2002	2 767	4 020	6 787	0.688
2003	2 114	3 212	5 326	0.658
2004	2 431	2 823	5 254	0.861
2005	3 260	4 234	7 494	0.770
2006	3 527	4 334	7 861	0.814
2007	4 855	5 512	10 367	0.881
2008	4 491	6 080	10 571	0.739
2009	4 131	6 639	10 770	0.622
2010	3 852	4 913	8 765	0.784
2011	5 678	3 642	9 320	1.559
2012	5 447	2 185	7 632	2.493
2013	5 519	1 440	6 959	3.833
Total	57 379	59 278	116 657	–

Source: own calculations.

As Figure 10.2 shows, the highest value for the ratio of the number of Polish inventors to foreign inventors for patents granted by the Polish Patent Office was reported in 2013, 3.833, while the lowest was recorded in 2009, 0.622. The results of calculations of the dynamics of change in the number of Polish inventors for patents granted by the Polish Patent Office is shown in Table 10.4.

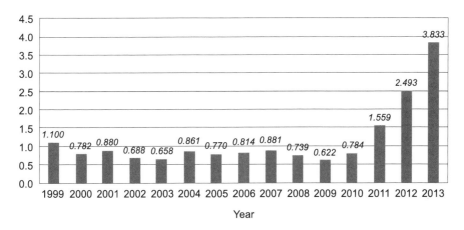

Figure 10.2. Ratio of the number of inventors from Poland to the number of non-Polish inventors for patents granted by the PPO
Source: own calculations.

On the basis of this analysis, it was found that the value of the average rate of change in the number of inventors from Poland for patents granted by the Polish Patent Office was 3.47%. This means that the number of inventors from Poland for patents granted by the PPO increased over the study period by an average of 3.47% year on year. Furthermore, the value for the average rate of change in the number of patents awarded by the PPO, $\bar{T}_p\bar{T}_p$, which was 0.39% (Table 10.2), is lower than the average rate of change for the number of inventors from Poland $\bar{T}_{tp}\bar{T}_{tp}$, which was 3.47% (Table 10.4), which means that the growth dynamic for the number of patent inventors year on year is greater than the growth dynamic for the number of patents. Hence it can be concluded that there is an increase in cooperation of Polish inventors in the creation of inventions that were under legal protection.

Table 10.4. Dynamic of change in the number of inventors from Poland for patents granted by the PPO during the period 1999–2013

Name of the variable analysed in the period 1999–2013	Value of the geometric mean – $\bar{y}_{tp}\bar{y}_{tp}$	Value of the average rate of change – $\bar{T}_{tp}\bar{T}_{tp}$ (%)
Number of inventors from Poland for patents issued by the PPO	1.035	3.47%

Source: own calculations.

The value of the average rate of change for the ratio of the number of Polish inventors to the number of non-Polish inventors was 9.32%. This means that the ratio of the number of Polish inventors to the number of inventors from outside Poland increased over the study period, averaging 9.32% year-to-year. In addition, this means a greater increase in the number of Polish inventors compared to the number of non-Polish inventors. A significant increase in the ratio of the number of Polish inventors to the number of non-Polish inventors was recorded in the years 2011–2013 (Figure 10.2). The inventors' collection does not specify separate information regarding gender. The structure of Polish inventors divided into women and men is shown in Table 10.6.

The total number of women – Polish inventors who are listed in the description of patents granted by the Polish Patent Office during the period 1999-2013 was 9 663 (Table 10.6). While the total number of men –Polish inventors was 47 005. The characteristic feature of the patent description, for the inventors, is the predominant number of men and women, and therefore individuals, in relation to other actors and institutions. The total number of women and men from Poland was 56 668 people, while the number of other entities and institutions totalled 711 for the entire study period.

Table 10.5. Dynamic of change in the number of inventors from Poland and the number of non-Polish inventors for patents granted by the PPO during the period 1999-2013

Name of the variable analysed in the period	Value of the geometric mean – $\bar{y}_{tpz}$	Value of the average rate of change – $\bar{T}_{tpz}$ (%)
Dynamic of change in the number of inventors from Poland and the number of non-Polish inventors for patents granted by the PPO	1.093	9.32%

Source: own calculations.

Table 10.6. The structure of Polish inventors of patents granted by the PPO

Year/ variable	Number of women – z_{kt}	Number of men – z_{mt}	Other entities and institutions	Number of inventors from Poland – total	Ratio of number of women to number of men from Poland who were inventors of patents granted by the PPO – z_{tkp}
1999	407	2 977	38	3 422	0.137
2000	363	2 735	20	3 118	0.133
2001	329	2 414	24	2 767	0.136
2002	379	2 363	25	2 767	0.160
2003	322	1 781	11	2 114	0.181
2004	392	2 017	22	2 431	0.194
2005	540	2 681	39	3 260	0.201
2006	545	2 933	49	3 527	0.186
2007	908	3 870	77	4 855	0.235
2008	788	3 655	48	4 491	0.216
2009	646	3 432	53	4 131	0.188
2010	542	3 262	48	3 852	0.166
2011	1 072	4 525	81	5 678	0.237
2012	1 257	4 111	79	5 447	0.306
2013	1 173	4 249	97	5 519	0.276
Total	9 663	47 005	711	57 379	–

Source: own calculations.

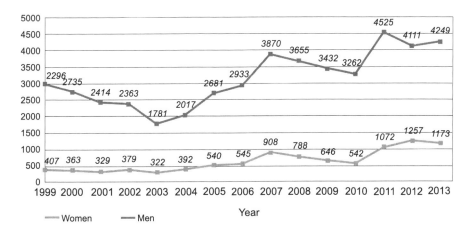

Figure 10.3. Polish women and men who are inventors of patents
Source: own calculations.

As Figure 10.3 shows, men greatly outnumber women in the source patent descriptions, identified as inventors from Poland. What, then, is the change dynamic of these variables? The calculated values of the average rate of change are shown in Tables 10.7 and 10.8.

Table 10.7. Dynamic of change in the number of women inventors from Poland for patents granted by the PPO during the period 1999-2013

Name of the variable analysed in the period 1999–2013	Value of the geometric mean – $\bar{y}_{kt}\bar{y}_{kt}$	Value of the average rate of change – $\bar{T}_{kt}\bar{T}_{kt}$ (%)
Women inventors from Poland for patents granted by the PPO	1.078	7.85%

Source: own calculations.

Table 10.8. Dynamic of change in the number of male inventors from Poland for patents granted by the PPO during the period 1999-2013

Name of the variable analysed in the period 1999–2013	Value of the geometric mean – $\bar{y}_{mt}\bar{y}_{mt}$	Value of the average rate of change – $\bar{T}_{mt}\bar{T}_{mt}$ [%]
Male inventors from Poland for patents granted by the PPO	1.025	2.57%

Source: own calculations.

The average rate of change of for Polish women inventors was 7.85%. This means that the number of women inventors from Poland for patents granted by the PPO increased over the study period by an average of 7.85% year on year. The average rate of change for Polish men inventors was 2.57%. This means that the number of men inventors from Poland for patents granted by the PPO increased over the study period by an average of 2.57% year on year.

Since $\overline{T}_{kt}\overline{T}_{kt} > \overline{T}_{mt}\overline{T}_{mt}$, and both sizes are positive, we can conclude that among the population of Polish inventors, the growth rate of creative patent activity for women is about 3-fold higher than the growth of creative activity among Polish men. This conclusion is also confirmed empirically by the average rate of change of the ratio of the number of women inventors to men inventors (Table 10.9).

Table 10.9. Dynamic of change in the ratio of the number of women to the number of men from Poland who created patents granted by the PPO during the period 1999-2013

Name of the variable analysed in the period 1999–2013	Value of the geometric mean – $\overline{y}_{tkp}\overline{y}_{tkp}$	Value of the average rate of change – $\overline{T}_{tkp}\overline{T}_{tkp}$ [%]
The ratio of women to men from Poland who are inventors of patents awarded by the Polish Patent Office	1.051	5.15%

Source: own report.

The average rate of change in the ratio of women to men inventors from Poland was 5.15%. This means that the ratio of women to men inventors from Poland increased over the study period by an average of 5.15% year on year. In addition, this means a greater increase in the number of women in comparison to the number of men who are inventors from Poland within the study period.

10.3. Cumulative creative patent activity of men and women in the Polish economy in the years 1999–2013

The cumulative creative patent activity of men and women in the sectors of the economy described by the NACE classification, for the entire study period was analysed and evaluated based on the use of the IPC/NACE concordance tables. The results are shown in Table 10.10.

The descriptions of the NACE Subsections, representing the various sectors of the economy are given in Appendix 10.2. The greatest cumulative number of women (Table 10.10) and men was noted in Subsection DG – Manufacture of chemicals, chemical products and man-made fibres, 5 389 women and 11 697 men. This is therefore the branch of the economy which represents the largest accumulation of creative activity for both women and men identified in the description of the inventors of patents granted by the Polish Patent Office throughout the period 1999–2013.The smallest number of women was observed in subsection CD – Mining and quarrying of non-energy raw materials, 2. This is the branch of the economy which represents the smallest accumulation of creative activity for women from Poland identified in the description of the inventors of patents granted by the Polish Patent Office throughout the period 1999-2013. The lowest number of men, on the other hand, was noted in Subsection DC – Manufacture of leather and leather products, 52. This is the branch of the economy representing the smallest accumulation of creative activity of Polish men, identified in the description of the inventors of patents granted by the Polish Patent Office throughout the period 1999–2013. Table 10.10 also includes the calculated value of the ratio of women to men from Poland. Figure 10.4 shows the values of this variable graphically.

Table 10.10. Cumulative creative patent activity of men and women from Poland in the economy in the years 1999–2013

NACE/ variable	Number of women	Number of men	Ratio of the number of women to the number of men
AA	24	207	0.116
BA	4	69	0.058
CA	78	3 280	0.024
CB	2	244	0.008
DA	966	1 556	0.621
DB	346	685	0.505
DC	12	52	0.231
DD	36	152	0.237
DE	43	161	0.267
DF	576	2 330	0.247
DG	5 389	11 697	0.461
DH	15	105	0.143
DI	247	1 013	0.244
DJ	252	3 414	0.074
DK	381	7 305	0.052
DL	858	8 961	0.096
DM	54	2 732	0.020
DN	161	962	0.167
FA	219	2 080	0.105
Total	9 663	47 005	–

Source: own calculations.

The highest number of women in relation to the number of men from Poland who are the inventors of patents granted by the Polish Patent Office throughout the period 1999–2013 was recorded in Subsection DA – Manufacture of food products; beverages and tobacco products, 0.621. This is also a joint area of creative activity for men and women, where their numbers are closest to each other. The lowest number of women in relation to the number of men from Poland who are the inventors of patents granted by the Polish Patent Office during the period 1999–2013 was noted in subsection CD – Mining and quarrying of raw materials other than for energy, 0.008.

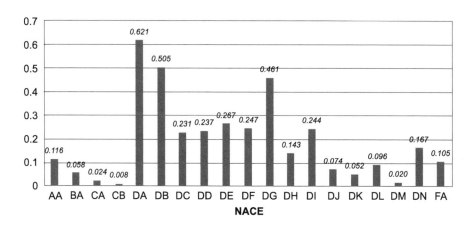

Figure 10.4. Ratio of the number of female to the number of male inventors from Poland during the period 1999-2013
Source: own calculations.

The cumulative creative patent activity of men and women in the sectors of the economy for the entire study period, was analysed and evaluated based on the use of the WIPO IPC/TECH concordance tables. The results are shown in Table 10.11. The descriptions of the technology areas of the economy are presented in Appendix 10.3. The greatest accumulation of the number of women (Table 10.11) and men was recorded in the area of organic chemistry, respectively 2351 and 4339. This is therefore the technological area of the economy, representing the largest accumulation of creative activity of women and men identified in the description of the inventors of patents granted by the Polish Patent Office throughout the period 1999–2013. In the area of IT methods for management in general, there were no men and women who were inventors from Poland. However, the area of microstructures and nanotechnologies recorded the lowest number of men who are the inventors from Poland, 12.

Table 10.11 also indicates the calculated value of the ratio of women to men coming from Poland who created patents granted by the Polish Patent Office during the period 1999-2013. Figure 10.5 shows a graphic representation of this variable.

As is clear from the data presented in Figure 10.5, the highest number of women in relation to men from Poland who created patents granted by the Polish Patent Office during the period from 1999 to 2013 was recorded in the field of biotechnology. This is the only area in which the number of Polish women inventors outnumber men.

Table 10.11. Cumulative creative patent activity of men and women from Poland in technical fields in the economy in the years 1999–2013

TECH area / variable	Number of women	Number of men	Ration of women to men
1	163	2 285	0.071
2	10	101	0.099
3	29	389	0.075
4	1	28	0.036
5	8	200	0.040
6	6	114	0.053
7	0	0	0.000
8	54	215	0.251
9	56	378	0.148
10	252	3 316	0.076
11	136	458	0.297
12	10	308	0.032
13	210	1 219	0.172
14	2 351	4 339	0.542
15	617	574	1.075
16	361	446	0.809
17	896	1 870	0.479
18	381	702	0.543
19	1 357	4 216	0.322
20	621	2 756	0.225
21	149	764	0.195
22	0	12	0.000
23	220	1817	0.121
24	246	1684	0.146
25	64	1513	0.042
26	211	1839	0.115
27	17	892	0.019
28	339	684	0.496
29	353	2479	0.142
30	65	1525	0.043
31	34	1629	0.021
32	28	1763	0.016
33	43	716	0.060
34	97	495	0.196
35	209	5251	0.040
Total	9 594	46 977	–

Source: own calculations.

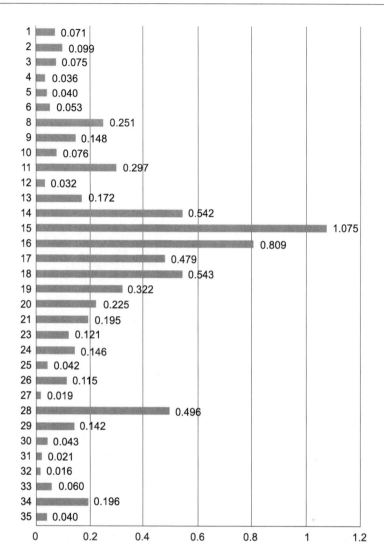

Figure 10.5. Ratio of the number of female to the number of male inventors from Poland during the period 1999–2013 in technological areas of the economy
Source: own calculations.

Conclusions

Based on the analysis and evaluation of selected components of the description of patents granted by the Polish Patent Office in the study period 1999-2013, the following conclusions have been formulated.

1. There has been an increasing trend in the number of patents granted by the Polish Patent Office over the study period.
2. The number of inventors from Poland for patents granted by the PPO increased over the study period by an average of 3.47% year to year.
3. The average rate of change in the number of patents granted by the Polish Patent Office $\overline{T}_p T_p$ was 0.39%, which is less than the average rate of change in the number of Polish inventors $\overline{T}_{tp} T_{tp}$, which amounted to 3.47%. Since $\overline{T}_{tp} T_{tp} > \overline{T}_p T_p$, Where both values are positive, it can be concluded that there has been an quantitative increase in the cooperation of Polish inventors in the creation of patents.
4. The average rate of change of the ratio of the number of Polish inventors to the number of non-Polish inventors was 9.32%, which means a greater increase in the number of Polish inventors in comparison to the number of non-Polish inventors.
5. The number of women inventors from Poland increased over the study period by an average of 7.85% year on year.
6. The number of men inventors from Poland increased over the study period by an average of 2.57% year on year.
7. Since the average rate of change of women inventors from Poland is greater than the average rate of change of men who are inventors from Poland ($\overline{T}_{kt} T_{kt} > \overline{T}_{mt} T_{mt}$), it can be concluded that in the community of Polish inventors, there was approx. a 3-fold higher growth rate of creative patent activity among women than men. The empirical confirmation of this conclusion is the average rate of change in the ratio of women to men inventors from Poland, which amounted to 5.15%. This means that the ratio of women to men inventors from Poland increased over the study period by an average of 5.15% year on year.
8. The NACE Subsection DG – Production of chemicals, chemical products and man-made fibres is the branch of the economy which represents the largest accumulation of creative activity for both women and men identified in the description of the inventors of patents granted by the Polish Patent Office throughout the period 1999–2013.
9. The NACE Subsection CD – Mining and quarrying of raw materials other than for energy – is the branch of the economy which represents the smallest accumulation of creative activity for women from Poland identified in the description of the inventors of patents granted by the Polish Patent Office throughout the period 1999–2013.
10. The NACE Subsection DC – Manufacture of leather and leather products – is the branch of the economy representing the smallest accumulation of creative activity of Polish men, identified in the description of the inventors of patents granted by the Polish Patent Office throughout the period 1999–2013.
11. NACE Subsection DA – Manufacture of food products; beverages and tobacco products – has the highest number of women in relation to the number of Polish men, who are the inventors of patents granted by the Polish Patent Office

throughout the period 1999–2013. It is also a joint area of creative activity for men and women, where their numbers are closest to each other.

12. NACE Subsection CD – Mining and quarrying of raw materials other than for energy – was characterized by the lowest number of women in relation to the number of men from Poland who were the inventors of patents granted by the Polish Patent Office during the period 1999–2013.

13. Organic chemistry is the branch of the economy which represents the largest accumulation of creative activity for both women and men identified in the description of the inventors of patents granted by the Polish Patent Office throughout the period 1999–2013.

14. IT methods for management is the technology area of the economy that recorded no men and women who are the inventors from Poland.

15. The area of microstructures and nanotechnologies is the technological area of the economy which marked the lowest level of creative activity among men who are inventors from Poland.

16. This is the only area in which the number of women Polish inventors outnumber men.

Literature

Chesbrough, H. (2011), *Open Services Innovation: Rethinking Your Business to Grow and Compete in a New Era*, San Francisco: Jossey-Bass.

Christensen, C., Anthony, D., Roth, E. (2004), *Seeing What's Next. Using the Theories of Innovation to Predict Industry Change*, Boston: Harvard Business School Press.

Davila, T., Epstein, M., Shelton, R. (2006), *Making Innovation Work: How to Manage It, Measure It, and Profit from It*, Upper Saddle River, NJ, USA: Wharton School Publishing.

DeGraff, J., Quinn, E. (2007), *Leading Innovation*, New York: McGraw-Hill.

Dyer, J., Gregersen, H., Christensen, C. (2011), *The Innovator's DNA*, Boston: Harvard Business Review Press.

European Commission, Eurostat Database (2014), available at: http://ec.europa.eu/eurostat/data/database [accessed June 2014].

European Union (2014), *Innovation Union Scoreboard 2014*, Brussels, http:/-/ec.europa.eu/enterprise/policies/innovation/files/ius/ius-2014_en.pdf [accessed 19.06.2014].

Griliches, Z. (1990), "Patent statistics as economic indicators: A survey," *Journal of Economic Literature*, Vol. 28, pp. 1661–1707.

McGowan, P. (1987), "Creativity and innovation," [in:] D. Steward (ed.), *Handbook of Management Skills*, London: Gower Publishing Ltd.

Morris, L. (2006), *Permanent Innovation*, Acasa, www.permanentinnovation.com [accessed June 2014].

OECD (2005), *Oslo Manual: Guide to Measuring Innovation*, Brussels: OECD Publishing.

OECD (2009), *Guide To Measuring The Information Society*, Paris.

OECD (2011), *Guide to Measuring the Information Society 2011*, OECD Publishing, http://browse.oecdbookshop.org/oecd/pdfs/free/9311021e.pdf [accessed 19.06.2014].

Okoń-Horodyńska, E., Wisła, R., Sierotowicz, T. (2012), *Measuring Patent Activity of Economic Branches with the Use of Concordance Tables*, Warsaw: Patent Office of The Republic of

Poland, http://jbc.bj.uj.edu.pl/Content/2-29315/Measuring%20patent%20%28...%29.pdf [accessed 19.06.2014].

Rothwell, R. (1994), "Industrial innovation: Success, strategy, trends," [in:] R. Rothwell, M. Dogson (eds.), *The Handbook of Industrial Innovation*, London: Edward Elgar Publishing.

Schmoch, U. (2008), *Concept of a Technology Classification for Country Comparisons. Final Report to the World Intellectual Property Organisation*, Karlsruhe: Fraunhofer Institute for Systems and Innovation Research.

Schumpeter, J. (1932), *The Theory of Economic Development*, New York: Galaxy Books.

Sobczyk, M. (2002), *Statystyka*, Warszawa: PWN.

Stern, S., Porter, M., Furman, L. (2000), "The determinants of national innovative capacity," Working Paper No. 7876, Cambridge: National Bureau of Economic Research.

Sternberg, R. (1999), *Handbook of Creativity*, Cambridge: Cambridge University Press.

Sundbo, J. (1999), *The Theory of Innovation: Entrepreneurs, Technology and Strategy (New Horizons in the Economics of Innovation)*, London: Edward Elgar Publishing.

Thomson Reuters (2007), *Global Patent Sources*, London: Thomson Scientific.

Thomson Reuters (2014), *Patent Fields and Tags*, http://www.thomsoninnova-tion.com/tip--innovation/support/help/index.htm#patent_fields.htm [accessed 19.06.2014].

Tidd, J., Bessant, J., Pavitt, K. (2005), *Managing Innovation: Integrating Technological Market and Organizational Change*, West Sussex: John Wiley & Sons, Ltd.

Twiss, B.C. (1994), *Managing Technological Innovation*, London: Pitman Publishing.

UPRP (2014), *Międzynarodowa Klasyfikacja Patentowa*, http://www.uprp.pl/miedzynarodowa--klasyfikacja-patentowa-mkp/Lead03,203,2800,1,index,pl,text/ [accessed 19.06.2014].

WIPO (2014a), http://www.wipo.int/classifications/ipc/en/ITsupport/Version2011-0101/trans-formations/viewer/index.htm [accessed 19.06.2014].

WIPO (2014b), *IPC – Technology Concordance Table*, http://www.wipo.int/ipstats-/en/statistics/technology_concordance.html [accessed 19.06.2014].

Appendix 10.1. List of industries described by NACE subclasses 1.1

NACE Class	Description
AA	Agriculture, hunting and forestry
BA	Fishing
CA	Mining and quarrying of energy producing materials
CB	Mining and quarrying, except of energy producing materials
DA	Manufacture of food products, beverages and tobacco
DB	Manufacture of textiles and textile products
DC	Manufacture of leather and leather products
DD	Manufacture of wood and wood products
DE	Manufacture of pulp, paper and paper products; publishing and printing
DF	Manufacture of coke, refined petroleum products and nuclear fuel
DG	Manufacture of chemicals, chemical products and man-made fibres
DH	Manufacture of rubber and plastic products
DI	Manufacture of other non-metallic mineral products
DJ	Manufacture of basic metals and fabricated metal products
DK	Manufacture of machinery and equipment n.e.c.
DL	Manufacture of electrical and optical equipment
DM	Manufacture of transport equipment
DN	Manufacturing n.e.c.
FA	Construction

Source: Eurostat, http://ec.europa.eu/eurostat/ramon/nomenclatures/index.cfm?TargetUrl=LS-T_NOM_DTL_LINEAR&StrNom=NACE_1_1&StrLanguageCode=EN [accessed 19.06.2014].

Appendix 10.2. Summary of technological areas in WIPO IPC/TECH concordance table

Label	Description
1	Electrical machinery, apparatus, energy
2	Audio-visual technology
3	Telecommunications
4	Digital communication
5	Basic communication processes
6	Computer technology
7	IT methods for management
8	Semiconductors
9	Optics
10	Measurement
11	Analysis of biological materials
12	Control
13	Medical technology
14	Organic fine chemistry
15	Biotechnology
16	Pharmaceuticals
17	Macromolecular chemistry, polymers
18	Food chemistry
19	Basic materials chemistry
20	Materials, metallurgy
21	Surface technology, coating
22	Micro-structural and nano-technology
23	Chemical engineering
24	Environmental technology
25	Handling
26	Machine tools
27	Motors, turbines, pumps
28	Textile and paper machines
29	Other special machines
30	Thermal processes and apparatus
31	Mechanical elements
32	Transport
33	Furniture, games
34	Other consumer goods
35	Civil engineering

Source: WIPO (2014b), *IPC – Technology Concordance Table*, http://www.wipo.int/ipstats-/en/statistics/ technology_concordance.html [accessed 19.06.2014].

Appendix 10.3. IPC designation assigned to technological areas in the WIPO IPC/TECH concordance table

Label	IPC Code[41]
1	F21H, F21K, F21L, F21S, F21V, F21W, F21Y, H01B, H01C, H01F, H01G, H01H, H01J, H01K, H01M, H01R, H01T, H02B, H02G, H02H, H02J, H02K, H02M, H02N, H02P, H05B, H05C, H05F, H99Z
2	G09F, G09G, G11B, H04N0003, H04N0005, H04N0007, H04N0009, H04N0011, H04N0013, H04N0015, H04N0017, H04N0101, H04R, H04S, H05K
3	G08C, H01P, H01Q, H04B, H04H, H04J, H04K, H04M, H04N0001, H04Q
4	H04L, H04N0021, H04W
5	H03B, H03C, H03D, H03F, H03G, H03H, H03J, H03K, H03L, H03M
6	G06C, G06D, G06E, G06F, G06G, G06J, G06K, G06M, G06N, G06T, G10L, G11C
7	G06Q
8	H01L
9	G02B, G02C, G02F, G03B, G03C, G03D, G03F, G03G, G03H, H01S
10	G01B, G01C, G01D, G01F, G01G, G01H, G01J, G01K, G01L, G01M, G01N0001, G01N0003, G01N0005, G01N0007, G01N0009, G01N0011, G01N0013, G01N0015, G01N0017, G01N0019, G01N0021, G01N0022, G01N0023, G01N0024, G01N0025, G01N0027, G01N0029, G01N0030, G01N0031, G01N0035, G01N0037, G01P, G01Q, G01R, G01S, G01V, G01W, G04B, G04C, G04D, G04F, G04G, G04R, G12B, G99Z
11	G01N0033
12	G05B, G05D, G05F, G07B, G07C, G07D, G07F, G07G, G08B, G08G, G09B, G09C, G09D
13	A61B, A61C, A61D, A61F, A61G, A61H, A61J, A61L, A61M, A61N, H05G
14	A61K0008, A61Q, C07B, C07C, C07D, C07F, C07H, C07J, C40B
15	C07G, C07K, C12M, C12N, C12P, C12Q, C12R, C12S
16	A61K0006, A61K0009, A61K0031, A61K0033, A61K0035, A61K0036, A61K0038, A61K0039, A61K0041, A61K0045, A61K0047, A61K0048, A61K0049, A61K0050, A61K0051, A61K0101, A61K0103, A61K0125, A61K0127, A61K0129, A61K0131, A61K0133, A61K0135, A61P
17	C08B, C08C, C08F, C08G, C08H, C08K, C08L
18	A01H, A21D, A23B, A23C, A23D, A23F, A23G, A23J, A23K, A23L, C12C, C12F, C12G, C12H, C12J, C13B0010, C13B0020, C13B0030, C13B0035, C13B0040, C13B0050, C13B0099, C13D, C13F, C13J, C13K
19	A01N, A01P, C05B, C05C, C05D, C05F, C05G, C06B, C06C, C06D, C06F, C09B, C09C, C09D, C09F, C09G, C09H, C09J, C09K, C10B, C10C, C10F, C10G, C10H, C10J, C10K, C10L, C10M, C10N, C11B, C11C, C11D, C99Z
20	B22C, B22D, B22F, C01B, C01C, C01D, C01F, C01G, C03C, C04B, C21B, C21C, C21D, C22B, C22C, C22F
21	B05C, B05D, B32B, C23C, C23D, C23F, C23G, C25B, C25C, C25D, C25F, C30B
22	B81B, B81C, B82B, B82Y
23	B01B, B01D0001, B01D0003, B01D0005, B01D0007, B01D0008, B01D0009, B01D0011, B01D0012, B01D0015, B01D0017, B01D0019, B01D0021, B01D0024, B01D0025, B01D0027, B01D0029, B01D0033, B01D0035, B01D0036, B01D0037, B01D0039, B01D0041, B01D0043, B01D0057, B01D0059, B01D0061, B01D0063, B01D0065, B01D0067, B01D0069, B01D0071, B01F, B01J, B01L, B02C, B03B, B03C, B03D, B04B, B04C, B05B, B06B, B07B, B07C, B08B, C14C, D06B, D06C, D06L, F25J, F26B, H05H
24	A62C, B01D0045, B01D0046, B01D0047, B01D0049, B01D0050, B01D0051, B01D0052, B01D0053, B09B, B09C, B65F, C02F, E01F0008, F01N, F23G, F23J, G01T
25	B25J, B65B, B65C, B65D, B65G, B65H, B66B, B66C, B66D, B66F, B67B, B67C, B67D

---

2   Full description of the IPC designations is available at: http://www.wipo.int/classifications/ipc/ en/ [accessed 19.06.2014].

Label	IPC Code[41]
26	A62D, B21B, B21C, B21D, B21F, B21G, B21H, B21J, B21K, B21L, B23B, B23C, B23D, B23F, B23G, B23H, B23K, B23P, B23Q, B24B, B24C, B24D, B25B, B25C, B25D, B25F, B25G, B25H, B26B, B26D, B26F, B27B, B27C, B27D, B27F, B27G, B27H, B27J, B27K, B27L, B27M, B27N, B30B
27	F01B, F01C, F01D, F01K, F01L, F01M, F01P, F02B, F02C, F02D, F02F, F02G, F02K, F02M, F02N, F02P, F03B, F03C, F03D, F03G, F03H, F04B, F04C, F04D, F04F, F23R, F99Z, G21B, G21C, G21D, G21F, G21G, G21H, G21J, G21K,
28	A41H, A43D, A46D, B31B, B31C, B31D, B31F, B41B, B41C, B41D, B41F, B41G, B41J, B41K, B41L, B41M, B41N, C14B, D01B, D01C, D01D, D01F, D01G, D01H, D02G, D02H, D02J, D03C, D03D, D03J, D04B, D04C, D04G, D04H, D05B, D05C, D06G, D06H, D06J, D06M, D06P, D06Q, D21B, D21C, D21D, D21F, D21G, D21H, D21J, D99Z
29	A01B, A01C, A01D, A01F, A01G, A01J, A01K, A01L, A01M, A21B, A21C, A22B, A22C, A23N, A23P, B02B, B28B, B28C, B28D, B29B, B29C, B29D, B29K, B29L, B99Z, C03B, C08J, C12L, C13B0005, C13B0015, C13B0025, C13B0045, C13C, C13G, C13H, F41A, F41B, F41C, F41F, F41G, F41H, F41J, F42B, F42C, F42D
30	F22B, F22D, F22G, F23B, F23C, F23D, F23H, F23K, F23L, F23M, F23N, F23Q, F24B, F24C, F24D, F24F, F24H, F24J, F25B, F25C, F27B, F27D, F28B, F28C, F28D, F28F, F28G
31	F15B, F15C, F15D, F16B, F16C, F16D, F16F, F16G, F16H, F16J, F16K, F16L, F16M, F16N, F16P, F16S, F16T, F17B, F17C, F17D, G05G
32	B60B, B60C, B60D, B60F, B60G, B60H, B60J, B60K, B60L, B60M, B60N, B60P, B60Q, B60R, B60S, B60T, B60V, B60W, B61B, B61C, B61D, B61F, B61G, B61H, B61J, B61K, B61L, B62B, B62C, B62D, B62H, B62J, B62K, B62L, B62M, B63B, B63C, B63G, B63H, B63J, B64B, B64C, B64D, B64F, B64G
33	A47B, A47C, A47D, A47F, A47G, A47H, A47J, A47K, A47L, A63B, A63C, A63D, A63F, A63G, A63H, A63J, A63K
34	A24B, A24C, A24D, A24F, A41B, A41C, A41D, A41F, A41G, A42B, A42C, A43B, A43C, A44B, A44C, A45B, A45C, A45D, A45F, A46B, A62B, A99Z, B42B, B42C, B42D, B42F, B43K, B43L, B43M, B44B, B44C, B44D, B44F, B68B, B68C, B68F, B68G, D04D, D06F, D06N, D07B, F25D, G10B, G10C, G10D, G10F, G10G, G10H, G10K
35	E01B, E01C, E01D, E01F0001, E01F0003, E01F0005, E01F0007, E01F0009, E01F0011, E01F0013, E01F0015, E01H, E02B, E02C, E02D, E02F, E03B, E03C, E03D, E03F, E04B, E04C, E04D, E04F, E04G, E04H, E05B, E05C, E05D, E05F, E05G, E06B, E06C, E21B, E21C, E21D, E21F, E99Z

Source: WIPO (2014b), *IPC – Technology Concordance Table*, http://www.wipo.int/ipstats-/en/statistics/ technology_concordance.html [accessed 19.06.2014].

Chapter 11

The diversity of creative activity of men and women in Germany, France, UK and Italy on the basis of patents filed at the EPO in the period 1999–2013

Tomasz Sierotowicz

Abstract

Patent statistics are currently one of the research areas being intensively explored. Patent activity, measured by the number of patents, is one of the recognized measures of creativity and innovation, not only among countries and regions but also business entities. Patent statistics include a rich and detailed description of the patent, not only in terms of its content. This description includes information about the inventors of the patent, as well as the International Patent Classification (IPC). A new chapter in the exploration of patent statistics is their use to assess the creative diversity of patent activity for men and women. This variation applies not only to the total number of patents. It is crucial to indicate the areas of science, technology and the economy in which different patent activity for men and women appears. Therefore, in this study two main research tasks were formulated: analysis of the differences in the dynamics of changes in creative patent activity of men and women and identification of the diversity of creative accumulation of patent activity for men and women for the entire study period 1999–2103 in the countries under study: Germany, France, the UK, and Italy. In order to obtain uniform conditions for obtaining patent protection for the inventions of all inventors, the data source was the database European Patent Office (EPO). The diversity of accumulation of creative patent activity for men and women was achieved by using the IPC/NACE concordance table.

Key words: inventions and innovations, research and development, intellectual property, comparative analysis of countries

Introduction

Patent statistics is a diverse area of research exploration. In the literature, it is seen as a measure of: innovation (Griliches, 1990; OECD, 2005; Wisła, 2014; European Union, 2014), competition, specialization (RIS3 Guide, 2012), creativity (Fischer and Varga, 2003), intellectual property, effects created by the outlays on research and development (R&D), and the level of technological advancement of countries, regions and individual traders. Patent activity is also recognized as a component of innovation potential. It can also serve as a measure of the creative involvement of women and men in building countries' innovative potential. In this study two research tasks were formulated: the first is to analyze the differences in the dynamics of changes in creative patent activity of men and women in selected countries. The second task is to identify the diversity of accumulation of creative patent activity for men and women for the entire study period in the selected countries. Patents are a legal protection granted for inventions, in particular as regards to the exclusive rights to their business use by developers. Individual countries have their own patent offices which grant legal protection in accordance with the laws which are valid in a given country regarding protection of intellectual property. For making a comparative analysis of patent statistics from different countries, it is necessary to preserve the identity of the legal principle of the rules for granting patents. This is possible thanks to the legal protection granted by the European Patent Office (EPO). Thus, the source of the data in this study was the EPO Patent statistics for the countries under study. In particular, information selected from the patent description such as: the IPC designation, and the list of inventors of each patent. The objects of the study of the diversity of patent activity were the countries belonging to the European Union that were seen as leaders in patent activity: Germany, France, the UK, and Italy. The research period adopted was 1999–2013 due to the availability of as complete patent specifications as possible, in particular relating to the inventors of patents obtained in the EPO. The first research goal was achieved through the use of a statistical tool – the average rate of change of the studied phenomenon in time (Freedman, Pisani, Purves, 2011). The second research goal was achieved by the use of the IPC/NACE concordance table (Okoń-Horodyńska et al., 2012).

11.1. Method of evaluating the creative diversity of patent activity for men and women

In this study two research tasks were formulated:
1. Analysis of the differences in the dynamics of changes in creative patent activity of men and women in selected countries.
2. Identification of the diversity of accumulation of creative patent activity for men and women for the entire study period in the selected countries.

The scope of the study was determined by the use of the EPO patent database, which was the source of the data, and the IPC/NACE concordance table (Okoń-Horodyńska et al., 2012), which was the tool used to achieve the second

objective. The study adopted the research period 1999–2013, due to the complete-
ness of the descriptions provided in the EPO database, determined by the date of
the grant of the patent. Since the source data does not specify separate information
on gender, the number of women and men have been identified on the basis of
male and female names identified in the description of the inventors.

Achievement of the first objective of the research the average rate of change
was used (Freedman et al., 2011). Its use enabled the analysis and assessment of
the dynamics of changes in patent activity of creative men and women in the given
research period. The calculations of the average rate of change were made based
on equations 1 and 2:

$$log_{\bar{y}_v} = \frac{1}{n-1} \times \sum_{i=2}^{n} log \frac{v_i}{v_{i-1}} \qquad \text{(Equation 1)}$$

where:
$\bar{y}_v$ − the geometric mean of the chain base indexes of the variable analysed
      over the entire study period,

v_i – the successive annual value of the time series of the variable analysed,

$\frac{v_{(i)}}{v_{(i-1)}}$ – the annual value of the chain base index of the variable analysed,

i – the successive values for chain base index,

N_z – number of elements in the time series of the variable analysed.

$$\bar{T}_v = (\bar{y}_v - 1) \times 100 \qquad \text{(Equation 2)}$$

where:
$\bar{T}_v$ − the average rate of change of the variable analysed throughout the study
      period,

$\bar{y}_v$ – the geometric mean of the chain base indexes of the variable analysed
      over the entire study period.

The procedure for calculating the average rate of change has been applied to
the individual calculation of variables listed in Table 11.1.

Achieving the second objective of the research required the use of the IPC/
NACE concordance table (Okoń-Horodyńska et al., 2012). This is based on the
description of industries by NACE Subsections 1.1 (Table 11.2).

The limitations of the research method include the fact that the study concerned
the analysis and assessment of the diversity of creative activity of men and women,
so only individuals were taken into account in the description of the inventors. All
other entities, such as companies, universities, research & development and other
institutions were not taken into account. Another limitation is the accuracy of the
concordance tables used. The point of their construction is to express one classification by describing another different classification. IPC describes areas of science

Table 11.1. Summary of the variables analysed, applied separately to relationships 1 and 2

Name of the variable analysed in the period 1999–2013	Type designation – v_i for the time series of the variable analysed	Designation of the average rate of – $\bar{T}_V$ for the variable analysed
Number of patents obtained in the EPO by Germany	v_{DE}	$\bar{T}_{DE}$
Number of patents obtained in the EPO by France	v_{FR}	$\bar{T}_{FR}$
Number of patents obtained in the EPO by the UK	v_{GB}	$\bar{T}_{GB}$
Number of patents obtained in the EPO by Italy	v_{IT}	$\bar{T}_{IT}$
Number of inventors from Germany for patents obtained in the EPO	v_{DET}	$\bar{T}_{DET}$
Number of inventors from France for patents obtained in the EPO	v_{FRT}	$\bar{T}_{FRT}$
Number of inventors from the UK for patents obtained in the EPO	v_{GBT}	$\bar{T}_{GBT}$
Number of inventors from Italy for patents obtained in the EPO	v_{ITT}	$\bar{T}_{ITT}$
Number of patents obtained in the EPO by women inventors from Germany	v_{DETW}	$\bar{T}_{DETW}$
Number of patents obtained in the EPO by men inventors from Germany	v_{DETM}	$\bar{T}_{DETM}$
Number of patents obtained in the EPO by women inventors from France	v_{FRTW}	$\bar{T}_{FRTW}$
Number of patents obtained in the EPO by men inventors from France	v_{FRTM}	$\bar{T}_{FRTM}$
Number of patents obtained in the EPO by women inventors from the UK	v_{GBTW}	$\bar{T}_{GBTW}$
Number of patents obtained in the EPO by men inventors from the UK	v_{GBTM}	$\bar{T}_{GBTM}$
Number of patents obtained in the EPO by women inventors from Italy	v_{ITTW}	$\bar{T}_{ITTW}$
Number of patents obtained in the EPO by men inventors from Italy	v_{ITTM}	$\bar{T}_{ITTM}$

Source: own report.

and technology, while NACE describes the classification of economic activities. Hence the difficulty of building concordance tables. In the literature more different types of concordance table are detailed. For the purposes of this study the above table was created whose mutual mapping spectrum of classification is the broadest.

In the cognitive layer of this study, we can specify the acquisition of new knowledge on the difference in the creative patent activity between men and women patent in the selected countries, based on the EPO patent database for the period 1999–2013, in the form of quantitative determination of: diversity and dynamics of changes in the patent activity and the diversity of the accumulation of patent activity in the individual NACE sections and technological areas.

Table 11.2. List of industries described by NACE subclasses 1.1

NACE Designation	Description
AA	Agriculture, hunting and forestry
BA	Fishing
CA	Mining and quarrying of energy producing materials
CB	Mining and quarrying, except of energy producing materials
DA	Manufacture of food products, beverages and tobacco
DB	Manufacture of textiles and textile products
DC	Manufacture of leather and leather products
DD	Manufacture of wood and wood products
DE	Manufacture of pulp, paper and paper products; publishing and printing
DF	Manufacture of coke, refined petroleum products and nuclear fuel
DG	Manufacture of chemicals, chemical products and man-made fibres
DH	Manufacture of rubber and plastic products
DI	Manufacture of other non-metallic mineral products
DJ	Manufacture of basic metals and fabricated metal products
DK	Manufacture of machinery and equipment n.e.c.
DL	Manufacture of electrical and optical equipment
DM	Manufacture of transport equipment
DN	Manufacturing n.e.c.
FA	Construction

Source: Eurostat, http://ec.europa.eu/eurostat/ramon/nomenclatures/index.cfm?TargetUrl=LS-T_NOM_DTL_LINEAR&StrNom=NACE_1_1&StrLanguageCode=PL [accessed 08.12.2014]. NACE Subsections were described in the concordance table with the appropriate IPC designation.[1]

11.1. Identification of the leading countries in the European Union in terms of patent activity

Selecting the leading countries required an examination of the patent activity of all EU countries in the given research period. The leading EU countries were selected on the basis of the share of patenting granted by the EPO per 1 million averaged population of each country throughout the study period. The results for this are shown in Figure 11.1.

According to the survey, the largest share of registered patents granted by the EPO was recorded in Germany 48.04%, followed by France 16.85%, Britain 12.67% and Italy 6.82% from all EU countries throughout the study period. The total value of the share of these countries is 84.38%, and the remaining 15.62% is the share of the other 24 EU countries. Thus, further studies included the selected group of four leading EU countries in terms of registered patents granted by the EPO.

---

1   The detailed description of the concordance table in this study with IPC designations is located at: Okoń-Horodyńska et al., 2012, pp. 31–39, 118–212.

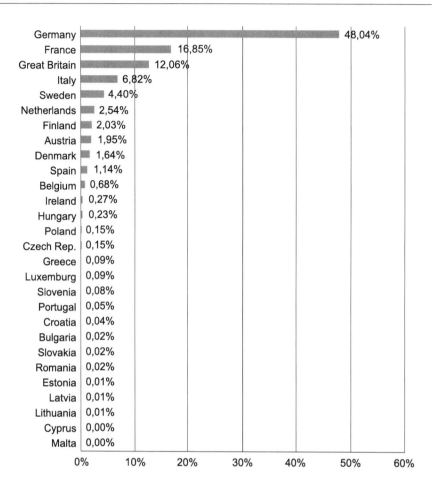

Figure 11.1. The share of applicants per 1 million inhabitants in the period 1999–2013
Source: own calculations.

11.2. The diversity of creative activity of men and women in the countries covered by the analysis

Creative patent activity was analysed and evaluated for Germany, France, the UK and Italy. The data source was the EPO Patent database. First the time series of annual values for the eight variables were identified (Table 11.3).

The most patents approved in the study period were received by Germany – 169 729 (Table 11.3), with the largest number of inventors – 417 133. The fewest patents were granted to Italy – 23 133, with the smallest number of inventors – 44 136. For the listed variables (Table 11.4) the geometric mean and the average rate of change were calculated separately. The results are shown in Table 11.4.

Table 11.3. Number of patents and inventors obtained from the EPO

Year/country/ variable	Number of patents granted by the EPO				Number of inventors of patents granted by the EPO			
	v_{DE}	v_{FR}	v_{GB}	v_{IT}	v_{DET}	v_{FRT}	v_{GBT}	v_{ITT}
1999	7 740	2 920	2 443	1 034	18 594	6 087	5 208	1 919
2000	5 718	2 134	1 924	847	13 698	4 511	4 208	1 648
2001	8 423	2 808	2 068	1 002	20 465	6 044	4 598	1 925
2002	11 551	3 786	3 148	1 473	28 326	8 139	6 831	2 559
2003	13 719	4 674	3 888	1 877	33 667	10 050	8 929	3 339
2004	13 787	4 176	3 637	1 868	33 724	9 020	8 568	3 379
2005	12 631	3 498	3 197	1 598	31 136	7 637	7 593	2 934
2006	14 333	4 143	3 472	1 927	35 213	9 079	8 248	3 535
2007	11 450	3 616	2 902	1 561	28 460	7 971	7 164	2 872
2008	12 825	4 323	3 000	1 752	31 971	9 615	7 264	3 202
2009	10 791	3 691	2 509	1 542	26 830	8 280	6 302	2 832
2010	11 598	4 208	2 587	1 714	28 432	9 405	6 623	3 225
2011	11 985	4 237	2 706	1 772	29 673	9 771	6 526	3 390
2012	11 706	4 081	2 783	1 832	28 639	9 318	6 947	3 525
2013	11 472	4 189	2 702	1 972	28 305	9 731	6 561	3 852
Total	169 729	56 484	42 966	23 771	417 133	124 658	101 570	44 136

Source: own calculations.

Table 11.4. The calculated values for the average rate of change for the entire period 1999–2013

Variable	Average rate of change
$\overline{T}_{DE}$	2.85%
$\overline{T}_{FR}$	2.61%
$\overline{T}_{GB}$	0.72%
$\overline{T}_{IT}$	4.72%
$\overline{T}_{DET}$	3.05%
$\overline{T}_{FRT}$	3.41%
$\overline{T}_{GBT}$	1.66%
$\overline{T}_{ITT}$	5.10%

Source: own calculations.

As follows from the calculations (Table 11.4), the largest value for the average rate of change was recorded for $\overline{T}_{ITT}$, which amounted to 5.10%, which is Italian inventors of patents obtained in the EPO. This means that the number of inventors from Italy for patents obtained in the EPO increased throughout the study period, from year to year by an average of 5.10%. Italy also achieved the highest average rate of change in the number of patents obtained in the EPO $\overline{T}_{IT}$, which amounted to 4.72%. This means that the number of patents at the EPO obtained by Italy increased from year to year by 4.72% on average. The lowest average rate of change was recorded for $\overline{T}_{GBT}$, which amounted to 1.66%, which is UK inventors of patents obtained in the EPO. This means that the number of inventors from the UK for patents obtained in the EPO increased throughout the study period, from year to year by an average of 1.66%. The UK also recorded the lowest average rate of change in the number of patents obtained in the EPO $\overline{T}_{GB}$, which amounted to 0.72%. This means that the number of patents at the EPO obtained by the UK increased from year to year by 0.72% on average.

The numbers of inventors for patents obtained in the EPO including the gender are shown in Table 11.5.

Table 11.5. The number of men and women who are the inventors of patents obtained in the EPO

Country	Germany		France		The UK		Italy	
Year/ variable	v_{DETW} [number]	v_{DETM} [number]	v_{FRTW} [number]	v_{FRTM} [number]	v_{GBTW} [number]	v_{GBTM} [number]	v_{ITTW} [number]	v_{ITTM} [number]
1999	721	17 808	522	5 537	299	4 671	200	1 684
2000	491	13 157	374	4 128	303	3 736	189	1 432
2001	884	19 509	594	5 425	304	4 089	181	1 704
2002	1 244	27 011	720	7 362	521	5 936	264	2 251
2003	1 626	31 931	906	9 066	720	7 669	400	2 856
2004	1 752	31 871	863	8 067	612	7 287	420	2 835
2005	1 573	29 470	809	6 774	615	6 235	336	2 492
2006	1 843	33 241	992	7 979	689	6 671	436	2 995
2007	1 603	26 741	832	7 070	621	5 685	362	2 404
2008	1 766	30 091	983	8 555	593	5 845	386	2 650
2009	1 516	25 220	870	7 355	603	5 087	355	2 361
2010	1 590	26 773	1 077	8 268	572	5 329	482	2 645
2011	1 708	27 911	1 009	8 725	579	5 486	491	2 842
2012	1 705	26 899	1 031	8 256	598	5 995	564	2 914
2013	1 785	26 484	1 025	8 681	606	5 677	661	3 150
Total	21 807	394 117	12 607	111 248	8 235	85 398	5 727	37 215

Source: own calculations.

The greatest number of women inventors for EPO patents was obtained for Germany, 21 807, and the lowest for Italy, 5 727, throughout the study period (Table 11.5). The greatest number of male inventors of patents obtained in the EPO was recorded for Germany, 394 117, and the lowest for Italy 37 215. The values for of the geometric mean and the average rate of change for female and male inventors of EPO patents obtained are shown in Table 11.6.

Table 11.6. Calculated values for the average rate of change of male and female inventors of EPO patents obtained in the period 1999–2013

Variable	Value of the average rate of change
$\overline{T}_{DETW}$	6.69%
$\overline{T}_{DETM}$	2.88%
$\overline{T}_{FRTW}$	4.94%
$\overline{T}_{FRTM}$	3.26%
$\overline{T}_{GBTW}$	5.18%
$\overline{T}_{GBTM}$	1.40%
$\overline{T}_{ITTW}$	8.91%
$\overline{T}_{ITTM}$	4.57%

Source: own calculations.

The highest average rate of change was recorded for Italian female inventors of EPO patents obtained, 8.91% (Table 11.6). This means that the number of female inventors from Italy for patents obtained in the EPO increased throughout the study period, from year to year by an average of 8.91%. The lowest average rate of change was observed for UK male inventors of EPO patents obtained, 1.40%. This means that the number of male inventors from the UK for patents obtained in the EPO increased throughout the study period, from year to year by an average of 1.40%.

11.3. Differentiation of the cumulative creative activity of men and women

The cumulative creative patent activity was analysed and calculated for the entire period of the study, based on the IPC/NACE concordance table (Okoń-Horodyńska et al., 2012) for each country in the analysis. The results are shown in Tables 11.7 and 11.8.

The NACE Subsection descriptions are given in Table 11.2. The highest number of male and female inventors throughout the study period was recorded in Germany, respectively 392 980 and 21 758, and the lowest in Italy, 37 136 and 5 717. Figures 11.2 and 11.3 show the accumulation of patent activity for men and women of the countries surveyed, over the entire study period, in particular areas of the economy.

The highest patent activity of female inventors (Figure 11.2), from all the countries surveyed, for patents obtained in the EPO, was noted in Subsection DG – Manufacture of chemicals, chemical products and man-made fibres, 45.56% of all women who are the inventors of patents. The second area is DL – Manufacture of electrical and optical equipment, which saw 19.95% of all female inventors.

Table 11.7. The number of men and women who are the inventors of patents obtained in the EPO in the whole period from 1999–2013 in NACE Subsections

Country	Germany		France		The UK		Italy	
NACE/ variable	Women [number]	Men [number]	Women [number]	Men [number]	Women [number]	Men [number]	Women [number]	Men [number]
AA	101	822	65	421	57	461	23	144
BA	13	129	32	181	23	277	16	46
CA	13	705	21	329	27	1 454	10	80
CB	0	0	0	0	0	0	0	0
DA	1 248	8 750	944	3 284	937	4 202	250	1 200
DB	367	6 144	133	1 430	105	933	102	1 363
DC	40	673	27	395	19	129	41	397
DD	43	1 231	18	190	8	88	8	126
DE	244	6 818	230	2 675	122	1 670	92	616
DF	119	1 344	175	1 121	48	506	26	164
DG	9 806	87 887	5 617	22 443	4 427	26 270	2 126	8 019
DH	161	3 155	136	1 932	50	973	109	806
DI	459	5949	319	2 310	78	1 120	76	791
DJ	908	25 971	390	6 882	103	3 130	273	2 904
DK	1 981	74 140	845	15 247	316	8 870	902	7 579
DL	4 126	93 856	2 786	33 586	1 676	27 488	1 036	6 783
DM	1 607	61 768	551	13 479	97	4 805	410	4 194
DN	248	5338	128	2047	56	1 292	117	911
FA	274	8 300	159	2 839	34	1 338	100	1 013
Total	21 758	392 980	12 576	110 791	8 183	85 006	5 717	37 136

Source: own report.

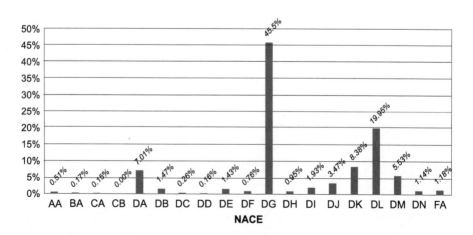

Figure 11.2. Accumulation of creative patent activity for women from all countries surveyed throughout the study period
Source: own calculations.

Men's patent activity is somewhat more diverse in terms of the spectrum of economic areas. The highest patent activity of male inventors (Figure 11.3), from all the countries surveyed, for patents obtained in the EPO, was noted in Subsection DL – Manufacture electrical and optical equipment, 25.84% of all men who are the inventors of patents. The second area is DG – Manufacture of chemicals, chemical products and man-made fibres, 23.11% of all men who are the inventors of patents. Other areas are DK – Manufacture of machinery and equipment n.e.c. and DM – Manufacture of transport equipment, where the share of male inventors are respectively 16.91% and 13.46%.

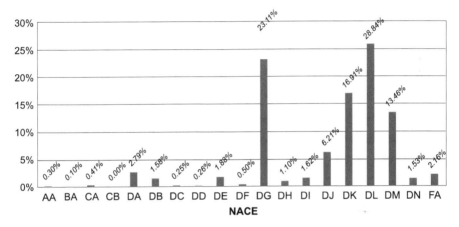

Figure 11.3. Accumulation of creative patent activity for men from all countries surveyed throughout the study period
Source: own calculations.

No patent activity at all throughout the study period, among both women and men, was noted in Subsection CB – Mining and quarrying of raw materials other than energy producing. Table 11.8 shows the results of calculation of the ratio of the number of women to the number of men in each NACE Subsection, in order to identify the sub-section in which the highest and lowest patent activity was recorded for men and women at the same time.

The higher the ratio of women to men (Table 11.8), the more women compared to men were involved in patent activity in the given NACE area. A value ratio greater than 1 indicates a greater number of women than men. In contrast, a value less than 1 indicates a greater number of men. The area of cooperation which marked the highest ratio of women to men in patent activity in Germany, France and the UK is DA – Manufacture of food products; beverages and tobacco, where it is respectively 0.143, 0.287 and 0.223.But the area for Italy is BA – Fishing, 0.348. The lowest value of the ratio of women to men in patent activity was recorded for Germany and the UK in CA – Mining and quarrying of energy for energy producing materials, 0.018, and 0.019, respectively, France 0.041 in the area of DM – Manufacture of transport equipment, and Italy 0.063 in the area of DD – Manufacture of wood and wood products.

Table 11.8. The number of men and women who are the inventors of patents obtained in the EPO in the whole period 1999–2013 in NACE Subsections

NACE/country	Germany	France	The UK	Italy
AA	0,123	0,154	0,124	0,160
BA	0.101	0.177	0.083	0.348
CA	0.018	0.064	0.019	0.125
CB	0	0	0	0
DA	0.143	0.287	0.223	0.208
DB	0.060	0.093	0.113	0.075
DC	0.059	0.068	0.147	0.103
DD	0.035	0.095	0.091	0.063
DE	0.036	0.086	0.073	0.149
DF	0.089	0.156	0.095	0.159
DG	0.112	0.250	0.169	0.265
DH	0.051	0.070	0.051	0.135
DI	0.077	0.138	0.070	0.096
DJ	0.035	0.057	0.033	0.094
DK	0.027	0.055	0.036	0.119
DL	0.044	0.083	0.061	0.153
DM	0.026	0.041	0.020	0.098
DN	0.046	0.063	0.043	0.128
FA	0.033	0.056	0.025	0.099

Source: own calculations.

Conclusions

Based on the analysis and the evaluation of the creative diversity of patent activity in Germany, France, the UK and Italy over the study period 1999-2013, the following conclusions may be formulated.

1. The largest increase in patent activity in the period 1999-2103, measured by the average rate of change in both the number of patents obtained in the EPO, as well as the number of inventors was reported for Italy. The number of patents increased from year to year by an average of 4.72%, while the number of inventors increased from year to year by an average of 5.10%.

2. The lowest average rate of change in the number of patents obtained in the EPO was recorded for the UK The number of patents increased from year to year by an average of 0.72%. Also, the lowest growth in the number of inventors was recorded for the UK. The number of patents increased from year to year by an average of 1.66%.

3. The number of female creators from Italy for patents obtained in the EPO increased most rapidly throughout the study period, from year to year by an average of 8.91%. The lowest average rate of change was observed for UK male inventors of EPO patents obtained, 1.40%. This means that the number of male inventors from the UK for patents obtained in the EPO increased throughout the study period, from year to year by an average of 1.40%.

4. In all the countries surveyed, the average rate of change in the number of women artists is positive and significantly higher than the average rate of change in the number of men who are inventors of patents granted by the EPO in the period 1999-2013.This means that women in the countries concerned exhibit significantly higher creativity than men in terms of patent activity.

5. The area of cooperation which marked the highest ratio of women to men in patent activity in Germany, France and the UK is DA – Manufacture of food products; beverages and tobacco, where it is respectively 0.143, 0.287 and 0.223. For Italy this area is BA – Fishing, at 0.348.

6. The area of cooperation, which recorded the lowest proportion of women to men in patent activity in Germany and the UK is CA – Mining and quarrying of energy materials, respectively 0.018, and 0.019, for France, 0.041, it is the area of DM – Manufacture of transport equipment and for Italy, 0,063, it is area DD – Manufacture of wood and wood products.

Literature

Chesbrough, H. (2011), *Open Services Innovation: Rethinking Your Business to Grow and Compete in a New Era*, San Francisco: Jossey-Bass.

Christensen, C., Anthony, D., Roth, E. (2004), *Seeing What's Next. Using the Theories of Innovation to Predict Industry Change*, Boston: Harvard Business School Press.

Davila, T., Epstein, M., Shelton, R. (2006), *Making Innovation Work: How to Manage It, Measure It, and Profit from It*, Upper Saddle River, NJ, USA: Wharton School Publishing.

DeGraff, J., Quinn, E. (2007), *Leading Innovation*, New York: McGraw-Hill.

European Commission (2012), *Guide to Research and Innovation Strategies for Smart Specialisations (RIS 3 Guide)*, Luxembourg: Publications Office of the European Union.

European Union (2014), *Innovation Union Scoreboard 2014*, Brussels, http:/-/ec.europa.eu/enterprise/policies/innovation/files/ius/ius-2014_en.pdf [accessed 19.06.2014].

Fischer, M., Varga, A. (2003), "Spatial knowledge spillovers and university research: Evidence from Austria," *The Analysis of Regional Science*, Vol. 37(2), pp. 303–322.

Freedman D., Pisani R., Purves R. (2011), *Statistics*, New Delhi: Viva Books.

Griliches, Z. (1990), "Patent statistics as economic indicators: A survey," *Journal of Economic Literature*, Vol. 28, pp. 1661-1707.

McGowan, P. (1987), "Creativity and innovation," [in:] D. Steward (ed.), *Handbook of Management Skills*, London: Gower Publishing Ltd.

Morris, L. (2006), *Permanent Innovation*, Philadelphia: Morris Publisher.

OECD (2005), *Oslo Manual: Guide to Measuring Innovation*, Brussels: OECD Publishing.

OECD (2009), *Guide To Measuring the Information Society*, Paris.

OECD (2011), *Guide to Measuring the Information Society 2011*, OECD Publishing, http://browse.oecdbookshop.org/oecd/pdfs/free/9311021e.pdf [accessed 19.06.2014].

Okoń-Horodyńska, E., Wisła, R., Sierotowicz, T. (2012), *Measuring Patent Activity of Economic Branches with the Use of Concordance Tables*, Warsaw: Patent Office of The Republic of Poland, http://jbc.bj.uj.edu.pl/Content/2-29315/Measuring%20patent%20%28...%29.pdf [accessed 08.12.2014].

WIPO (2014a), http://www.wipo.int/classifications/ipc/en/ITsupport/Version2011-0101/transformations/viewer/index.htm [accessed 19.06.14].

WIPO (2014b), *IPC – Technology Concordance Table*, http://www.wipo.int/ipstats-/en/statistics/technology_concordance.-html [accessed 19.06.14].

Wisła, R. (2014), *Regional Patterns of Technical Knowledge Accumulation in the Countries of Central and Eastern Europe*, Warsaw: Polish Scientific Publishers PWN.

Chapter 12

Psychological aspects of innovation

Magdalena Jaworek, Anna Dyląg

Abstract

The purpose of this study is to analyse the most important psychological factors that impact on the innovation process. In psychology, the determinants of innovation are usually considered at three levels: individual, group/team and organization. When it comes to individual factors, research indicates that the variables associated with innovation are to some extent intelligence, personality traits such as openness to experience, low agreeableness and conscientiousness, and intrinsic motivation. The factors discussed at team level are group norms underlying the organizational climate and the composition of the team, with a focus on group roles. At the organizational level, the main role in the innovation process is played by the appropriate leadership and organizational factors such as autonomy, and the level of workload. This very brief overview will only serve to familiarize readers without any knowledge of psychology with the complexity of the issues facing innovation in this field.

Key words: psychology, innovation process, individual, group, organization

Introduction

Innovation is a concept most often dealt with in the field of economics and the economy, usually considered a technological phenomenon, although the latest definitions also take social innovation into account. Nevertheless, the human factor and the role of psychology in this area are often marginalized or even ignored (Kożusznik, 2010). And yet the person plays a key role in the innovation process – s/he is the author of the concept, which s/he after several stages ultimately puts into effect, but also the person is often a major barrier and obstacle to the creation and implementation of innovative ideas. Therefore, the study of innovation, and the search for the factors determining it, as well as affecting it inhibitorily must be interdisciplinary and take psychological factors into account.

Innovation issues in psychology are often considered at three levels: (i) the individual and individual resources, such as defined personality traits and cognitive abilities; (ii) the group, especially in terms of its structure, composition, standards and atmosphere; and (iii) the organization, where special emphasis is placed on the working environment, the climate and organizational culture, and leadership (e.g. Kożusznik, 2010; Trompenaars, 2010; Patterson et al., 2009). In addition, job-level factors are discussed which relate to the contextual characteristics of the everyday work (job structure, tasks and resources) and their influence on employee motivation and innovative behaviours (Parzefall et al., 2008).

Kożusznik (2010) further distinguishes thematic areas in which research is conducted in the field of innovation in psychology, such as:
- diagnosis of psychological characteristics with particular emphasis on creativity,
- study of innovation diffusion and transfer, i.e. the analysis of the route from concept to implementation and dissemination of the inventions,
- the uptake of innovations, with emphasis on factors of resistance to change, risks and fears occurring among workers in an innovative situation, or
- the stages of assimilation of innovation.

In the traditional view, creativity and innovativeness were characteristics of a few select individuals. Nowadays, these capacities are believed inherent in every person, although this potential may remain closed or hidden in some settings, meaning that certain traits or features which fuel innovativeness in one environment may not be very helpful in another. Also different individual/team factors may be required at different stages of the innovative process (see Mathisen et al., 2008). Innovativeness is believed to be a complex issue, thus an understanding of the creative processes and innovation need a multi-level perspective – from individual, job, through team, to organizational. The role of human resources management may be critical in enhancing employee innovativeness (Parzefall et al., 2008).

The significant achievements of psychology (and management) in this area make it impossible to discuss the topic comprehensively in such a short paper. Therefore, the authors focus on the analysis of the psychological and organizational factors associated with innovation selected most often by other researchers.

12.1. Innovativeness – individual level factors

The innovations that have been used by generations over the world have thus far tended to be the work of brilliant individuals. Today, there is an era of discoveries and inventions behind which whole teams work, but that does not mean that the outstanding and creative minds in the field have ceased to matter (see: *Innovation and teamwork*). What is the difference between those people on whom the progress and development of civilization largely depends from conventionally-minded people? How do they feel and perceive reality; how do they process information? Do they perhaps have some personality traits common to creative individuals that allow them to realize often seemingly crazy ideas? Psychologists have been trying to answer these questions and researching the root causes of human genius for over a century. Their areas of research on issues of creativity can be grouped into cognitive factors associated with the personality of the individual and their motivation.

12.1.1. Cognitive resources

One of the forefathers of research on intelligence is the brilliant, although very controversial, Sir Francis Galton, who also dealt with issues of genius. He believed, rightly, that what connects the highly gifted individuals is their high level of intelligence. Initially it was thought that intelligence is strongly associated with creativity, as indicated by some theories, e.g. Guilford or Sternberg (in: Nęcka, 2005). Later, research results slightly revised this view. Intelligence has to do with creativity only to a certain level – 115-120 IQ. Above that limit its importance is negligible (Feist and Barron, 2003), which means that among people with very high intelligence there is relatively the same number or slightly fewer creative people than among just above average intellect. These results also show that a certain level of intelligence is necessary in creative thinking to master a particular area of study. In conclusion, creativity is definitely a different research construct. Patterson, Kerrin and Gatto-Roissard (2009) made an apt analogy, comparing the relationship of intelligence and creativity more to cousins than siblings.

So what is creativity or creative thinking? The definitions of innovativeness and creativity have a lot in common, which is why in psychological studies it is often considered as a determinant of innovativeness.[1] Although researchers do not entirely agree on what exactly it is and how to treat it – is it a final product, a process, or perhaps as a feature of a person, and which criteria to adopt so that a given idea can be considered creative – many of them consider that creativity can be reduced to the production of new and useful ideas or solutions (e.g. Oldham and Cummings, 1996).

One of the first concepts of creativity was the theory by Guilford (1978), one of the greatest scholars of human intelligence. He identifies creativity with divergent thinking, which involves finding multiple solutions to one problem; however, subsequent studies have not confirmed this relationship (Barron and Harrington, 1981; Runco, 2004). Guilford also distinguished the criteria for creative thinking: fluidity, meaning the ease of generating ideas and adding to their number, flexibility, understood as the ability to change the direction of thinking, as reflected in the diversity of solutions (number of categories), and originality, or the uniqueness, singularity and inimitability of these solutions.

Because the research on the relationship of creativity and intelligence has been fairly inconsistent and has not confirmed a strong correlation between them, attention turned towards cognitive styles, or ways of processing information, of approaching and solving problems, or the "preferred way of performing cognitive functions" (Nęcka,

---

1   However, the relationship of creativity to innovation, despite appearances, it is not at all clear. For example, Sohn and Jung's research (2010) conducted in Korean companies showed that, although the organizational variables have a bearing on creativity, its bearing on innovation in them – not.

2001, p. 125). The most common approach is Kirton's theory, which distinguishes two styles: innovative and adaptive. Adapters are described as people who "do things better;" they prefer to improve the group and/or organisation within the status quo. Kirton defines them as: those who seeking accepted solutions, maintaining high precision performance for long periods of time, or providing a secure base for the risky activities of the innovators. The innovators are people who "do things differently;" they are less focused on operating within existing structures. Kirton describes them as seemingly undisciplined, approaching problems from an unforeseen perspective, able to carry out specific tasks only in short bursts, and having a low level of doubt when generating ideas (Stum, 2009; Bagozzi, 1995). Kirton emphasizes that to achieve the objectives of the group both those presenting innovative and adaptive cognitive styles are required. The first is responsible for coming up with and introducing innovations, the second – consolidating and improving these changes.

An interesting relationship with innovation/creativity has been observed in the range of knowledge related to the subject of innovation – no or too little knowledge, but also too high a level disadvantageously affects the generation of innovative solutions (in: Patterson et al., 2009). This relationship may be due on the one hand to the inability to create something out of nothing, and on the other hand, too much information can be a kind of psychological barrier that locks the individual into the statement: "I know this like no other, and I know that in this matter, there's nothing more to think of." Such an approach may result in not making any effort in the direction of generating new solutions.

12.1.2. Personality

Is the creative mind itself enough to create something that nobody has previously invented? What distinguishes creative individuals from the rest, not only in terms of processing information, but also mode of action, relationships with others, etc.? Nęcka (2001) gives three qualities that characterize creative people: openness, independence, and perseverance. The importance and role of these characteristics depend on the phase of the creative process. These features partially overlap with the results of research on the relationship of creativity and personality traits. Of these, the most commonly taken into consideration is the Big Five Model, according to which personality can be described by five dimensions: openness to experience, extraversion, conscientiousness, agreeableness, and neuroticism. Openness to experience is also mentioned by Nęcka (2001), and means cognitive curiosity, tolerance for the new, unconventional thinking, independence of views, or the tendency to challenge authority (Zawadzki et al., 1998), and seems to be the best predictor of innovation. According to Nęcka (2001) it is particularly important in the latent phase of the innovation process, when an entity is observing, seeking, learning, verifying, analysing and synthesizing information related to the product of creativity – the result of these operations is a novel idea.

Another dimension showing a relationship with innovation is agreeableness, manifested in trust for others, sensitivity to human affairs, and cooperative behaviour. Low agreeableness means self-centeredness, competition, and scepticism about other people (Zawadzki et al., 1998). Interestingly, studies indicate that innovation is more associated with low agreeableness, which explains the fact that innovators are guided by the principle of social independence, otherwise they would not penetrate with their innovative ideas, which tend to cause resistance among the "conventional thinking." Therefore, some researchers believe that this independence of thought and action is particularly desirable, or even necessary, in the later stages of the innovation process, in bringing ideas to life. The role of autonomy in the innovation process is also mentioned by Nęcka (2001).

Conscientiousness – the next dimension of the Big Five, means scrupulousness, integrity in the performance of duties, a strong will, high motivation, and perseverance in action (Zawadzki et al., 1998), i.e. the features of an ideal employee. However, people with high conscientiousness are more resistant to change and more willing to submit to social norms, which is contrary to behaviour aimed towards creative solutions. And this dependence is confirmed by some studies that observed a relationship between low conscientiousness and innovation (Barron and Harrington, 1981; Gelade, 1997; Runco, 2004).

For the last two dimensions – extraversion and neuroticism – their relationship with innovation is much less clear. Some researchers (Feist, 1998) believe that introversion, or reserve in social interaction, lack of optimism, and a preference to be alone (Zawadzki et al., 1998) is positively correlated with innovation, as solitude and isolation may contribute to the generation of new ideas. In contrast, other studies (Patterson et al., 2009) suggest that it is the polar opposite – extraversion can be a predictor of innovative solutions. It seems that the relationship of this dimension to innovation may depend largely on the context in which the innovation process takes place. In art introversion promotes the formation of works, but in the field of management – where human contact is the essence of the work – extraversion may be a better predictor, although further studies are indicated in this direction (Patterson et al., 2009). Similarly, the relationship of innovation with neuroticism, which is experiencing negative emotions, such as fear, frustration, resentment, guilt, low stress tolerance (Zawadzki et al., 1998), is not clear and seems to depend on the areas in which new solutions are generated.

12.1.3. Motivation

A separate factor to be taken into consideration when examining innovativeness is the motivation of the individual. Crucially important here is intrinsic motivation, which in one's behaviour means the internal energy generated through positive emotions such as joy or satisfaction from performing a given activity. External incentives, such as material benefits, recognition in the eyes of others, and even those of an altruistic character of higher order, play a supporting role here. In contrast, the action itself, whether in the form of physical or intellectual activity, brings the individual joy and is the source of broader creativity having much to do with innovativeness. It seems that intrinsic motivation is crucial in the early stages of the innovation process, such as generating ideas, but further, when the first ardour may dim somewhat, the voice of external motivators comes in the form of recognition for their efforts (Eisenberg and Cameron, 1996; Patterson et al., 2009). It is also important here to mention perseverance, which Nęcka lists (2001) as the third feature of creative people.

In summary, creative individuals are persons endowed with high intelligence, but not outstanding, broad-minded, showing considerable independence of opinion, unruly in action, not really attaching importance to any standards, rules, and legal and social regulations; driven by internal motivation consisting roughly of "satisfaction with the work being done" without any external reinforcements.

12.2. Innovativeness – job level factors

The job level factors, frequently described as job-level determinants of innovativeness are autonomy (within clearly defined goals) combined with a sufficient level of challenge and time. Stimulating and non-routine jobs are naturally positively associated with innovativeness, although too high a level of task complexity may lead to over-stimulation, exhaustion and stress, thereby overwhelming the employee and killing creativity (Parzefall et al., 2008, p. 171). This mechanism is discussed below from the perspective of Karasek's model of stress, in which a dynamic balance between situational demands and resources is recommended, as it is believed to provide opportunities for personal growth which in turn help to promote innovativeness.

Interesting findings have been cited in relation to the availability of material and time resources as a prerequisite for innovative outcomes. Although it seems important to have access to sufficient material resources in order to test different solutions, sometimes this may prevent employees from more creative behaviours. In reference to time constraints, however, it seems that lack of time pressure is positively related to creative solutions. Employees prefer to have enough "time to think," to learn and experiment and to test new ways (see Parzefall et al., 2008).

12.3. Innovation and teamwork

It is believed that the era of inventions and discoveries made individually has passed. Currently, humanity is entering a more complex reality, impossible to grasp by one even mentally brilliant individual. In science interdisciplinarity has long been promoted, and in the area of management, due to the implementation of increasingly larger and more complex, often international, projects, the emphasis is on teamwork skills. Therefore, it is important to understand the mechanisms of the group, both those that are favourable and inhibit teamwork, and especially their creative potential, which is the task of psychology and sociology. The factors that may play a role in the innovation process in the context of the team include the group norms that underpin organizational/group climate and the team roles in the context of Meredith Belbin's theory of team roles (2003, 2009).

12.3.1. Group norms

One of the basic group mechanisms determining the creation of innovative solutions are appropriate group norms that underpin the climate or culture. Norms and values provide clues for the members of the group about what is good and bad, which behaviours can expect acceptance, and which will ostracize them from the rest of the team. On the one hand, they are a kind of cement for the group, bringing a certain order, as well as a sense of security and predictability, on the other hand, too much attachment to the prevailing standards inhibits the growth of the group and may adversely affect the achievement of the purpose for which it was established (unless the norm in a team is breaking the rules). Norms may relate to the treatment of "renegades," people who have a different point of view on issues discussed from the rest of the team. Are their opinions respected, seen as an opportunity to solve the problem in an unconventional way, or just the opposite – "stepping out of line" is not welcome. In the literature a subject often discussed is the issue of the role of minorities in the group. Nemeth's studies (1986) show that a minority in the group (e.g. in terms of choice of solution options other than the remainder of the group) influences a view of the problem from another perspective by the other members and encourages them to think creatively.

12.3.2. Organizational/group climate

Group norms and values form the basis of organizational climate, defined e.g. as "characteristic of a given set of norms conditioning company employee behaviour ... and determines the framework of conduct for employees in a given organization"(Potocki, 1992, p. 32). Although the literature mainly talks about organizational climate, the very definition of the construct allows that the group may have a climate, except that the group climate is due to norms, and norms are one of the main attributes of the group (whether a few or several dozen members, which may then already be the organization).

West and Richter (2008) have identified six characteristics of the organizational climate that affect innovation at the level of the group (in: Patterson et al.,

2009). These included minority (and conflict) management in a constructive manner; and also: commitment that results from intrinsic motivation and identification with the group, participation in decision-making leading to greater cohesion within the group, the involvement of individual members, but also taking responsibility for their own actions, as well as promoting innovative ideas, and the development of a sense of security and trust within the group and "reflexivity."

12.3.3. Group roles

An entirely different matter which may be of importance in the process of innovation for the team is its proper construction. Meredith Belbin, work and organizational psychologist, for nine years has studied a variety of factors – including personality, intelligence, and the roles in the group of individual team members – that affected the efficiency and effectiveness of their work. Eventually he came to the conclusion that the most important, and practical, is the last factor, which is to build effective teams based on the capabilities and abilities of the individuals to perform specific roles in the group. He distinguished nine of them and called them: the practical organizer, the leader, the locomotive, the evaluator, the group man, the perfectionist, the specialist, the contactor, and the creator. From the standpoint of this study the latter two roles are of paramount importance. Belbin's long-term observations led him to conclude that the performance of the group, especially when it comes to its innovativeness, depends to a large extent on the presence of a person who has a predisposition to act as a creator, i.e. an individualist with a rich imagination, great knowledge, an unconventional look at the problems, and an introverted disposition, and a seeker of sources – the inquisitive individual, responsive to change, with the need to explore new territories, and, unlike the predecessor – with the characteristics of an extrovert. Interestingly, the number of innovators in the group has little effect on the final result in the form of innovative solutions implemented in life. Too many creative ideas are not best handled by the rest of the members of the group, which Belbin quite aptly likens to excessive use of even the best ingredient in the dish. A similar effect was observed in groups of people with above-average intelligence, called the Apollo effect (Belbin 2003, 2009).

In summary, the creative potential of individuals has a chance to develop if it falls on fertile ground in the group in which they have to work. In such a group the appropriate standards and a climate supporting innovation should dominate, through respect and tolerance of different views of all members of the group. The same group has a chance for a novel approach to the problem, provided that there are creative individuals in their ranks assisted by other members of the team, complementing the deficiencies and low levels of skills and abilities that creators and seekers of sources do not have, but needed, or even essential to the whole process of innovation.

12.4. Innovation and the organization

Current projects of an innovative nature generally require adequate funding and coordination of the efforts of many people. These conditions can only be met by organizations. However, not all organizations are innovative. What differentiates them from those that do not implement innovative ideas? The factors related to the innovation and creativity of individuals at the level of the organisation most commonly taken into account and analysed by researchers are primarily appropriate leadership, and also organizational factors, such as a sense of control, and workload. It should be emphasized that the same variables are important at the level of the group.

12.4.1. The role of leadership

Leadership in the group and the organization plays an important, not to say essential, role. The climate in the group depends largely on the leader; this is so because of their power – they select their colleagues, forms the group norms, and finally, the leader is the one who is the example for other employees to follow. Anderson and King (1991) proposed a model in which, depending on the phase of the innovation process, the leaders perform different roles (for details, see Figure 12.1).

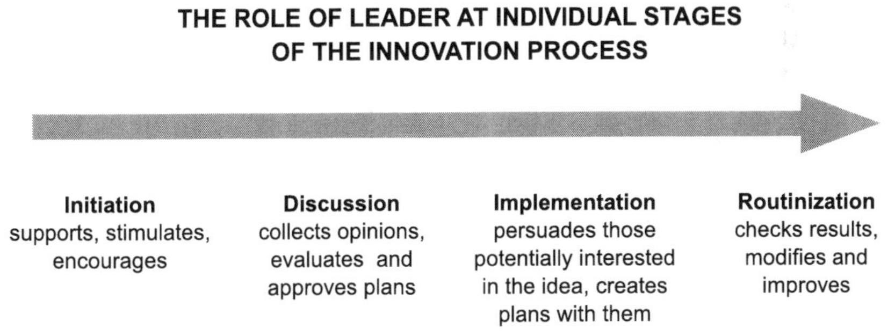

**THE ROLE OF LEADER AT INDIVIDUAL STAGES
OF THE INNOVATION PROCESS**

Initiation	Discussion	Implementation	Routinization
supports, stimulates, encourages	collects opinions, evaluates and approves plans	persuades those potentially interested in the idea, creates plans with them	checks results, modifies and improves

Figure 12.1. Model of the leadership role in the innovation process
Source: based on N. Anderson, N. King (1991), "Managing innovation in organizations," *Leadership and Organization Development Journal*, Vol. 12, pp. 17–21.

At the early stages of the innovation process, the basic role of the leader is to support their subordinates and colleagues, encouraging them to analyse the problem and come up with solutions. Then, it is important to create the right atmosphere in the group, in which there is no place for fear of criticism, and workers can share their ideas without interruption. After the selection and arrangement of the details of the solution of the problem, the tasks of the leader are to bring the idea to life, which involves convincing people outside the project group. At the final stage, the role of the leader is to check the results, control and introduce possible improvements in the solution. This model is consistent with contemporary theoretical approaches to leadership, according to which not only the specific personality or intellectual traits play a role in effective and efficient leadership, but more the ability to adapt to different situations and respond appropriately depending on the circumstances (see typology of leadership styles by Boyatzis et al., 2002).

12.4.2. Organizational factors

Another factor associated with innovation at the level of the organization is the work environment and its organization. The results show that a moderate level of workload, sometime pressure, as well as giving employees more autonomy, all promote innovation. These results almost perfectly fit into the theory of job requirements – Karasek control (Widerszal-Bazyl, 2003), which assumes that employees are best motivated to work when they have a lot of responsibilities, but also control over their execution. The worst situation, increasing the risk of depression and burnout, is the case of a heavy workload with low control. Autonomy, and a sense of control are the subjects of psychological research in conjunction with many aspects of life, and the results are clear – everyone likes to control their situation, to have their "field for cultivation," for which they will be responsible and will occupy themselves with at their own discretion. Even more important is a sense of control in the context of innovation. As indicated by the study (see above), creative individuals are those who have their own opinions and are not afraid to express them (low agreeableness), do not like to submit to standards (low conscientiousness), have broad horizons, and have a high tolerance for change (openness to experience). Most likely, these people will not feel comfortable in an environment fortified by rules, regulations and standards where only the leader/manager is right, and the work/product is to be made according to fixed rules.

In summary, innovative ideas, especially those that require large amounts of money, are only likely to see the light of day if they are implemented by organizations. These, in turn, if they want to be innovative, should ensure a culture of innovation, whereby on the one hand they place high demands upon their employees, on the other – give them a large degree of autonomy in carrying out their work. It is also important to hire the appropriate managers, able to exploit the creative potential of their subordinates.

12.5. Multiple level summary of findings

Nowadays, when tasks are increasingly complex and the turbulence of the environment is one of its main features, it is impossible to effectively discuss issues related to innovativeness from one perspective or level. Employees interact and work within teams – not only with group members, but also contacting people from outside, such as clients. Teams are nested within organizations, thus determinants and inhibitors from each level may strongly impair others.

In the table below the findings are summarized on multiple level factors related to innovativeness, based on the literature review.

Table 12.1. Multiple level factors related to innovativeness

Level of analysis	Factors	Effect on innovativeness
Individual	Personality (Big Five Model) – openness to experience	+
	Personality (Big Five Model) – conscientiousness/extraversion/neuroticism/agreeableness	Mixed
	Goal orientation, proactivity	+
	Values – congruence of values, creativity, trust	+
	Values – conformity	–
	Thinking styles – systematic thinking	–
	Motivation – intrinsic motivation	+
	Risk avoidance (expected image of risk)	–
	Psychological states – negative affect/negative moods/emotional ambivalence	Mixed
Job	Job complexity, job required innovativeness	+
	Time pressure	Mixed
	Rewards	+
	Task and goal interdependence	+
Team	Leadership – transformational leadership, – supervisory support/supervisory empowerment behaviours/ supervisory benevolence, – supervisory expectations for creativity, – supervisory developmental feedback and non-close monitoring	+
	Co-workers – co-worker support/ creativity expectations by co-workers	+
	Presence of creative co-workers	Mixed
	Team composition – heterogeneity (diversity)/cognitive style/multidisciplinary	Mixed
	Expertise/experience/membership change	+
	Team climate participative safety/vision/support for innovation/task and goal orientation/conflict	Mixed
	Team climate – climate for excellence	+
	Team processes – information exchange/problem solving style/team participation	+

Organization	Management related factors – HR practices, – top managers' demographic characteristics (e.g., ownership, racial and gender diversity)	Mixed
	Leadership – transformational and transactional leadership/management support/top management leadership/cooperative conflict management	+
	Knowledge utilization and networks – knowledge search and spillover (transfer)/knowledge stock/social network	Mixed
	Absorptive capacity/intellectual capital	+
	Organization strategy – innovation strategy	+
	Availability of resources	Zero
	Exchange of resources/resource diversity and quality	+
	Climate Innovation climate/reflexivity climate/climate for psychological safety and personal initiative	+
	Culture – national culture (power distance, masculinity, uncertainty avoidance, individualism, social face)/empowerment	Mixed
	External environment – geographic distribution of R&D activity/environmental uncertainty/turbulence/dynamism/urbanization/community wealth/population growth/unemployment	Mixed
	Bureaucratic practices	–
	Corporate entrepreneurship as innovation	mixed

Source: literature review mainly based on: N. Anderson, C.K.W. De Dreu, D.A. Nijstad (2004), "The routinization of innovation research: A constructively critical review of the state-of-the-science," *Journal of Organizational Behavior*, Vol. 25, pp. 147–172; M.-R. Parzefall, H. Seeck, A. Leppanen (2008), "Employee innovativeness in organizations: A review on the antecedents," *Liiketaloudellinen Aikakauskirja, Finnish Journal of Business Economics*, Vol. 2, pp. 165-182.

Conclusion

The summary of this study is the model by the repeatedly cited research team here: Patterson, Kerrin and Gatto-Roissard (2009), who reviewed the study for factors that were primarily psychological in nature associated with innovation. The factors analysed were grouped into individual resources, primarily personality and intellectual traits related to the motivation of the individual and their level of knowledge in a given field, then – social, which included a network of contacts, an appropriate leadership style depending on the phase of the innovation process (see: Anderson and King, 1991), organizational, like climate and organizational culture, ways of managing human resources, as well as the working environment, which includes autonomy and external factors, independent of the people directly involved in the innovation process, e.g. state policy, the presence or absence of competition, etc. These groups of factors fulfil different roles depending on the stage of the innovation process, of which the authors mention five, i.e. the ability to identify the problem, initiation and generation of ideas, development and the search for solutions, implementation and stage "after," in which any possible changes and improvements are effected. Of course we may argue with the authors on the merits of assessment of some factors to one group and not another, though no doubt this model is an attempt to organize the existing research results in the field of psychology, sociology, and management for the determinants of innovation and innovativeness in contemporary organizations.

It should be noted that the authors of this model emphasize that the process of innovation does not always pass through all the stages delineated, and may not necessarily be linear, because the individual phases may overlap, and some not occur at all. Also, a given resource need not be relevant in every case. The weakness of the model is not taking into account the barriers and obstacles emerging in the way of innovative ideas.

Kożusznik (2010) cites examples of barriers which were detected after analysis of interviews with more than 500 executives of Polish enterprises. These barriers included on an individual basis, such as anxiety associated with expressing their own opinions and judgments, and the lack of a sense of security and confidence in the success of any changes; team obstacles associated with low soft competences such as an inability to conduct group discussions and group problem solving. A significant barrier to innovation focuses on managers themselves, who treats their subordinates as people who do what they are told, and not as a potential, an opportunity, involving the use of their knowledge, skills and experience to create some change. Other barriers included the communication problems related to difficulties with the clear transfer of information, organization of meetings, where issues related to the work can be discussed and clarified. The last obstacle concerns the implementation of an appropriate incentive system, involving just rewards for employees' efforts, and sometimes even noticing them by management.

The process of innovation is a very complicated phenomenon where its practitioners and researchers have more questions than answers. To be better understood, and thus, more easily and quickly run, we need to know all the determinants that condition it, as well as barriers to innovativeness, including those that are economic, political, and psychological. Psychology plays a special role because, as was mentioned in the introduction, the individual in the innovation process is the most important, along with their ability to change the surroundings/environment in which they live, as well as fear and resistance against what is new, because unknown and untested. This very brief overview will only serve to familiarize readers do not have any knowledge of psychology to the complexity of the issues facing innovation in this field.

Literature

Anderson, N., King, N. (1991), "Managing innovation in organizations," *Leadership and Organization Development Journal*, Vol. 12, pp. 17-21.

Anderson, N., De Dreu, C.K.W., Nijstad, D.A. (2004), "The routinization of innovation research: A constructively critical review of the state-of-the-science," *Journal of Organizational Behavior*, Vol. 25, pp. 147-172.

Bagozzi, R.P. (1995), "Construct validity and generalizability of the Kirton Adaptation-Innovation Inventory," *European Journal of Personality*, Vol. 9, pp. 185-206.

Barron, F.B., Harrington, D.M. (1981), "Creativity, intelligence, and personality," *Annual Review of Psychology*, Vol. 32, pp. 439-476.

Belbin, M. (2003), *Twoja rola w zespole*, Gdańsk: Gdańskie Wydawnictwo Psychologiczne.

Belbin, M. (2009), *Zespoły zarządzające. Sekrety ich sukcesów i porażek*, Kraków: Oficyna Wolters Kluwer.

Boyatzis, R., Goleman, D., McKee, A. (2002), *Naturalne przywództwo. Odkrywanie mocy inteligencji emocjonalnej*, Wrocław-Warszawa: Jacek Santorski – Wydawnictwo Biznesowe.

Eisenberg, R., Cameron, J. (1996), "The detrimental effects of reward: Myth or reality?," *American Psychologist*, Vol. 51, pp. 1153-1166.

Feist, G.J. (1998), "A meta-analysis of personality in scientific and artistic creativity," *Personality and Social Psychology Review*, Vol. 2, pp. 290-309.

Feist, G.J., Barron, F.X. (2003), "Predicting creativity from early to late adulthood: Intellect, potential, and personality," *Journal of Research Personality*, Vol. 37, pp. 62-88.

Gelade, G. (1997), "Creativity in conflict: The personality of the commercial creative," *Journal of Genetic Psychology*, Vol. 165, pp. 67-78.

Guilford, J.P. (1978), *Natura inteligencji człowieka*, Warszawa: Państwowe Wydawnictwo Naukowe.

Kożusznik, B. (2010), "Kluczowa rola psychologii we wspieraniu i stymulowaniu innowacyjności," [in:] B. Kożusznik (ed.), *Psychologiczne uwarunkowania innowacyjności*, Vol. 2(35), Katowice: Wydawnictwo Uniwersytetu Śląskiego, pp. 21-50.

Mathisen, G.E., Martinsen, O.M., Einarsen, S. (2008), "The relation between creative personality composition, innovative team climate and team innovativeness: An input process – output perspective," *The Journal of Creative Behaviour*, Vol. 42, pp. 13-31.

Nemeth, C.J. (1986), "Differential contributions of majority and minority influence," *Psychological Review*, Vol. 93, pp. 23-32.

Nęcka, E. (2001), *Psychologia twórczości*, Gdańsk: Gdańskie Wydawnictwo Psychologiczne.

Nęcka, E. (2005), *Inteligencja. Geneza, struktura, funkcje*, Gdańsk: Gdańskie Wydawnictwo Psychologiczne.

Oldham, G.R., Cummings, A. (1996), "Employee creativity: Personal and contextual factors at work," *Academy of Management Journal*, Vol. 39, pp. 607-634.

Parzefall, M-R., Seeck, H., Leppanen, A. (2008), "Employee innovativeness in organizations: A review on the antecedents," *Liiketaloudellinen Aikakauskirja, Finnish Journal of Business Economics*, Vol. 2, pp. 165-182.

Patterson, F., Kerrin, M., Gatto-Roissard, G. (2009), *Characteristics and Behaviours of Innovative People in Organizations. Literature Review*, A paper prepared for the NESTA Policy & Research Unit (NPRU), London: NESTA, pp. 1-63, http://www.nesta.org.uk/sites/default/files/characteristics_behaviours_of_innovative_people.pdf [accessed 1.06.2014].

Potocki, A. (1992), *Wybrane metody humanizacji pracy*, Wrocław: Ossolineum.

Runco, M. (2004), "Creativity," *Annual Review of Psychology*, Vol. 55, pp. 657-687.

Sohn, S.Y., Jung, Ch.S. (2010), "Effect of creativity on innovation: Do creativity initiatives have significant impact on innovative performance in Korean firms?," *Creativity Research Journal*, Vol. 22(3), pp. 320-328.

Stum, J. (2009), "Kirton's adaptation-innovation theory: Managing cognitive styles in times of diversity and change," *Emerging Leadership*, Vol. 2(1), pp. 66–78.

Trompenaars, F. (2010), *Kultura innowacji*, Warszawa: Oficyna Wolters Kluwer.

Widerszal-Bazyl, M. (2003), *Stres w pracy a zdrowie, czyli o próbach weryfikacji modelu Roberta Karaska oraz modelu: wymagania–kontrola–wsparcie*, Warszawa: CIOP-BIP.

Zawadzki, B., Strelau, J., Szczepaniak, P., Śliwińska, M. (1998), *Inwentarz osobowości NEO-FFI Costy i McCrae. Adaptacja polska. Podręcznik*, Warszawa: Pracownia Testów Psychologicznych Polskiego Towarzystwa Psychologicznego.

Chapter 13

From Innovation to Innovative Gender

Ewa Okoń-Horodyńska

Abstract

Of interest in this chapter is the search for the wider sourcing of creative ability because traditional methods have failed to solve a variety of problems – social, political, daily life, family, economic, cultural, and religious – which as unconventional and practical applications become innovations. How multidimensional the abilities to tackle them are also depends on the ability to develop innovation. In view of the growing importance of gender studies, the conditions indicated should include another one, namely gender. And the concept of Innovative Gender has been accepted, ascribing to women and men equal measure, opportunities and situations included in the model of the innovation genome. The starting point of the Innovative Gender study is to build four dedicated matrices filled with information (variables) describing a given area including gender, among which the crucial one is cooperation.

Key words: creativity, innovation, innovativeness, innovative gender

Introduction

In spite of the diagnosis that the European Union is burdened with a triple crisis – of substance, trust and power (Kukliński, 2011) – leading to its institutional weakening on the global stage as an innovator, the growing predominance of thinking via procedures, and the expansion of the overwhelming control limiting freedom of choice, more offensives and strategies to intensify the development of research and innovation in all Member States are constantly being created. The failure to achieve the goals of the Lisbon Strategy is explained by a lack of political will and the conviction of heads of state that the objectives were too ambitious and that they lacked a cohesive policy between the whole European Union and the strategies of individual Member States, which is further compounded by the poor state of public finances in many EU countries and the crisis of 2008. A kind of "extension" of the Lisbon strategy is the Europe 2020 Innovation Union, and in particular the use of the procedure to shift the trust and support of innovative activity to the regions. Will yet another programme free EU innovation from its "straitjacket" (*Green Paper on Innovation*, 1995)? Entrepreneurs argue that EU regulations harm innovation, and universities that the use of EU support, which, it is true, has enabled a leap forward in improving the quality of infrastructure, in the long run will lead to the financial collapse of institutions that dramatically take out loans necessary for their own contribution to projects and maintaining this infrastructure, and they are already no longer sufficient for the research. Of interest in this chapter is the search for the wider sourcing of creative ability, because traditional methods have failed to solve a variety of problems – social, political, daily life, family, economic, cultural, and religious – which as unconventional and practical applications become innovations. How multidimensional the abilities to tackle the mare, both those inherent in people, motivated by the market, organized or elemental, as well as those aided or impeded by state policy in different countries or regions, also depends on the ability to achieve innovation. In view of the growing importance of gender studies, the conditions indicated should include another, namely gender. This article is a contribution to the research project now underway at the Jagiellonian University in Kraków; a presentation of proposals for research areas in which the role of gender in the innovation process can be captured. On this basis, it will be possible to develop research methods which will enable assessment of the strength of this relationship symbolically defined in the InnoGend project.

13.1. Innovation, innovativeness – the driving force for development

Although the literature contains many and increasingly diverse definitions of innovation, just as in the process of innovation the literature contains many proposals for models that were created over the last 30 years of the previous century, there is no way not to refer to these once again; however, the keynote is this time to seek changes in the economy and society, denoting innovation, in which gender may be of particular importance. Driven by the probably Latin origin of the word innovation – *innovare* or "creating something new" – the definitions formulated by many famous scientists emphasize that innovation is "the process of converting existing possibilities into new ideas and putting them into practical use. It is, briefly speaking, the introduction of new products, processes or procedures to broad use" (Allen, 1966, p. 7). In this trend, for example, industrial innovations and specific steps towards their formation could be pointed at (Freeman, 1982), or, specific abilities, skills, competences of entrepreneurs (Drucker, 1985). Companies achieve competitive advantage through innovation if they introduce innovation in a broad sense (Porter, 1990). In the same vein, Fagerberg writes about innovation as "the application of new ideas in practice (2006), and the conversion of ideas

into activities which bring benefits" (Stachell, 1998, pp. 33–34).The importance of the commercialization of ideas and concepts is particularly exposed by the point that "… the commercialization of innovation does not necessarily imply only the highest technological achievements (radical innovation), but also includes the use and practical application of know-how, even on a small scale (incremental improvement, innovation)" (Rothwell and Gardiner, 1985, p. 168) as in practice not all innovation is based on inventions (Jasiński, 1997). For some researcher innovation is about creating value out of ideas, concepts Soete (2006), when the ideas are brought to the market in the form of new products, better designs, better manufacture or distribution and when it all takes place within the institutional environment of the national innovation system. In this context, just as in Freeman (1987), which decided to locate the concept of a "national system of innovation" in economic theory, the scale of elements describing the concept of innovation greatly expands, emphasizing the importance of qualitative changes in the development of innovation, such as changes in the system of education, science, engineering and technology, the intensity of cooperation between the actors involved in the innovation process; there is also a causal investigation of these changes that in different ways activate or destructively influence people's behaviour. Schumpeter, considered one of the forerunners of innovation theory, emphasized that innovation is virtually in the centre of all phenomena, difficulties and problems of the economic life of the capitalist community. The sense of innovation here is "the formation of a new production function" (Schumpeter, 1939, p. 87). The entrepreneur is characterized by dynamism and innovativeness and thus creates new businesses, new products, introduces a new organization of production and new production technologies. The entrepreneur-innovator therefore decides on the driving force for economic development and the concept of innovation refers to broader creative human activity. Schumpeter's marking of the special role in the development of the economy through innovation by entrepreneurs has over the years been the basis for many researchers to seek a definitional basis and modelling within this conception. Innovations make a "new combination of factors," which may be caused by (Schumpeter, 1960, p. 128):
- introducing new or improving existing products,
- using new or improving previous production methods,
- opening a new market (expansion into a new market),
- introducing new ways of buying and selling,
- gaining a new source of raw materials (using new raw materials or semi-finished products),
- introducing a new method of organization (changing the current method of organizing the production process).

This definition is regarded as a classic, and began the discussion on the importance of innovation in economic development, both in a positive sense, providing a jump in the growth of economic efficiency, as well as negative, because it is capable of inducing economic crises. It is true that many flaws are attributed to it (Czerniak, 2013, pp. 14–15) such as its too broad scope, tautology, open nature, and lack of usefulness in practice, so from the point of view of the considerations here we need to underline its usefulness. Schumpeter's, one might say theory, of innovation, is invariably a reference to establishing the importance of innovation as a driver of economic growth, which in particular is also emphasized in the current policy of the European Union (Europe 2020, 2010). The broad approach to innovation also enables us to capture areas in which the importance of gender would be possible to determine. Particularly important here is the whole sphere of innovative entrepreneurship, in the assessment of which the significance of gender and the resulting specific predispositions already constitute a significant range (mazowia.eu). In addition, this definition implies a clear and strict reference to the commercial dimension of innovation, in which the processes of production and distribution are of decisive importance, hence considerations should apply only to the appropriate competences to these processes. In this view, the technical changes and organizational changes required and only partly social ones underlie innovation and are identified with the new, or with the modified, which has been brought forward to modern, institutional definitions of innovation (Oslo Manual, 2005). Alongside the digressions as to its too broad and general treatment of innovation, there is also the question of the scale of newness as the essence of innovation. Within the broad understanding of innovation, the reference to the new, as the basal characteristic of innovation is sometimes regarded subjectively. For example, Kotler (1978, p. 224) believes that "… the concept of innovation refers to any good, which is seen by some as new," while, within a narrow understanding of innovation, Mansfield, says to the contrary, that "An invention which has been used for the first time is an innovation" (Mansfield, 1968, p. 99, introducing a reservation as to the understanding of new). There is certainly no doubt in this case about Freeman's definition, from which it follows that not every novelty can be considered an innovation, but only that which is "… the first commercial introduction (application) of a new product, process, system or device" (Freeman, 1982, p. 7). In any case, it may not be necessary to discern definitional compliance as to the scale of the key fact that determines innovation, which is "novelty." Does the scale relate to individuals, companies, the economy or the global market, or to producers or consumers. Here radical definitions, declaring innovation to be "novelty" at the scale of the economy (Schmookler, 1966), collide with decidedly weaker definitions in which, to be able to talk about innovation, "novelty" merely refers to a product, process, organization of the company, work, or enterprise-scale marketing (OECD, 2005, pp. 46–47), disregarding the requirement of absolute novelty and originality on the global market (Hall, 1994, p. 17). The practice, however, drastically verifies this approach, in fact, it is the leaders of innovation who count in the world; all the rest are only "followers." Invariably the catalogue of innovation characteristics distinguished, and therefore the processes in which they are born, may include (Okoń-Horodyńska, 1998):

1. Combining the intellectual elements with material. Every innovation must be preceded by mental work containing creative elements, and triggering creativity. This connection implies today, often ineffectively (as in Poland) by regulation, the

institutionalization of mediation at the interface between the industrial sphere and R&D facilities (e.g. higher education, research and development bodies, research institutes), and requirements apply here to professional solving of both theoretical and methodological and practical problems.

2. The increase in the role of the intellectual element, which together with industrial development has become an essential factor in any progress (knowl-edge-based economy, creative economy). An external expression of increasing the role of the theoretical and methodological preparation for changes in industrial production is the creation of a variety of scientific and research and development institutions (an increase the number of places where knowledge is created and where creativity is taught), specializing in intellectual, pre-production, innovation activity, and expansion of the scale of specific education, as well as technology transfer.

3. The accelerated increase in mixing the complexity of the relationships be-tween intellectual and material elements, as well as the internal complexity of these components, due to the turbulent changes in the technosphere, the increasing complexity of systems, new data, incomplete knowledge, new issues, people, and risks. The practical work is combined with the necessity of a multidisciplinary and interdisciplinary (holistic) approach to solving problems related to the operation of the innovation process. There is also a need to integrate practical activities, and the continuous interpenetration of intellectual and material elements carried by specialized cells in the production process, determined by the social environment.

4. Innovation is characterized by a degree of risk and uncertainty higher than in other ventures (incomplete knowledge) in the process of creating innovation and obtaining the desired scale of innovations as results of innovative activity.

5. The need to ensure the leading participation of the best cells of human poten-tial in a given system, its multidimensional skills and tangible economic research facilities ensuring that innovative changes are carried through. This best potential functions as a paradigm for other entities involved in innovation processes.

6. Innovations force a growing relationship between the degree of maturity of the innovation processes and the dynamics of the development of industry, economy and society, forcing innovation on society, a culture of innovation, the growing involvement of the public in innovative activity takes on a permanent character. Lack of innovation entails the inefficiency of the economy to solve com-plex problems hitherto unknown, which ultimately results in a waste of manpower and resources and inhibits growth.

7. Although technological innovation, regarded as a determinant of the process of taking a lead in the global economy, is still considered decisive in modern com-petition, approaches that focus on social innovation are being developed with great intensity. Hence, the European Commission has also strongly verified its approach to innovation by introducing a definition of social innovation understood as: "The development and implementation of new ideas (products, services and models) to meet social needs and the creation of new social relations and cooperation" (European Commission, 2013).

8. Innovation is a business tool, it requires the creation of better jobs, which, according to Schumpeter's approach, means that it provides resources with new opportunities to create wealth.

9. Innovations determine the competitiveness of a company and an economy, which means that they decide on the presence of a company in the market and the position of the economy on the global scale.

10. Innovations have the ability to polarize entities and sectors of the economy, and also countries and regions of the world, in terms of the level of innovation in the economy. Because the innovativeness of an economy entails creativity, creative capabilities, the formation of new social relations and motivation for traders towards innovative activity, comprising a constant search for new results for scientific research, R&D work, new concepts and ideas, to develop and launch the production of new or improved materials, products, equipment, services, processes or methods devoted to the market or to meet the variety of social needs necessary in practice.

Following the aforementioned features the following two constitutive elements of innovation should be distinguished:

- Innovative change – which, in contrast to unintended changes is at least to some extent prepared and developed in an intentional way in the process of innovation.
- Actual innovation – a feature that should characterize the baseline of innovation as an intentional process. The degree of novelty imposes on the innovation development process an additional risk that arises from the possibility of not achieving economic success. Thus the problem of measuring the sources and effects of innovation becomes more justified because not every product, service or process that meets the criteria of innovation brings tangible benefit for the company just because it meets the criteria of innovation.

It seems that one of the more useful sources for Innovative Gender from the point of view of the search for approaches to innovation, is the one that selects the scale of innovation on the basis of the consumer and the manufacturer (Hirsh and Peters, 1978, p. 9). Through innovation the consumer stabilizes or changes the consumption patterns and the following have an impact here (Jasiński, 1997, p. 12):

- Continuous innovation determined, for example, by tastes, a fashion for colours, sizes, shapes, etc.,
- Dynamic continuous innovations triggered by a wave of some technical changes, e.g. the electric toothbrush, knife, comb, massage device, still current today and even solar powered,
- Discontinuous innovation – extremely rare, different from anything known before, and requiring the consumer to lean to use and enjoy.

The manufacturer, on the other hand, assesses the degree of novelty commercially and technologically. So, it is important to improve the product, replace it, make minor physical changes, expand the product lines, and diversify. It is hard not to see that it is the consumer point of view on innovation in the process of creating a model of consumption and even a consumption strategy may be a good field of research for the assessment of the significance of gender in innovation activity. Even general observation allows us to show that women subordinate decisions about choosing consumption patterns to tastes or fashion, and men technical usability, to a much higher degree.

Since, as demonstrated with a significant sample, innovation is defined in different ways, further agonizing over definitions can be omitted for now, knowing there is a large literature on the subject. Another issue, however, seems to be worth signalling. The increasing complexity of productive life as a fundamental element of the management process creates fewer and fewer opportunities to give birth to an ad hoc innovation as a sudden "miracle" solution. Although, as Drucker states, there is more innovation based on "brilliant ideas" than all the rest put together – about seven out of every ten patents – they are the most risky and least effective source of opportunity to innovate, and are characterized by the greatest "mortality" (Drucker, 1985, pp. 143-145). Therefore, today the essence of innovation should be seen rather in its permanent, systematic and consistent character. This approach has also been adopted, for example, by the European Union, which has been trying for years to implement a European innovation policy (Okoń-Horodyńska, 2013), as schematically shown below. Unfortunately, the institutional environment for expanding innovation policy in the EU through the multiplication of programmes and regulation stifles people's creativity and strengthens the bureaucracy and waste of public funds. This is one example of how even the best formulated programmes are converted into economic failures due to lack of strategy.

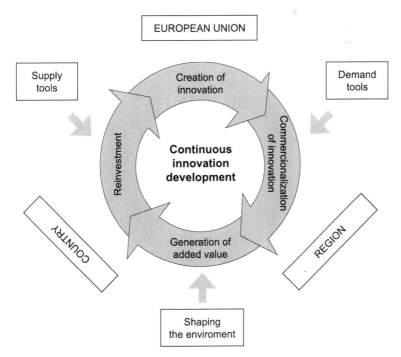

Figure 13.1. EU innovation policy environment
Source: own elaboration.

The philosophy determining the development of innovation of regularity and continuity of innovative activity is certainly associated with the security companies and economies in the unique resources as a source of not only innovation but also sustainable competitive advantage. This concept, developed in the resource approach to innovation, even assumes that a company is a collection of such rare material resources (production and technology) and intangibles (managerial knowledge, intellectual property rights, organizational culture) so difficult to imitate and replace, that have an impact on the business' results (Mizgajska, 2013). In particular, however, thanks to a specific set of resources, enterprises have a dynamic ability to integrate and reconfigure internal and external competencies in a rapidly changing environment, which allows them to create and innovate. However, this resource approach has also not avoided a kind of criticism, although interesting conclusions from research on the impact of workers' experience, competence, ability to co-operate, and knowledge in R&D as one of the indicators of innovation activity remain valid today. A company's and an economy's innovativeness depends on the state of originality and also availability of resources for innovation, considered to be one of the most progressive factors of socioeconomic development, even at the local level. Innovativeness is the ability and willingness of economic entities/regions to constantly seek and use in business practice different types of resources, such as the results of research and R&D, new concepts, ideas, inventions, improvement and development of technologies for producing material and non-material (services) goods, business models, skills and abilities of people, the introduction of new methods and techniques in organization and management, and the improvement and development of infrastructure and knowledge. Innovation and its sources are subject to a detailed measurement process acting on the place of a given company in the market in global competition or rankings of innovation leaders (IUS, 2013). In this thread we must also see the research field for the assessment of gender roles as the characteristics of one of the resources in achieving dynamic ability to innovative activity in the business, the economy, and society.

13.2. Dualism of innovation: creativity and commercial viability as a source of exploration of the importance of gender

Although the set of ideas presented on innovation and innovativeness does not in any way exhaust the definitional proposals contained in the rich literature on the subject, each in its own way shows that the sense of innovation should be seen in the driving force resulting in change in all its surroundings. And though they may have different natures, extents, and directions, starting from minor adjustments and ending in "upheavals," and that they are able to both facilitate and hinder our lives by constantly complicating the environment, they can also affect national security, or seriously affect the system of values, institutions and decision-making processes. So every element of that driving force, including gender, requires careful discernment and proper harvesting. In this sense, the best, definition, closing the discussion, is that innovations are hard, deliberate, focused work that requires knowledge, diligence, creativity, perseverance, and commitment; they require the use of the innovators' strongest points, and they are the effect induced in the economy and society, as they cause changed behaviour for both businesses and consumers (Drucker, 1985, pp. 152–153). There is no doubt, however, that the concept of "innovation" is used in a double sense:

1) on the one hand, it describes a process involving research, design and development, creating new relationships between people and also the organization of manufacture of a new product, process or system, which is often called the " innovation process," which lies at the basis of human creativity,

2) on the other hand, it describes the first use of a new product, process or system, achieved by commercialization.

The dimension of creativity indicates the potential of knowledge and skills at the same time to create something new. Although this is a thought process it leads to new, original ideas, concepts, associations and new ways of solving problems in practice. It is a process that is difficult to define, thus escaping simple schemata. For example, Einstein said that if he had an hour to solve a problem on which his life depended, he would devote 55 minutes to asking the right question and then even less than 5 minutes would be enough to solve the problem itself (http://www.ideachampions.com/weblogs/, accessed 15.02.2014). The creation of something new can occur because both as a result of painstaking research and quite by accident, and also as a result of intuitive impulses and imagination, unconventionally, as Einstein emphasized. Intuition and imagination are mostly conducive to knowledge and deep reflection, predispositions to explore the knowledge and the ability to use it. Creativity's uniqueness lies in the fact that it is actually inexhaustible: "You can't use up creativity. The more you use, the more you have" (Angelou, 2010). Let the exemplification of this thesis be the interesting set of quotes posted defining creativity on the website functioning under the slogan: *The Head of Innovation* (2010). And so:

–   "The things we fear most in organizations – fluctuations, disturbances, imbalances – are the primary sources of creativity." – *Alfred North Whitehead*
–   "The chief enemy of creativity is 'good sense.'" – *Pablo Picasso*
–   "Everyone who's ever taken a shower has had an idea. It's the person who gets out of the shower, dries off and does something about it who makes a difference." – *Nolan Bushnell*
–   "As competition intensifies, the need for creative thinking increases. It is no longer enough to do the same thing better … no longer enough to be efficient and solve problems." – *Edward de Bono*

- "I make more mistakes than anyone else I know, and sooner or later, I patent most of them." - *Thomas Edison*
- "Creativity is thinking up new things. Innovation is doing new things." - *Theodore Levitt*
- "The secret to creativity is knowing how to hide your sources." - *Albert Einstein*
- "Creativity is allowing yourself to make mistakes. Art is knowing which ones to keep." - *Scott Adams*
- "Don't think. Thinking is the enemy of creativity. It's self-conscious, and anything self-conscious is lousy. You can't try to do things. You simply must do things." - *Ray Bradbury*
- "Creativity is the sudden cessation of stupidity." - *Edwin Land*
- "There's room for everybody on the planet to be creative and conscious if you are your own person. If you're trying to be like somebody else, then there isn't." - *Tori Amos*
- "The key question isn't 'What fosters creativity?' But it is why in God's name isn't everyone creative? Where was the human potential lost? How was it crippled? I think therefore a good question might be not why do people create, but why do people not create." - *Abraham Maslow*
- "To live a creative life, we must lose our fear of being wrong." - *Joseph Chilton Pierce*
- "By believing passionately in something that still does not exist, we create it. The non-existent is whatever we have not sufficiently desired." - *Nikos Kazantzakis*
- "Creativity is discontent translated into arts." - *Eric Hoffer*
- "A truly creative person rids him or herself of all self-imposed limitations." - *Gerald Jampolsky*
- "Things are only impossible until they're not." - *Jean-Luc Picard*
- "Anxiety is the hand maiden of creativity." - *T.S. Eliot*
- "Creativity is piercing the mundane to find the marvellous." - *Bill Moyers*
- "The new meaning of soul is creativity and mysticism. These will become the foundation of the new psychological type and with him or her will come the new civilization." - *Otto Rank*
- "The more original a discovery, the more obvious it seems afterwards." - *Arthur Koestler*
- "It's not what you look at that matters, it's what you see." - *Henry David Thoreau*
- "If you have nothing at all to create, then perhaps you create yourself." - *Carl Jung*
- "I can't understand why people are frightened of new ideas. I'm frightened of the old ones." - *John Cage*

Creativity often escapes the canons of rationality which, in the commercial dimension in turn, are critical, and at first glance it apes the absurd, yet it can lead to the invention of something new, thanks to the unconventional imagination.

Defining precisely, but also identifying and measuring creativity as a process of creating something new is very difficult. If only because the "new" is often very variously understood and perceived, and sometimes, too, ignored. Creativity may indeed serve to improve the quality of social and economic life, but manipulated by a few it can reduce this quality. In recent years, the global crisis has exposed this spectacularly, where the substrate is primarily the creation of new financial instruments, including fraudulent pyramid schemes, toxic derivatives and other financial pseudo innovations. Another example is activities, highly detrimental to consumers and the environment (but driving the profits of producers), aimed at producing products on the market whose life span is short, or that forces the need for additional, complementary services and products (an example of this power supplied matching only one type of device, such as a computer, telephone, etc.). No coincidence that more and more researchers point to a new social phenomenon appearing – progress fatigue. This also ties in in practice with the decreasing marginal utility of progress. Difficulties in assessing and measuring creativity are also related to the scarcity of statistics on the subject and its meanders. In addition, a variety of social stereotypes and prejudices are superimposed on it, often erroneous assessment, which is highly correlated with gender stereotypes. Therefore, an important field of research for assessing the role of gender in creative activity would be the sphere of creative thinking and analysis of the defining elements of this skill.

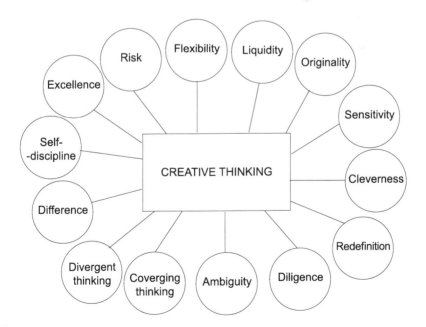

Figure 13.2. Key features of creative thinking
Source: own elaboration.

Bearing in mind that natural creativity reaches its peak in preschool, then definitely decreases – so that we can ensure these declines are not drastic we must constantly use different formulas to support it. Thus, for example, as a result of education, the acquisition and accumulation of knowledge can improve creative efficiency, which, however, left without improving the knowledge and application in education, life and work, techniques creativity have also been declining. Creativity techniques and deliberate raising awareness allows us to expand the scale of the characteristics of creative thinking, for example, excellence, self-discipline, openness to risk, otherness, and so on. Shaping these features is in essence determined by individual psychosocial and cultural predispositions, including gender. And, the scale of the use of these features determines the quality of our thinking (Figure 13.3) and the loss of creativity.

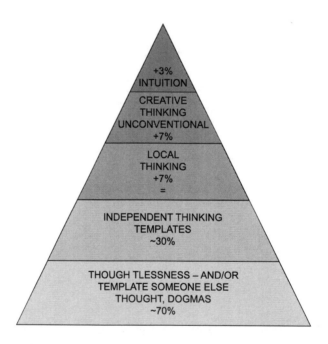

Figure 13.3. Pyramid of the quality of human thinking
Source: J. Chafee (2001), *Potęga twórczego myślenia*, Warszawa: Bertelsmann, p. 487, za: Cempel (2012).

Looking at the figure and taking the approach of Einstein, only 3% of thinking is the source of problem solving in an unconventional breakthrough way. It is thus hardly surprising that creativity, identified with the ability to look more broadly, bravely meeting challenges and with the ability to cope with any situation, is considered to be one of the most desirable features in today's job market. For some, creativity is an innate trait, others argue that the development of creativity can and should be taught (education and creativity techniques) and it is triggered primarily by (Tracy, 2010):

- clearly defined objectives – here first and foremost continuity of planning and focus on the benefits that realization of these objectives will bring us is emphasized. It is believed that achievement of the benefits constitute motivation and mobilization of our mind to look for new solutions and ideas, which can significantly facilitate the achievement of planned objectives,
- urgent problems – here it is important to have a reference to the ability to cross barriers, master obstacles, and transform them into challenges. Growing excitement and commitment to meet the challenges, increases the scale of creativity in action,
- specific questions – as already indicated in the quotation from Einstein, a well-constructed, sometimes uncomfortable, or provocative question can trigger a real volcano of creativity providing a rapid solution to a problem.

In the above context, creativity is also a base for research and development (basic research, applied, and experimental development) involving the pursuit of systematic conduct of creative work, undertaken to increase the stock of knowledge, including knowledge of humanity, culture and society, as well as for finding new uses for this knowledge.

According to official statistics, women are much less represented in the field of creativity, innovation, invention and scientific achievements. This is reflected, inter alia, by statistics for the Nobel Prize. Women Nobel Prize winners are less than 5% of the total awarded this prize. Men dominate decisively. There is a slightly more favourable image according to data on the number of double Nobel Prizes. This double prize has been awarded twice to four scientists so far, including one woman – Pole Maria Curie-Skłodowska (Nobel Prize for Physics in 1903 for her discovery of radioactivity, and Nobel Prize for Chemistry in 1911 for obtaining pure radium). However, in assessing the true role of women in the field of creativity we cannot in any event settle only on the figures. This is aptly captured by sentence from Albert Einstein: "Not everything that can be counted counts, and not everything that counts can be counted" (http://izquotes.com/quote/56404, accessed 21.02.2014). But attempts to measure creativity are commonly taken (Table 13.1), although gender issues are not included in them.

Although the examples of indicators measuring creativity presented give rise to a certain institutional assessment of the level of creativity in general, the ingenuity and creativity of women in solving many difficult issues of everyday life is not to be underestimated, nor in the major areas of social and economic life, including education, design, fashion, medicine, media, tourism, social communication, and in the sphere of culture (the creative industries). This is extremely important, but very difficult to measure, because it is not as spectacular as the great scientific discoveries, for example. In this sense, women are great but silent inventors. The Polish proverb "where the devil fails, you can send a woman there" exposes the great creative potential of women. Certainly better exploitation of the potential of women's creativity will be supported by growing segments of the information

Table 13.1. How to measure creativity

Indicator	Range	Source of information
European Creativity Index	Human capital, technology, institutional environment, openness and diversity, social environment	The contribution of culture to creativity, KEA, 2009
Hong Kong Index	A set of interacting variables which make up the creative environment	Home Affairs Bureau of the Hong Kong Special Administrative Region Government, A study on a Hong Kong Creativity Index, 2004
Euro-Creativity Index	Set of characteristics that attract the "creative class" – technology, tolerance, and talent	Europe in the creative age; Florida, 2004
Flemish Index	Technological innovation, entrepreneurship, openness of society. It is used for inter-regional comparisons	A Composite index of the Creative Economy, the Catholic University of Leuven, 2006
UNCTAD Global Data Base on the Creative Economy	International trade in creative-sector goods and services (export/import)	Creative Economy Reports 2008 and 2010, UNDP, UNESCO, UN
Indicators for innovativeness		
EIS, IUS	Technological innovation. It is used for comparisons between countries, the version poorer in variables (ERIS) also for interregional comparisons.	The European Innovation Scoreboard, The Innovation Union Scoreboard, European Commission

Source: own elaboration.

society, in this area there is definitely a growing demand for female staff. Through the use of their potential favourable conditions are created for the implementation of "social futurism," proposed by Alvin Toffler, primarily through the creation at all possible social and economic levels of centres focused on interdisciplinary "brain activation," in order to discover the social consultants of the future. Social futurism may be a remedy for the narrow economic technocracy and economic myopia, the more so because the progress and rate of change are rendering the traditional objectives of enterprises obsolete (Toffler, 2000), and foresight studies form the basis for building development strategies at various levels of the economy and society, and other institutions (Okoń-Horodyńska, 2011).

Creativity is a term that has left the field of theoretical discussion (Florida, 2002) and permanently placed itself in the economy, providing the basis for the formation of creative industries, experimentally in the UK (Department of Culture, Media and Sport, 1997), to awaken the desire for a creative economy in many other countries (Creative Economy 2008). Creative industries can be defined as those that have their origin in individual creativity, skill and talent and which have the potential to create wealth and jobs through the generation and exploitation of intellectual property. Originally, the areas falling within the creative industries were advertising, the antiques trade, architecture, crafts, design, fashion, film, video and computer games (programs for entertainment), music, the performing arts, publishing, software, and TV and radio; but today the scale is gradually broadening (Creative Economy, 2013, p. 22). The transition from intellectual discussion about creativity to its materialization may be the characteristics included in the definition that "Creativity is a holistic process by which ideas are generated, developed and transferred to value." And in this sense, creativity involves what people usually understand by the concept of innovation and entrepreneurship; it includes both the art of creation (birth) of new ideas and the discipline that gives these ideas shape and development until it is a realised value"(Kao, 1997, p. 17). "In the process of transformation of knowledge into value, the decisive variable is creativity" (Kao, 1997, p. 7). It should probably be added, however, that this is about the transformation of knowledge into an exchange value, and then it is already a transition from making the creative process in the laboratory or workshops, often ending in an invention, which is commercialized via the process of products and services whose place is on the market. In this context, the subject of interest is definitions that clearly define the need to focus on the dimension of commercial innovation. For example:

- "Commercial innovation is the result of the application of ingenuity associated with a business model, technology, or market to create a new product, process or service that will be successfully introduced to the market" (Alic et al., 1992, p. 43),
- "Innovation is the process by which an invention or idea is translated into the economy" (US Department of Commerce in 1967, p. 8),
- "Innovation requires at the same time close coordination of the relevant technical expertise and excellent knowledge and assessment of the market in order to achieve economic, technological, or other success. Only when these factors occur simultaneously can innovation bring economic or technological success" (Kline and Rosenberg, 1986, p. 275),
- "The road of innovation requires a significant commitment from many entrepreneurs in both the private and public sectors" (Van de Ven et al., 1999, p. 149),
- "Innovative change is the creation and marketing of new goods, new technologies and the accompanying restructuring of the organization's systems" (Janasz, 2004, p. 29).

The combination of creative and commercial approaches to innovation is included in the statement, that "... the invention is the first appearance of an idea ... while innovation is the first attempt of practical application on the market" (Fageberg et al., 2006, p. 4). Both the creative and commercial dimensions of innovation require specific skills where gender may be a domain or a barrier. These skills should cover a broad area of activities, such as:

- effective learning and knowledge accumulation,
- converting different (and sometimes absurd) knowledge resources into ideas of a rational nature,
- practical transformation of ideas into new products, services, processes, systems, and social interaction,
- creating new value streams that satisfy the shareholders of the company and ensure sustainable growth,
- creating new jobs,
- offering a new service to customers,
- improving the quality of life and promoting the sustainability of society,
- building alliances, cooperation,
- managing innovation, or managing all activities that contribute to the introduction of innovations on the market (to life) (EFQM, 2005, p. 5).

The development of science and technology, and changes in the ecosphere, mean that the concept of innovation and also the formation of its relationship with creativity change (Table 13.2, Figure 13.4).

Table 13.2. The evolution in the perception of innovation

Past	Present
Developed one-dimensionally.	Developed multi-dimensionally.
A discontinuous process.	A continuous, systematic process.
A means to achieve your own success.	The transition from the perception of innovation as a means to achieve your own success to joint success with a co-operator through the joint development of innovation.
The invention.	Innovation as a process.
A linear model of innovation.	A nonlinear dynamic model of innovation.
Based on the requirements of forecasts.	Is the answer to the sense and expectations – is the solution to a problem. It is the result of anticipating future expectations of the business environment in the broad sense and opportunities for science and technology.
Independent.	Interdependent. Innovations increasingly require the use of knowledge of many fields of science and technology at the same time.
Occurs in individual disciplines of science and technology.	It occurs as a result of cooperation between team understood as global R&D team structures, cooperating continuously (24x7).

Source: own elaboration based on C. Harris (2006), "Applying innovation", *IBM Innovation Week*, Eindhoven, p. 6, http://ec.europa.eu/enterprise/policies/innovation/files/ius-2013_en.pdf [accessed January 2014].

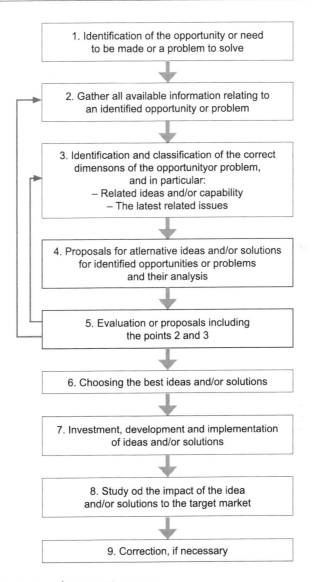

Figure 13.4. Creativity in the innovation process
Source: own elaboration based on P. McGowan (1987), "Creativity and innovation," [in:] D. Steward (ed.), *Handbook of Management Skills*, London: Gower Publishing Ltd., p. 490.

The process of globalization and the progressive computerization of the flow of information make the area of creativity and idea generation more important. Today's corporations use ideas management information systems, which are used to stimulate creative thinking and allow the acquisition, evaluation and selection of ideas for further development in the process of innovation. Acquisition of ideas, their management and the emergence of ideas for implementation has become an area in which many companies have arisen providing specialized services, included in the creative industries. The need for continuous, permanent (Morris, 2006) development of innovation in the enterprise and society also requires the exploration of ideas continuously, and is an extension of the supplier– recipient relationship in favour of partnership, to create a space for the exchange of information as to the ideas and suggestions from partners, buyers of the product who in this way gain influence on the shape of the product they purchase. The manufacturer gains a source of ideas, which they examine, and select those that will enter development as product innovation. In the group of partners, the manufacturer also gains a group of regular customers. This kind of phenomenon is observed increasingly frequently, e.g., in the practice of the functioning of IT companies, it refocuses the supplier–customer relationship for the provision of complex forms of services comprising the continuous development of innovative products. This leads to the concept of building an ecosystem of innovation in the corporation, whose central element is an innovation process that develops continuously. Because creativity is bears ideas, and these in turn are a source of innovation, therefore an important issue becomes their continuous acquisition. In the face of the increasing complexity of innovative products, a problem arises in the collaboration between professionals from different fields of science and technology as well as companies, universities and R&D centres. Looking at the economy as an environment for the development and deployment for innovation, where diverse knowledge is used, is at the same time concentrating on creativity, which is a catalyst for the development of science, technology, competence, abilities and skills, the more effective it is, the closer to balanced cultural characteristics, and therefore gender.

13.3. Why Innovative Gender

As has been mentioned earlier, innovation has been given a prominent role in the new Europe 2020 Strategy and in one of its "flagship initiatives," the Innovation Union. Recruiting and retaining women in scientific and technical fields is seen as a key to success for the 2020 Strategy. A number of studies and reports have stressed the acute problem of women's under-representation in science in the business enterprise sector. Whilst women represent over 35% of all researchers in the higher education and government sectors of most European countries, this is not the case for the corporate sector. The percentage of female researchers in the business enterprise sector is less than 25% in most countries (Europe, 2020). Yet another flagship initiative under the 2020 Strategy, the New Skills and Jobs Agenda, focuses on the need to modernize labour markets, increase labour participation and match labour market and skills. Studies show that the European labour shortage is likely to have more effect on female or male dominated occupations than on less divided sectors (European Commission, 2009). Occupations in healthcare and ICT are already affected by the shortage of professionals in Europe. For example, the rapidly growing demand for ICT specialists was one of the motivators behind the European Code of Best Practices for Women and ICT launched by the European Commission (Vinnova, 2011, p. 20). Organisations that have signed the Code include global corporations like Google, Cisco and Microsoft and research institutes like the Research Council of Norway. There is considerable interest in the design of new measures to get more women involved in technology as well as innovation processes in the business enterprise sector. This will tackle the demographic challenge and achieve innovation results. A European dialogue is underway linked to the innovation case for gender diversity. This dialogue is reflected in policy, practices and various programmes providing funding for cluster initiatives. Equal participation of men and women is essential for Europe to exploit the full potential of innovative strengths – not only for demographic reasons, but also in case of innovation processes and results. There is a need to clarify what (new) cluster policy relate measures can support the process to get more women involved in the innovation process of business and research.

Observation of many innovation exercises show that optimal innovation occurs when there is an equal mix of men and women using a systematic process (SIT, 2011). Because when a predominately male group tries to innovate, results are less impressive. And, when a predominately female group tries to innovate, results are less impressive. But put them together and the results are amazing. Research in this area may have some suggestions why (Millward and Freeman, 2002). The essence of the research is that, while men and women are equally innovative, their gender role within the context of an organization can affect how they are perceived and how they behave when innovating and sharing ideas. Men are perceived as more innovative and risk-taking, and women are perceived as more adaptive and risk-adverse. Thus, gender roles may interact with the role of the manager to inhibit (in the case of women) or facilitate (in the case of men) the likelihood of innovative behaviour. The results of the research suggest that innovative solutions were attributed more often to a male than a female manager, whereas adaptive solutions were attributed more often to a female than a male manager. Men are expected to take more risks when innovating and sharing ideas. Failure is less damaging to men because that's what's expected of them. Women are expected to be less risky, and this appears to limit or constrain both their degree of inno-vation and their willingness to share it. Failure is more damaging for women so they behave more adaptively in innovation exercises. There is both a negative and a positive side to this. On the one hand, innovation workshops need a process to assure that women feel they can innovate "bigger" and share those ideas with the group. If, as the research suggests, women are more likely to hold back, then the facilitation approach has to break through it. Otherwise, one can lose the inherent value of the (equal) innovation talent they bring to the table. On the positive side, these differences can be beneficial. This more adaptive behaviour in women and more risk-taking behaviour in men provides a certain balance or harmony during innovation, is a complementary effect that seems to yield better results. Means that

each partner holds the other accountable for ideas that are, at the same time, novel but adoptable. Working in pairs, men and women also do a better job of expressing jointly-developed new ideas that may help overcome risks that women may be feeling. Workshop processes that pair men and women up to take advantage of this are going to be more fruitful and differential role expectations did not have an impact on the production of actual solutions. The findings are discussed for their potential to complement existing research on role expectations and innovation as well as their implications for the development of a new research agenda. In this project the equal role of gender in the innovation process is called Innovative Gender. In simplest terms gender is *a concept that refers to the social differences between women and men that have been learned, are changeable over time and have wide variations both within and between cultures* (European Commission, 1998). The previously mentioned characterization of changes in the perception of innovation, strengthening the criterion of creativity, multidimensionality, and balancing the need for cooperation and balance, and also the gradual transition from a closed to open, leads to the concept of the innovation genome (DeGraff and Quinn, 2007), which may be a map of areas of research for Innovative Gender (Figure 13.5).The innovation genome is composed of four squares, which are the areas of the innovation system, such as:
  - cooperation,
  - creativity,
  - competition,
  - control.

In each of the squares practical ways are characterized to create various forms of value. The strengths and weaknesses in each of these areas and their mutual interaction determine the ability of an organization to create innovation in certain economic, social, and political conditions (DeGraff and Quinn, 2007, pp. 9-10). Each of the four areas has appropriate metrics for the measurement of the effects achieved, their own environment, recognized handling practices in the organization, and teams, or delegated leaders. The central element of the innovation of is to create value using people in all possible areas simultaneously, which is based on the following formula (DeGraff and Quinn, 2007, p. 11):

$$\boxed{\text{PEOPLE} + \text{PRACTICE} = \text{INTENTIONS}}$$

Where:
  - *intentions* – means the goals sought by the people,
  - *practices* – means any action and values considered important by those involved in the realisation of the intentions,
  - *people* – all the people involved in the efforts for the achievement of intentions.

In using the innovation genome model to study Innovative Gender, the starting point may be to build four dedicated matrices filled with information (variables)

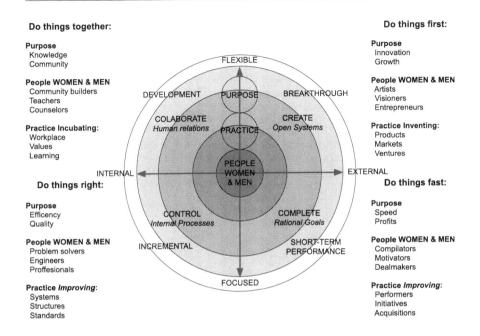

Do things together:

Purpose
Knowledge
Community

People WOMEN & MEN
Community builders
Teachers
Counselors

Practice Incubating:
Workplace
Values
Learning

Do things right:

Purpose
Efficiency
Quality

People WOMEN & MEN
Problem solvers
Engineers
Proffesionals

Practice *Improving*:
Systems
Structures
Standards

Do things first:

Purpose
Innovation
Growth

People WOMEN & MEN
Artists
Visioners
Entrepreneurs

Practice Inventing:
Products
Markets
Ventures

Do things fast:

Purpose
Speed
Profits

People WOMEN & MEN
Compilators
Motivators
Dealmakers

Practice *Improving*:
Performers
Initiatives
Acquisitions

Figure 13.5. The genome innovation model as a map of areas for Innovative Gender
Source: J. DeGraff, E. Quinn (2007), *Leading Innovation*, New York: McGraw-Hill, p. 12.

describing the area of gender. On the basis of the experience, it can be demonstrated that the key to creating value in the model of the innovation genome is one of its elements, namely cooperation. In the practice of economic, political and social life, the essence of cooperation between the sexes in the idea of the team has been lost, while subordination based on dependence dominates. The call by feminists for the introduction of quotas will not solve the problem, it can only structure the workers, political, or social groups; however, a group is not identical to a team. In a group, even with an equal number of women and men, functional subordination may still apply, while in a heterogeneous team the optimal potential accumulates, providing economies of scale and synergies at the same time. Millward's and Freeman's experiments cited above clearly showed how fruitful research involving men and women together in the research team, not just women or just men, can be.

Multidimensionality and the wide range of areas shown in the innovation genome demonstrate, it is true, that all members of the organization and selected experts from co-operating organizations are committed to the process of innovation; however, for the time being it does not take gender into account. It is possible to extend it with these aspects, and the innovation genome acting as a basis for Innovative Gender can then illustrate the innovation process model taking into account all aspects of such a broad spectrum, including the importance of gender. For now we have shown "the path to innovation," composed of seven stages, defined very broadly as the participation of all members of the organization in the pursuit of innovation, which takes into account the values associated with the culture of the organization, the individual, the creation of a vision, practices and behaviours, and traditions which are accepted by members of the organization. In this sense, the "path to innovation" is more in the nature of an agenda, but it is open to new research topics, according to the statement:

> What innovation is really about is questioning what is taken for granted – challenging the norms – and finding new pathways are things. In challenging the norm, we need a critical perspective and undoubtedly a gender perspective can be helpful (Vinnova, 2011).

Innovative Gender determines the equality of women and men in measurement, opportunities and situations included in the innovation genome model. The issue of gender is assumed in a general range as equality of access to education, equality before the law, equal pay, equal access to employment, equal access to training, equal access to career advancement, equality in working conditions, equality in social security, in the exercise of social and political roles, equality in job security, equality of access to maternity and parental leave, in a given socioeconomic system is already maintained, and any gaps in this area can be neutralized institutionally. It remains only to assess the involvement of the "gender resource" in the innovation process and its impact on the results. In this regard, however, there are significant multivariate differences created by gender, which should be considered only in a positive sense, because from them comes the possibility of achieving synergy as a result of cooperation of research or business teams in the innovation process. Focusing on the differences, usually in studies taken as the basis for claims arising out of the various dimensions of gender discrimination, is not under consideration here. In the Innovative Gender approach, it is more about process changes, in which the creation, implementation and dissemination involve various teams of cooperating men and women belonging to different social groups, whose participation in the team can be either professional (scientists, researchers, engineers, etc.) or quasi-professional, where participants in this process are social workers, creating changes and disseminating their results, or politicians securing such processes institutionally.

Literature

Alic, J., Branscomb, L., Brooks, H., Carter, A., Epstein, L. (1992), *Beyond Spinoff: Military and Commercial Technologies in a Changing World*, Boston: Harvard Business School Press.

Allen, J.A. (1966), *Scientific Innovation and Industrial Prosperity*, London: Longman.

Angelou, M. (2010), *Conversation with Maya Angelou by Jeffrey M. Elliot*, http://artquotes. robertgenn.com/getquotes.php?catid=65#.UwJETmeYaUm [accessed 15.02.2014].

Cempel, Cz. (2012), *Inżyniera kreatywności w projektowaniu maszyn i systemów techno i socjosfery*, Poznań: Politechnika Poznańska.

Chafee, J. (2001), *Potęga twórczego myślenia*, Warszawa: Bertelsmann.

Cordis (2006), CORDIS focus Newsletter, No. 272, November 2006, http://www.sciencebusiness. net, RCN: 26473 [accessed 10.10.2013].

Creative Economy (2008), *Report 2008*, New York: UNDP, United Nations.

Creative Economy (2013), *Report 2013 Special Edition, Widening Local Development Pathways*, Paris: UNDP, United Nations, UNESCO.

Czerniak, J. (2013), *Polityka innowacyjna w Polsce*, Warszawa: Difin.

DeGraff, J., Quinn, E. (2007), *Leading Innovation*, New York: McGraw-Hill.

Department of Culture, Media and Sport (1997), *Creative Industry Task Force*, London.

Drucker, P. (1985), *Innovation and Entrepreneurship*, London, New York: Harper & Row.

Drucker, P. (2007), *Innovation and Entrepreneurship*, Burlington, MA, USA: Elsevier.

Europe 2020 (2010), *A Strategy for Smart, Sustainable and Inclusive Growth*, European Commission, COM(2010)2020 final.

European Commission (1998), 100 words for equality. A glossary of terms on Equality between Women and Men, http://www.generourban.org/documentos/glossary_gender_equality/glossary_en.pdf [accessed January 2014].

European Commission (2009), *Gender segregation in the labour market. Root causes, implications and policy responses in the EU*, Directorate-General for Employment, Social Affairs and Equal Opportunities, Luxembourg: Publications Office of the European Union.

European Commission (2013), *Guide to Social Innovation*, http://s3platform.jrc.ec.europa.eu/documents/10157/47822/Guide%20to%20Social%20Innovation.pdf [accessed 15.02.2014].

European Foundation for Quality Management (EFQM) (2005), *Framework for Innovation*, Brussels: EFQM.

European Commission (1995), *Green Paper on Innovation*, http://europa.eu/documents/comm/green_papers/pdf/com95_688_en.pdf [accessed January 2014].

Fagerberg, J. (2006), "What do we know about innovation and socioeconomic change," [in:] L. Earl, R. Gault (eds.), *National Innovation, Indicators and Policy*, Cheltenham: EE Publishing.

Fagerberg, J., Mowery, D., Nelson, R. (eds.) (2006), *The Oxford Handbook of Innovation*, Oxford: Oxford University Press.

Florida, R. (2002), *The Rise of the Creative Class ... and How It's Transforming Work, Leisure, Community and Everyday Life*, New York: Basic Books.

Forum Akademickie (2013), *Finansowa zapaść*, Konferencja Rektorów Uniwersytetów Polskich, nr 9.

Freeman, Ch. (1982), *The Economics of Industrial Innovation*, London: Frances Pinter.

Freeman, Ch. (1987), *Technology Policy and Economic Performance: Lessons from Japan*, London: Pinter.

Freeman, Ch., Soete, L. (1997), *The Economics of Industrial Innovation*, 3rd edition, Milton Park: Routledge.

Hall P. (1994), *Innovation, Economics and Evolution. Theoretical Perspectives on Changing Technology in Economic Systems*, Hemel Hempstead: Harvester-Wheatsheaf.

Harris C. (2006), *Applying Innovation*, IBM Innovation week, Eindhoven, EU, http://ec.europa.eu/enterprise/policies/innovation/files/ius-2013_en.pdf.

Hirsz, R.D., Peters M.P. (1978), *Marketing a New Product. It's Planning, Development and Control*, California: Benjamin.

IUS (2013), *Innovation Union Scoreboard*, Brussels.

Janasz, W. (2004) (red.), *Innowacje w rozwoju przedsiębiorczości w procesie transformacji*, Warszawa: Difin.

Jasiński, A. (1997), *Innowacje i polityka innowacji*, Białystok: Wydawnictwo Uniwersytetu w Białymstoku.

Kao, J. (1997), *Jamming: The Art and Discipline of Business Creativity*, New York: HarperCollins Publisher.

Kline, S., Rosenberg, N. (1986), "An overview of innovation," [in:] R. Landau, N. Rosenberg, *The Positive Sum Strategy: Harnessing Technology for Economic Growth*, Washington, D.C.: National Academy Press.

Kotler, Ph. (1978), *Marketing Management, Analysis, Planning and Control*, New Jersey: Prentice-Hall.

Kukliński, A. (2011), "Europa quo vadis. Memorandum? Reconsidered," [in:] *Europa Quo Vadis?*, Wrocław: Lower Silesia.

Mansfield, E. (1968), *The Economics of Technological Changes*, New York: W.W. Norton Company, Inc.

Mazowia.eu (2013), *Przedsiębiorczość jest kobietą – fundusze unijne efektywnym wsparciem kobiecych biznesów*, Warszawa: Mazowiecka Jednostka Wdrażania Programów Unijnych.

McGowan P. (1987), "Creativity and innovation," [in:] D. Steward (ed.), *Handbook of Management Skills*, London: Gower Publishing Ltd.

Millward, L., Freeman, H. (2002), "Role expectations as constraints to innovation: The case of female managers, *Creativity Research Journal*, Vol. 14, Issue 1.

Mizgajska, H., (2013), *Aktywność innowacyjna małych I średnich przedsiębiorstw w Polsce – zmiany i uwarunkowania*, Wydawnictwo Uniwersytetu Ekonomicznego, Poznań.

Morris, L. (2006), *Permanent Innovation*, Acasa, www.permanentinnovation.com.

OECD (2005), *Oslo Manual 2005. Guidelines for Collecting and Interpreting Innovation Data*, OECD/European Commission.

Okoń-Horodyńska, E. (1998), *Narodowy system innowacji w Polsce*, Katowice: Wydawnictwo Akademii Ekonomicznej w Katowicach.

Okoń-Horodyńska, E. (2011), "Rola procesu *foresight* w badaniu nierówności rozwojowych," [in:] E. Okoń-Horodyńska, A. Zachorowska-Mazurkiewicz (eds.), *Współczesne wymiary nierówności w procesie globalizacji*, Kraków: Wydawnictwo Uniwersytetu Jagiellońskiego.

Okoń-Horodyńska, E. (2013), *Polityka innowacji w UE: przerost formy nad treścią?*, Kongres Ekonomistów Polskich, Warszawa: PTE.

Podręcznik Oslo (2008), *Zasady gromadzenia i interpretacji danych dotyczących innowacji. Pomiar działalności naukowej i technicznej*, 3rd edition, Warszawa.

Porter, M. (1990), *The Competitive Advantage of Nations*, London: McMillan.

Rothwell, R., Gardiner, P. (1985), "Invention, innovation, re-innovation and the role of the user. The case study of British hovercraft development," *Technovation*, Vol. 3, No. 2, June.

Schmookler, J. (1966), *Invention and Economic Growth*, Boston: Harvard University Press, http://briantracy.pl/profile/ebook-psychologia-osiagniec.pdf [accessed 15.02.2014].

Schumpeter, J. (1939), *Business Cycles*, New York-London: McGraw-Hill.

Schumpeter, J. (1960), *Teoria rozwoju gospodarczego*, Warszawa: PWN.

SIT (2011), *Systematic Inventive Thinking*, http://www.sitsite.com/ [accessed 19.02.2014].

Soete, L. (2006), *A Knowledge economy paradigm and its consequences*, MERIT Working Papers 001, http://www.merit.unu.edu/publications/wppdf/2006/wp2006-001.pdf [accessed 11.07.2014].

Stachell, P.M. (1998), *Innovation and Automation*, Ashgate: Brooksfield.

The Head of Innovation (2010), http://www.ideachampions.com/weblogs/archives/2010/11/25_awesome_quot.shtml [accessed 15.02.2014].

Toffler, A. (2000), *Szok przyszłości*, Poznań: Zysk i S-ka.

Tracy, B. (2010), *Psychologia osiągnięć*, e-book, http://briantracy.pl/profile/ebook-psychologia-osiagniec.pdf [accessed 17.02.2014].

US Department of Commerce (1967), *Technological Innovation*, New York: MD.

Van de Ven, A., Polley, D.E., Garud, R., Venkataraman, S. (1999), *The Innovation Journey*, New York: Oxford University Press.

Vinnova (2011), "Innovation & Gender," [in:] I. Danila, J. Grant Thorsuland (eds.), *Vasteras*, Sweden: Edita Vastara Aros AB.

List of Tables

List of Maps

List of Figures

List of Graphs

List of Appendixes

TECHNICAL EDITOR
Renata Włodek

PROOFREADER
Agnieszka Toczko-Rak

TYPESETTER
Tomasz Pasteczka

Wydawnictwo Uniwersytetu Jagiellońskiego
Redakcja: ul. Michałowskiego 9/2, 31-126 Kraków
tel. 12-663-23-80, 12-663-23-82, tel./fax 12-663-23-83